A SHORT HISTORY
OF ST GEORGE'S HOSPITAL
AND THE ORIGINS OF ITS WARD NAMES

A SHORT HISTORY OF
ST. GEORGE'S HOSPITAL

AND THE
ORIGINS OF ITS WARD NAMES

TERRY GOULD & DAVID UTTLEY

THE ATHLONE PRESS
London & Atlantic Highlands

First published 1997 by
THE ATHLONE PRESS LTD
1 Park Drive, London NW11 7SG
and 165 First Avenue,
Atlantic Highlands, NJ 07716

© T R Gould and David Uttley 1997

British Library Cataloguing in Publication Data
*A catalogue record for this book is available
from the British Library*

ISBN 0 485 11504 2 hb
0 485 12126 3 pb

Library of Congress Cataloging-in-Publication Data
Gould, Terry, 1931–
  A short history of St. George's Hospital and the origins of
its ward names / Terry Gould and David Uttley.
    p. cm.
  Includes bibliographical references and index.
  ISBN 0-485-11504-2 (hb). – ISBN 0 485-12126-3 (pbk.)
  1. St George's Hospital (London, England)--History. 2.
St George's Hospital (London, England)--Biography. 3. St
George's Hospital (London, England)--Buildings--Names.
4. Public hospitals--England--London--History.   I. Uttley,
David. II. Title.
  [DNLM: 1. St. George's Hospital (London, England) 2.
Hospital Units--history--England. 3. Hospitals, Public--his-
tory--England.
WX 28 FE5 L8SG2G 1996]
RA988.L8S344 1996
362.1'1'0942132--dc21
DNLM/DLC
for Library of Congress   96-39214
                                                      CIP

Typeset by
Bibloset, Chester

Printed and bound in Great Britain by
the University Press, Cambridge

*Dedicated to Shirley and Estelle for their patience and understanding
as we selfishly satisfied our curiosity for the past.*

Contents

Contents

Acknowledgements

The photograph of Lord Smith of Marlow is reproduced by kind permission of the President and Council of the Royal College of Surgeons of England and we are grateful to the British Orthopaedic Association for allowing us to reproduce the photograph of Sir Frank Holdsworth. We thank David and Margaret Myles for their kind permission to reproduce the photograph of Ruth Myles. The other pictures reproduced in this book are copies of paintings, sculptures, cartoons and photographs which are held in the Library of St. George's Hospital Medical School and the Archives Department of St. George's Hospital.

List of Illustrations

Foreword

The Special Trustees for St. George's Hospital were first appointed in 1974 at the time Boards of Governors were superseded by Area Health Authorities and District Management Teams. The Trustees were appointed to hold and administer the property that had been formerly held by the Board of Governors. Their prime responsibility is to manage and administer the Trust or old Endowment Funds that began to accumulate when St. George's Hospital was a voluntary hospital supported entirely by subscriptions and donations. The interest from the funds is now used for the benefit of patients and staff as well as supporting medical research. The Special Trustees also have the responsibility of taking care of the items of value and historical interest which were either given to or acquired by the hospital during its history which now spans over two hundred and fifty years. These include numerous paintings, furniture, sculptures and other memorabilia. The items however, which the Trustees most value are the various minute books which date from 1733 and are safely kept in the archives of the hospital. These books not only provide us with detailed information of the development of St. George's during its long history but give us an insight into the origins of its traditions and those who have played a major part in its evolution.

The Special Trustees firmly believe that the names of those who have contributed so much to St. George's should not be forgotten or lost. Some, among them are the governors and benefactors who gave vast fortunes in order to finance the further developments of the hospital including its rebuilding at Hyde Park Corner in the early 1830's. Others, include the Chairmen of the Boards of Governors and the Administrators who steered through the changes and of course, those clinicians who saw through the advances in medicine and surgery so ensuring that St. George's achieved international recognition as a hospital of excellence.

Terry Gould and David Uttley, former consultants to St. George's and the Atkinson Morley's Hospitals have long laboured to ensure that there is public awareness of these great names and clearly wish that they are not forgotten. The Special Trustees welcome this book which we have found to be both informative and engaging. We hope that an awareness of the past will inspire medical students and junior staff and will remind the older and more senior of the greatness and endeavour of their forebears. I am certain that this book will encourage us all to aim to overcome difficulties and reach for the highest standards so that St. George's maintains its position as a leader in the provision of healthcare yet remains a human and friendly place.

The love and care of one's fellow man and especially those we work with is clearly exemplified by our predecessors as outlined in this book. Their example is our heritage. It was their unselfish calling to medicine and their love of caring that exhilarated them and stimulated their successors which has led us to where we stand today.

This book has attempted to play its part in acknowledging our debt to the past and those great people who have paved the way. I am confident that it has achieved its objectives and I hope that it will be widely read and enjoyed by the present and many future generations.

Christopher J Bourne
Chairman of the Special Trustees for St. George's Hospital

Preface

St. George's Hospital was founded over two hundred and sixty years ago
in 1733, but it was not until 1866 that William Emmanuel Page, the
senior physician to the hospital at that time, wrote the first history of
the hospital entitled *Some Account of the Hospital and School.* In 1910
George C. Peachey published Part I of his *History of St. George's
Hospital* which he intended should be the definitive chronicle. In his
author's note he states that his history would be issued in twelve
parts, each part costing just 2/6d (25p). After labouring for another
four years Peachey had just reached Part VI, which only covered the
first twenty year period of the hospital's history, when he abandoned
his mammoth task. One cannot help wondering how Peachey planned
to cover the next one hundred and sixty years in his final six volumes,
and keeping to the original price structure at the same time! Joseph
Blomfield, the anaesthetist completed his peerless history *St. George's,
1733-1933* in time for the two hundredth anniversary of the hospital
foundation, and Alastair Hunter's sad death before he had completed
his account of the history of the hospital from 1933-1983, robbed us
of the full text, although that which he had finished was published
posthumously.

It is a great loss that the histories of Page, Peachey and Blomfield are
no longer in print; on these grounds alone there was a need for another
study to go back to the beginnings of the hospital, and then to bring the
record of the passing years up-to-date. There was a certain momentum
involved in the undertaking driven by the changing ethos in the hospital
service, where a serious imbalance is occurring, with undue stress being
laid on the balance sheet at the expense of healing and compassion. In
its own poor way this short book is an attempt to redress the balance

slightly, and restore a degree of equilibrium to the system, by dealing with a history of success stemming from the combined efforts of dedicated, selfless, hospital staff motivated by the altruistic goal of alleviating human suffering, which is something impossible to quantify!

We have no illusions that we could even begin to emulate the literary style of Blomfield, nor did we feel that there was a need to follow in the footsteps of Peachey and cover the passing years in exhaustive and exhausting detail. We were of the view that the casual reader with only a moderate interest in hospital matters would prefer a succinct account in the vein of Page so avoiding too much historical detail ; and this general sort of a book is the one that we set out to write. We invite those readers who feel that our work is devoid of historical minutiae to delve amongst the shelves of the Medical School Library where there are rich seams of archival material awaiting their attentions. Yet as we were researching this history we became acutely aware that a number of patients, visitors and staff were eager to learn something about the lives of those whose names have been used to denote wards at St. George's Hospital. So we have attempted to give the reader a concise history of St. George's Hospital, and, at the same time, provide a more detailed account of the origins of its ward, wing and block names. In some cases we have been able to use the names to illuminate some interesting aspect of the hospital's history, and in others we have attempted to give a short abridged biography of the individual concerned which we hope satisfies the curiosity, not only of the present readership, but also that of future generations. We hope that there is in the book a sufficiently positive account of various aspects of the never-ending struggle against disease, to give those still locked in it a feeling of modest encouragement.

We would like to express our grateful thanks to the Special Trustees of St. George's Hospital for giving us the opportunity and the encouragement to write this book. We gratefully acknowledge the help we have received from Andrew Rolland, the photographer, Debbie Lock, Terry Pickthorne, Philippa Rossdale, Tina Craig of the Royal College of Surgeons, Helen Snook of the British Orthopaedic Association, Barbara Lawrence of the British Geriatrics Association, David and Margaret Myles for the useful advice they have given us in our labours. Their help has greatly facilitated the preparation of this manuscript. We are also indebted to George Edwards for his literary gems which were published in the Medical School Gazette in the 1950s and 60s, William Page, George Peachey, Joe Blomfield, Alastair Hunter and the many earlier biographers whose writings have either been, or guided us to, the primary sources, and from whose writings we have plundered shamelessly. If we err by commission or omission the fault lies at our door, and we accept correction and reproof. As our characters are real we are unable to dodge behind the fictional formula that they bear no resemblance to anybody alive or dead, in the course of our account we may have given offence unintentionally by attributing to them motives which upset preconceived applecarts, for which we tender our apologies. Our opinions are our own. As usual.

1

The History of St. George's Hospital

Early 18th century London was no place to be poor let alone ill; there was no such thing as a National Health Service or Welfare State to help ease these oppressive and all too frequent burdens. Any poor relief that took place was under the aegis of private citizens with a conscience, and this was usually confined to old clothes and food given on a sporadic basis whenever the mood came upon them, which was usually when they had anything old and surplus. There was no systematic attempt to quantify the scale of the problem, let alone rectify matters other than on a piecemeal basis, indeed it would have been impossible, except in the grandest houses, for a single household to provide continuously for a large number of the indigenous poor. Those of the middling sort would often feed a servant who was unable to work by virtue of age, infirmity, or disability, but there was no compulsion upon them to do so, other than their sense of duty, and this, like most human attributes, was exercised in a very arbitrary fashion. Hospital treatment was woefully inadequate for the needs of the ordinary people who made up most of the population of the metropolis; and if provision did exist it was not necessarily where it was most needed, so it came about that large areas were not catered for at all. The few hospitals in being had grown up haphazardly, their siting was largely dependent on the whim of their founders several centuries earlier, and thus not related to current demands. That this happens in the wake of major demographic trends is something we are still learning at the end of the 20th century.

The local ramifications of this intolerable situation was addressed in 1716 when St. Dunstan's Coffee House in Fleet Street was chosen as the venue for an historic meeting that was to lead in time to the construction of two large hospitals in Westminster where none were present before. These were desperately required in a poverty stricken slum area of London which was ravaged by contagious disease. On the occasion of this meeting four gentlemen: Henry Hoare, a merchant banker, William Wogan, a writer on religious subjects, Robert Witham, a brewer, and Patrick Cockburn, a former curate, discussed the plight of the poor sick people of Westminster; as a result of their deliberations they published a *Charitable Proposal for Relieving the Sick and Needy, and other Distressed Persons*. The proposal was an appeal for money, clothes, linen and food on a continuing basis, which they could use to help these unfortunates.

Their efforts were quickly rewarded and soon they were able to ease some elements of the pervasive suffering, but increasing familiarity with the underlying circumstances revealed that there were many sick people in the area who needed hospital care for whom none was available. Encouraged by the success of their previous appeal the four went ahead to establish the Westminster Public Infirmary in Petty France in 1720. The Infirmary, supported in its entirety by voluntary contributions, became only the third voluntary general hospital to be built in London. The other two, St. Bartholomew's and St. Thomas's had been founded in the twelfth century, but, because of their religious origins and connections, they had been suppressed together with the monasteries by Henry VIII between 1536 and 1541. Along with the dissolution of the monasteries a large number of small hospitals attached to them also disappeared in company with their devoted and expert staff of infirmarians. Henry VIII allowed the refoundation of St. Bartholomew's in 1544, and at the same time he gave St. Mary's of Bethlehem, later to be known as The Bethlehem, which was eventually shortened to Bethlem (or Bedlam), to the City Merchants for the treatment of the insane. In 1551 Henry's son, Edward VI, allowed the citizens to repair St. Thomas's which they purchased and reopened. Two years later Edward in response to a report from the Bishop of London approved the foundation of Christ's

2

Hospital for Orphans, and Bridewell (St. Bride's) for the correction of idle vagabonds.

Like St. Bartholomew's and St. Thomas's, the Westminster Public Infirmary was rapidly inundated with patients, and Henry Hoare and his colleagues were forced to look for larger and more commodious premises. In 1724 they relocated their infirmary to Chapel Street, but by 1732 the Chapel Street establishment was found in turn to be inadequate for the growing needs of the charity. The vice president, a Mr. Green, very generously offered two larger houses of his own for consideration which were situated in James Street and Castle Lane respectively. A majority of the governors favoured the house in Castle Lane, but a minority, which included all the medical staff, preferred a third option, namely, that of Lanesborough House at Hyde Park Corner, which also happened to be available. The upshot being that whilst the majority agreed to take up Mr. Green's offer and adapt the Castle Lane premises, a sizeable minority decided that they would break away and open their own hospital at Hyde Park Corner. The arguments between the two groups 'grew in heat and acrimony', and ultimately entered the public domain.

Several open letters were exchanged setting out the irreconcilable views of the protagonists. These were given a wide circulation and copies of them exist in the possession of the British Museum. Although the dispute was carried out with considerable bitterness and wide publicity, which seemed to run directly counter to the philanthropic aims of the participants, the outcome, nevertheless, was enormously beneficial to the sick poor of London as the split lead to the establishment of two major voluntary hospitals in the same vicinity: the Westminster and St. George's.

St. George's opened in Lanesborough House in 1733. The house had been built in 1719 by James Lane, the second Viscount Lanesborough who wished to live in what was then the country surroundings of Hyde Park. Viscount Lanesborough had inscribed above the front door 'It is my delight to be, Both in the town and country'. Regrettably, the country air appears to have done his health little good as he died in 1724. The house was ideal as a hospital, situated on the outskirts of the capital, within easy access to the most populous areas, in a salubrious setting, and very close to the principle purveyors of

3

asses milk, then a very potent therapeutic commodity. The medical staff which included Claudius Amyand, William Cheselden, Ambrose Dickins, William Wasey, Alexander Stuart, Noel Broxholme, Simon Burton, David Ross, James Wilkie, and George Teissier, were pleased to contribute towards the rent which amounted to £60 annually, and they gave their services free of charge to the Westminster Hospital until new staff could be recruited, as a gesture of reconciliation. A further charge of £15 was made for the stables, dairy cowsheds and outbuildings. It is uncertain as to why St. George's received its name, probably it was because it was situated within the parish of St. George's, Hanover Square, it is less likely to have been in deference to the reigning monarch, George II, as there was no precedent for this type of designation at that stage, although it became common in later years.

The Westminster Infirmary refused to hand over any of its funds to St. George's, but the new hospital was not short of friends and well-wishers, so very quickly it attracted considerable sums in donations and subscriptions. The Board of Governors also agreed that no one would qualify as a trustee or governor, without paying an annual subscription of at least five guineas. Thus the Board were able to appoint a matron, Mrs. Johnson, at a princely salary of ten pounds a year, her husband was appointed messenger at six pounds a year, both had previously been employed by Lord Lanesborough as caretakers, another appointee was Mr. Thomas Aldridge as apothecary for one year: 'on trial and probation without payment or expense', but he was given his lunch. The Board also appointed two nurses and a cook, and purchased a clock and a sedan chair. Mr. Thompson made the bedsteads.

The hospital measured forty three by forty one feet and was comprised of three floors. The ground floor contained the matron's room, the secretary's and the treasurer's offices, the boardroom and the physicians' room. The surgeons were not given a room until 1751. The servants occupied the upper floor and the first floor accommodated thirty patients in two wards, one, female and the other, male. The patients diet was simple and consisted mainly of pottage, boiled mutton and boiled beef. Beer was supplied to both patients and staff by Thomas Rea of Knightsbridge, but gin was strictly forbidden. Huggitt, a cow-keeper was engaged to supply the hospital with milk.

In the early days no distinction was made between medical and surgical patients, and they lay side by side in the ward. Operations were carried out without anaesthetics in the ward itself, not an agreeable experience for either the patients or their neighbours, indeed to our tender susceptibilities it is hard to imagine anything more calculated to cause distress. Medical treatment was extremely limited, and as irrational in application as it was ineffective in practice. Some of the commoner remedies were: compounds of mercury, which loosened the teeth and caused excessive salivation; Dr Woord's pills – a concoction consisting mainly of camphor and pepper; dried horse's hoof; snake-root; Daffy's elixir; Sir Walter Raleigh's cordial; mint water; and whisky. The last two were at least relatively safe, though the last would need to have been taken in immoderate doses to expunge the horrors of 18th century medicine. Soldiers who were admitted with venereal disease were charged 4d a day, but otherwise patients were treated free of charge. Those patients who died, and this outcome was not unknown, were buried in the hospital's burial ground in Brompton which had been purchased for £400. Although a certain Mrs. Hoare was responsible for the burials, she was not paid directly for this service, but was paid for the vegetables which she grew on the land and supplied to the hospital. Conditions rapidly became so cramped and miserable that as early as 1735 it became necessary to consider extending the hospital.

The Board was concerned that it did not own the freehold of Lanesborough House. The Dean and Chapter of Westminster Abbey readily agreed to the purchase of the freehold for £500 which allowed the Board to plan for immediate extensions to Lanesborough House. At the same time the Board felt that it should plan also for development in the longer term which would require more land. The Grosvenor Estates were asked if it would sell the hospital two acres of its adjoining land. Negotiations were protracted and it was not until 1767 that Sir Richard Grosvenor agreed the lease of the two acres at a peppercorn rent.

Isaac Ware, an eminent architect working with His Majesty's Board of Works, was engaged to design the extension to the hospital. Ware's design was executed over a ten year period from 1734 to 1744, and when completed the hospital had fifteen wards with over two hundred and fifty beds. This was a much more considerable structure and it was now possible to place female and male patients in different wings and have separate 'salivating' and 'cutting' wards as well as accident wards. An operating room was placed over the boardroom but presumably no surgery was undertaken whilst the Board was meeting!

St. George's continued to develop over the next sixty years, and in doing so established itself as one of the leading teaching hospitals in London. Many distinguished medical names were elected to the staff including John Hunter, John Gunning, Charles Hawkins, William Bromfield, Matthew Baillie and William Heberden. and they attracted pupils who later achieved fame such as Jenner, Astley Cooper, Abernethey and Cline.

At the dawn of the nineteenth century eminent names such as: Everard Home, Robert Keate, Benjamin Brodie and Thomas Young were ranked amongst the physicians and surgeons on the staff of St. George's, but even their exploits were unable to deflect attention from the sorry state of the fabric of the building which was causing great concern. The roof was leaking, the baths and plumbing were unsatisfactory, the drains were infested with rats, and the windows were causing endless problems. Lewis Wyatt, the hospital architect, reported these matters to the Board and as a result it was resolved that 'the accommodations of the present hospital are totally inadequate to the wants of the public.' A building fund was set up and due to the indefatigable efforts of the Fuller family and others, considerable funds were raised to defray the cost of building a new St. George's Hospital.

Lewis Wyatt estimated that it would cost £50,000 to build a three hundred and fifty bedded hospital and submitted a plan. The Board rejected Wyatt's plan, much to his annoyance, and decided to hold a competition for the best design. At this Wyatt resigned. The competition was won by William Wilkins, who had been responsible for a number of college buildings in Cambridge, as well as University College and the National Gallery in London. Wilkin's estimate was forty thousand pounds, and the building work was to be carried out in three phases, the first of which was to cost £16,000. Work began on this first phase in 1827, but got off to a poor start during the digging of the foundations, when the builder found he had to go deeper than planned, as the ground had been previously excavated and filled with rubbish. In a strange coincidence during the building of the Atkinson Morley's Hospital nearly fifty years later a similar difficulty was encountered. Another minor difficulty arose when young Mr. Tattersall,[1] objected to bricks being piled against his premises and stables.

As William Wilkins began to supervise the work on the second phase of the building he noticed that Apsley House, which was being reconstructed at the same time, was being given an improved facade with Corinthian pillars similar to those he had designed for his new St. George's. Wilkins realised that this work was being overseen by the cousin of Lewis Wyatt, and suspecting that the latter was probably to some extent under the influence of his still embittered relative, immediately changed his planned facade to give the hospital its very distinctive Doric columns. The new St. George's was completed in 1844 at a cost just slightly in excess of Wilkins' original estimate. The old Lanesborough House was demolished as the new building was constructed and patients and staff were delighted to gradually move into new and modern facilities.

Nevertheless, the Governors found it difficult to meet the total cost out of the building fund, and decided to pay the difference from the general fund. Henry Holland, the treasurer, did not agree and promptly resigned.

As the fundamentals of physiology and pathology were being discovered, surgery and medicine began to undergo rapid development. Although repeated bleeding, cupping, leeching, together with liberal doses of mercury and antimony were still orthodox procedures in medicine, physicians were beginning to look towards more rational treatments, and with the introduction of anaesthesia, surgeons were able to undertake more complex procedures.

---

[1] Richard Tattersall (1724-1795) was born in Hurstwood, Lancashire and came to London as stud-groom to the Duke of Kingston. In 1776 Tattersall became an auctioneer and in 1766 took a ninety- nine year lease from the Grosvenor Estates of some ground in the yard behind the hospital. It was here that he set up his auction rooms which became celebrated mart of thoroughbred horses and a great racing centre. After Richard Tattersall's death his son carried on the business but transferred the centre of their operations to Knightsbridge in 1867. Interestingly, stables remained on the site of Tattersall's in Grosvenor Mews well into the 1960's.

From the very beginning physicians and surgeons in lieu of 'fee or reward' were allowed a small number of pupils, and the fees collected from these teaching activities were pooled and shared, but there was no formal or systematic teaching such as lectures, and the pupil only gained knowledge from his respective teacher, and this was very much at the latter's inclination or whim. Surgeons' pupils were called 'dressers' because they helped to dress wounds, whereas physicians' pupils were known as 'clerks' (terms which may still be heard in use today). John Hunter, one of the hospital's greatest surgeons, attempted to set medical teaching on a more formal basis, and invited all the pupils to attend the lectures given by him and his brother, William, at their academy in Windmill Street without charge. In 1783 Hunter made the daring suggestion that St. George's should have its own Medical School and each surgeon should give six lectures annually, but the idea was rejected by his colleagues. They, on the other hand, drew up their own plans in 1793, which when communicated to Hunter in the hospital, caused him to become so angry as to provoke a heart attack which lead to his sudden death in the boardroom of Lanesborough House. Ten years after Hunter's death his brother-in-law, Everard Home, gave the first recorded formal lecture at St. George's in 1803.

From the beginning of the nineteenth century medical training became more structured, and pupils at St. George's were required to learn anatomy at either Hunter's, Lane's, Carpue's or Brookes' schools of anatomy, which were in effect private academies set up for this purpose; and chemistry was taught at the Royal Institution in Albermarle Street, in addition to their clinical subjects which were dealt with at the hospital.

On the opening of Wilkin's new St. George's, a school of medicine and surgery was formally opened, but pupils continued to study anatomy at the private schools. It was the intense dislike that Benjamin Brodie nursed for Samuel Lane and his 'School of Anatomy and Surgery adjoining St. George's Hospital' that led him to purchase a house in Kinnerton Street, which he then leased back to St. George's for use as an anatomy theatre, a lecture room and a museum. At last, St. George's had its own complete medical school. Lane's school closed down in 1863. In 1868 the Kinnerton Street school was moved into buildings adjoining the hospital, but by the beginning of the twentieth century, with space at a premium, students were forced to undertake their preclinical training at King's College in the Strand, University College, London, or outside the capital altogether at either Cambridge or Oxford Universities. It was not until 1976, when the new Medical School was opened at Tooting, that all pre- and clinical training could be accommodated on the hospital campus.

During the nineteenth century St. George's was fortunate to count amongst its medical staff such eminent men as John Snow, who was appointed as anaesthetist to the outpatient department, Henry Gray, who sadly died at the age of thirty four from smallpox just before he was appointed surgeon, Henry Bence Jones, Robert Lee, Robert Barnes, Sir William Dalby, James Hope, William Howship Dickinson, Thomas Tatum, Sir Prescott Hewett, Timothy Holmes, Thomas Whipham, John Cavafy, Sir William Bennett, Henry Champneys, John Warrington Haward, and Thomas Pickering Pick.

By 1859 the ever-increasing demand for beds was desperate, so in order to cater for this situation an attic floor designed by A. P. Mee, a well-known architect, was added which regrettably spoilt the grand and balanced lines of Wilkin's original design. It was hoped that the third floor would give space for the increasing numbers of convalescent patients but this failed to be realised because of the unfulfilled need for acute beds. Fortunately, one of the governors, Mr. Atkinson Morley, a wealthy hotel owner, left the bulk of his estate to St. George's in 1859, specifically for the purpose of building a convalescent hospital. The trustees of the hospital received £150,000, and purchased twenty eight acres of land in Wimbledon, with the result that Atkinson Morley's Hospital was opened in 1869.

In recognition of her great contribution to nursing, Florence Nightingale was elected a governor to St. George's in 1880, so becoming the first woman to hold such a position in our hospital, or indeed any other hospital. She immediately repaid the compliment by insisting upon more space between the beds. About this time the Duke of Westminster leased sufficient land to permit an extension of three additional wards.

A few years earlier St. George's suffered a major disaster when the cast iron water tank, situated in the roof, burst and five thousand gallons of water cascaded through the building. Two patients died as a result and one medical student who had jumped through a window to escape the flood sprained his ankle. Despite this tragedy St. George's moved forward to the beginning of the twentieth century with confidence.

This confidence stemmed from the general feeling that the hospital might again be rebuilt, and this created an optimistic climate in which it was thought that the ever increasing pressures on beds would be relieved. Interestingly enough it was at the very turn of the century when the suggestion that St. George's should be rebuilt away from its existing site was first mooted. It was recognised that the cost would be considerable, and the hospital would be hard pressed to obtain the same favourable terms that it was receiving presently from the Duchy of Westminster. The notion of rebuilding was temporarily shelved as the dark clouds of the Great War gathered over Europe.

St. George's was served at this time by such famous medical luminaries as Sir Isambard Owen, William Ewart, Sir Humphry Rolleston, James Collier, Clinton Dent, Sir George Turner, Marmaduke Shield, Radford Dakin, Charles Slater and Sir Frederick Hewitt.

It was during this period that St. George's students excelled in sporting pursuits. At rugby, a number of the hospital team including the Tuckers, the Turners, J. E. H. Mackinley, W. E. Collins, and H. H. Taylor, all played internationally. In rowing, with such names as Gardner, Muttlebury, Fison, Noble, Drury Pennington, Taylor, Orme, and Stiff, the hospital was unbeaten at Henley for a number of years. Clinton Dent was a superb climber, Monier Williams was a skater of renown, E. W. Lewis was amateur tennis champion in 1889, and I. McW. Bourke was amateur cycling champion at one and ten miles in 1898. Off the playing field ex-St. George's men achieved fame, Dr. E. B. Hartley was awarded the Victoria Cross in Basutoland in 1879, and many others have been decorated for bravery, services to their country, or to medicine. In later years some left medicine altogether, pursued totally different careers and achieved fame and acclaim. Louis Boyd Neel founded an orchestra and became Dean of the Royal Conservatory of Music in Toronto and recently Sam Hutt has become popular as the Country and Western singer, Hank Wangford.

After the Great War was over St. George's was in the hands of such doctors as James Torrens, Anthony Feiling, Hugh Gainsborough, Ivor Back, George Ewart, Sir Terence Crisp English, Philip Jory, and others, who, with the Board of Governors, were uncertain whether St. George's should be rebuilt at Hyde Park Corner or somewhere in the suburbs. Some like Crisp English were adamant that the hospital should not move outside central London, others, such as Gainsborough and Ewart, favoured the suburban option. The governors played a cautious hand, and held a competition for a design for the new St. George's to be built at Hyde Park Corner. The competition was won by a young student architect, Alexander Gray, who was later a partner in the firm of Watkins and Gray, who, many years later, designed the new St. George's that was built ultimately on the Tooting site.

Considerable funds were raised by the rebuilding committee to pay for the proposed new hospital at Hyde Park Corner by donations, subscriptions, matinees, mannequin parades, and auctions. A mannequin parade at the Hyde Park Hotel featuring Nora Swinburne and Evelyn Laye, the actresses raised more money as did Captain Oswald Birley's offer to paint the portrait of the highest bidder. Jack Hulbert was the auctioneer. Another auction held in the boardroom of the hospital ended disastrously when Leslie Henson, the comedian, encouraged those present to drink to excess, with the result that they bid far more than they could afford. The auction was abandoned, and had to be held again the following day when everyone had sobered up. Wentworth hosted a ladies golf championship to raise more money and Rosenberg and Helf put on a Cezanne exhibition at their Bond Street Gallery. Sir Harry Oakes, the President of Lake Shore Gold Mine, Ontario, reputed to be one of the world's richest men proved to be the major subscriber when he gave nearly £100,000 to the rebuilding fund.

The general financial state of the hospital was not always so healthy but through the generosity of the Governors and the support of the public St. George's kept its head above water and was proudly able to boast that it was supported entirely by voluntary subscription. In fact, the wording placed high up on the northern facade of the hospital read 'Supported Entirely By Voluntary Subscription'.[1] The hospital was occasionally helped out of its financial plight by windfalls. A number of generous legacies were left to the hospital, flag days raised considerable sums and many events were held to reload the coffers. St. George's often resorted to ingenuous means to replenish its falling reserves. The front of the hospital was festooned with bunting and scaffolding to make colourful grandstands for State occasions and seats were sold at a substantial profit. It is told that on the occasion of the Coronation of Queen Elizabeth II in 1953 all the seats were sold in advance but on the eve of the ceremony the Ministry of Works ordered a number of seats to be removed. The hospital complied but mindful that the seats had been sold the resourceful hospital secretary replaced the seats just before the paying spectators arrived.

As the rebuilding fund accumulated Hitler was beginning to mobilise his forces in Germany, and, with the invasion of Poland, Britain became embroiled in the Second World War thus dashing any hopes of hospital rebuilding. As soon as war was declared many of the consultants enlisted in the armed forces. Those remaining at St. George's prepared themselves to care for the inevitable casualties of the aerial bombardment. Among the emergency measures taken was one to set aside a number of beds at Hyde Park Corner for the treatment of the victims of air raids, which limited the number of beds available for the medically ill, and in another, the governors, mindful of their responsibilities towards the young student nurses, decided to move the Preliminary Training School to the Atkinson Morley's Hospital. By the end of 1941, because of increased aerial attack the Ministry of Health asked the Board of Governors if St. George's could carry on some of its work outside London. It was suggested initially that the work should be transferred to the Windsor Emergency Hospital, but the governors and medical staff

---

[1] The wording 'Supported Entirely By Voluntary Subscription' was altered just after the Second World War before the introduction of the National Health Service when the government gave a number of subsidies to help the hospital out of a financial crisis to read 'Supported By Voluntary Subscription'. On the eve of the introduction of the National Health Service in 1948 some mischievous medical students altered the wording to read 'Supported By Involuntary Subscription'. The words were removed in the 1950's.

12

asked the Ministry whether the Atkinson Morley's could be adapted to deal with the general acute work. The Ministry readily agreed, and the total number of beds at the Atkinson Morley's was increased to 120, and an operating theatre, a radiology department and a sanitary tower were constructed. By the autumn of 1942 the Atkinson Morley's was ready to accept acute surgical and medical admissions. George Ewart, the surgeon and Eric Bellingham-Smith, the physician were appointed to be responsible for the patients. Two weeks before the first patients were due to be admitted George Ewart suffered a fatal coronary thrombosis and the plans were immediately shelved. Instead, it was agreed to use the Atkinson Morley's partly as a neurosurgical unit under the care of Wylie McKissock, partly for patients with gastro-intestinal disease and the remaining beds being retained for convalescent patients. At the end of the war it was decided to allow the Atkinson Morley's to develop as a neuroscience centre, and its use as a convalescent hospital to gradually reduce.

As soon as the Second World War came to an end the debate began again as to where St. George's should be rebuilt. By now most of the medical staff favoured a position outside central London, and this was long before the administrators began to take an interest in these matters, which culminated in them trying to claim the credit for the rebuilding of St. George's in the suburbs. Discussions were held with the Westminster Hospital to see if they should join forces and rebuild together, but nothing came of them. A number of possible positions were considered including the St. Mary Abbot's Hospital site, Mottingham, Fulham Palace, the Tooting area, the Springfield Hospital site, and on the Atkinson Morley's land. It was proposed that the new St. George's should have 1,250 beds. The Ministry of Health supported the Springfield proposal and agreed to open discussions with the Middlesex County Council.

On the introduction of the National Health Service in 1948 the Royal Dental Hospital, the Victoria Hospital for Children in Tite Street, Chelsea, the Broadstairs Convalescent Home and the Princess Beatrice Hospital, Fulham were designated as part of the St. George's Group. The responsibility for the latter two was quickly transferred but the Board of Governors recommended to the Ministry of Health that there should be a single contract for the rebuilding of the hospital and medical school which would now include a dental hospital and an undergraduate dental school. The Ministry's reply stated that the proposed hospital was too large and should be scaled down. In 1949 Aneurin Bevan, the Minister of Health at the time, ruled out the Springfield site on the grounds that a new hospital would overshadow St. James' Hospital, Balham, and in the event of a nuclear attack it would be undesirable for the two hospitals to be in such close proximity; and therefore the Grove Fever Hospital and the Fountain Hospital sites were by a process of elimination found to be the preferred site for the rebuilding of St. George's Hospital. Aneurin Bevan stated that the new St. George's would be built as soon as possible so that the existing wards at Tooting would not have to be used, as they were very much sub-standard. He added 'the sooner the wards are destroyed by bulldozer, the better'. At the time of writing, over forty five years later, some of those old wards are still in use!

Although nothing else had fundamentally changed it became clear by 1950 some of his earlier urgency appeared to have evaporated, which could have only come about by political machinations, as Bevan announced that he could not give a date when the rebuilding would begin, but suggested as an alternative that St. George's should use some of the wards in the Grove Fever Hospital, and should also undertake some refurbishment at Hyde Park Corner. The Grove Fever Hospital was designated to St. George's in 1953, and the latter immediately took charge of the pathological and catering services, and some St. George's nurses were sent to look after the poliomyelitis cases. By 1956 a number of clinical 'firms' and outpatient clinics were established at Tooting, and on the credit side a number of improvements were made to the hospital, and in parallel developments at Hyde Park Corner included the opening of a new operating theatre, a new outpatients department, and a new casualty department and several wards were upgraded.

In 1960 the Ministry of Health announced that it was to review the major hospital rebuilding programme, but it anticipated that the rebuilding of St. George's would begin in 1966. Later in the year Enoch Powell, the Conservative Minister of Health, requested the closure of Victoria Hospital for Children with the transfer of the beds to Tooting. The sorry chapter of muddle and delay was not yet over, and it was not

14

until 1973 that building began on Grove and Fountain site, some 24 years after the proposals had first been broached as a step which should brook no delay! Such are the tergiversations of the political process.

The first phase of the Medical School building, which comprised Hunter and Grosvenor Wings, was opened in 1976, by which time changes in the structure of the National Health Service, following its reorganisation in 1974, had lead to the Board of Governors being disbanded, and in their place was now the Merton, Sutton and Wandsworth Health Authority, although St. George's was directly managed by a District Management Team. This reorganisation had produced a three tier level of control: with the Region at the apex, the Area was the next level down, and several Districts responded to each Area. This ill-conceived measure produced a bureaucratic tangle of gigantic proportions. These were the days of consensus, which meant that if anything were to get done very often the strongest personality had to ride roughshod over the rest of the committee, leading to some bizarre and disastrous decisions. Responsibility was supposed to spread down the chain of command, and accountability up the way; sadly the pathways were almost totally obliterated at every level. These were the 'dog days' in terms of action. The District which concerns us included not only St. George's and the Atkinson Morley's Hospitals, but the South London Hospital for Women, the Weir Hospital, St. Benedict's Hospital, Birchlands, Springfield Hospital, St. James' Hospital, the Bolingbroke Hospital, and the Springfield Annex in Kingston. These links allowed a number of St. George's 'firms' to be based temporarily at St. James' and the Bolingbroke Hospitals, until Lanesborough Wing, the first ward block, was opened in 1980. This led to St. George's final departure from Hyde Park Corner after a sojourn of nearly two hundred and fifty years.

In 1982 a further reorganisation brought St. George's under the control of the Wandsworth Health Authority, and in the years that followed the Weir, the South London Hospital for Women, St. Benedict's, and the Springfield Annex were closed; responsibility for Birchlands was transferred to the Hospital for Aged Jews; and the Bolingbroke Hospital was adapted for the care of the elderly.

Gradually further ward blocks were erected at Tooting: Jenner Wing was opened in 1984, and St. James' Wing was completed in 1988, when it became possible to close St. James' Hospital in Balham. In the early 1990's, with what promises to be the greatest reform of the Health Service since its inception as it alters not only the way in which it is administered but also its basic philosophy, St. George's, the Atkinson Morley's and the Bolingbroke Hospitals became part of St. George's Healthcare NHS Trust. This convulsion in the NHS started off well with much to recommend it, but its implementation has alienated many of the professionals who work in it, and it is probably not unfair to say that the balance is now tilted in favour of management. Few would deny that it needs benign adjustments, and a reshaping of its emphasis to a kinder profile. The jury is still out on these matters. Until more is known it would be unwise to prophesy what the future holds for St. George's in the next millennium; though its contribution to the alleviation of human suffering over the years must have earned for it our hopes that it will continue to fulfil the same role for the foreseeable future.

2

The Naming of Wards and Buildings – Historical Aspects

When first founded the majority of the voluntary hospitals were small units with at most two or three wards. As the hospitals were enlarged to increase bed numbers, so it became necessary to identify the wards, in order to make it easier for patients, relatives and staff to find their way around. Some hospitals chose to number their wards, and to give an alphabetical letter to each floor or block. This simple system has the merit that it is very easy to follow, and is used today in such hospitals as University College Hospital, and the Hospital for Sick Children in Great Ormond Street. Some chose to name wards after flowers, shrubs, trees, actors, artists, places, poets, or other notable people. From its very inception St. George's Hospital chose to name its wards as a way of commemorating a distinguished benefaction, royal patronage, or outstanding service to the hospital. Over the years this tradition has at times caused embarrassment, doubtless led to jealousy and envy, as well as given rise to offence, all of which has prompted frequent change, and led to confusion for patients and staff. And this makes a good story.

The names chosen for the four wards to be opened in Lanesborough House where St. George's Hospital was first founded in 1733 were: *Richmond*, after an early benefactor, the Duke of Richmond and Lennox, *Newcastle*, after the Duke of Newcastle, another early benefactor, *Prince's*, after HRH Frederick, the Prince of Wales, who was President of the

Hospital from 1734 until 1751, and *Talbot,* after Lord Chancellor Talbot, who was Vice President in 1734.

Such was the fame of the infant St. George's Hospital that almost immediately after it was opened, Isaac Ware, the architect to HM Board of Works, was engaged for the purpose of substantially extending the hospital in order to increase the number of wards to eleven, and the bed numbers, from the original thirty, to over two hundred and fifty. The names chosen for the first four additional wards to be opened in 1736 were as follows. *Winchester,* which was named after either Dr. Richard Willes, Bishop of Winchester, who was the first President of St. George's in 1734, or his son, Hoadly, who in turn also became Bishop of Winchester, and was a Vice President and governor of the hospital from 1734 until 1749. *Kings,* after the unpopular, quick tempered and foul mouthed, King George II, the reigning monarch, whose name it has been suggested may also have been chosen as the name of the hospital, although this seems most unlikely in view of his unpopularity, and it seems more tenable that the hospital owes its name to the fact that it was situated within the parish of St. George's, Hanover Square. *Princesses,* after their Royal Highnesses, Anne, Amelia and Caroline, and lastly, *Ratcliffe,* after Dr John Radcliffe, the highly successful and distinguished physician, whose name is usually more closely associated with the Infirmary and Library at Oxford. Dandridge, who was Radcliffe's apothecary, and who himself was worth £50,000 when he died, said that 'Radcliffe had not been in London more than a year before he was making more than twenty guineas a day'. It was said that many people feigned illness in order to be entertained by Radcliffe's urbane and witty conversation. John Radcliffe found both favour and disapproval with the Royal Family; on the whole he was well regarded, but he was severely criticised for not attending Queen Anne before her death. Radcliffe became a Member of Parliament for Buckingham in 1713, but died a year later after a 'fit of apoplexy'. Although St. George's Hospital received £1000 from the Radcliffe Trust it never did get around to using the correct spelling of its benefactor's name!

By 1738 Isaac Ware had completed another five wards. Three of these were named after benefactors, *Marlborough* (Charles, Duke of Marlborough), *Thanet* (Earl of Thanet), and *Burlington* (Richard,

Earl of Burlington). The other two names chosen were *Queen's* after Her Majesty Queen Caroline, and *Oxford* after Edward, the Earl of Oxford and Mortimer, who was a Vice President of the Hospital.

Ware completed his final two wards in 1744 and these were named *Uxbridge* and *Sherard.* Uxbridge marked the benefaction of the Earl of Uxbridge, and Sherard was named after Sir Brownlow Sherard, who was a governor of the hospital from 1733 to 1744.

In 1825 the Board of Governors resolved that 'the accommodations of the present hospital are totally inadequate to the wants of the public' A public meeting to encourage support was held in King Street, St. James' 'for the purpose of considering the propriety of forming a fund for adding to or rebuilding partly or altogether the present hospital'. The meeting was successful in its aims, and a committee was formed to push forward the rebuilding scheme. The committee included Henry Holland, the treasurer, W. W. Pepys, a governor, and Dr H. P. Fuller, the visiting apothecary to the hospital. Fuller was entrusted with the responsibility for collecting the funds required to bring the enterprise to fruition. All three were eventually to have wards named after them in the new St. George's Hospital, which was opened in 1834, and built by William Wilkins very near to the initial costing of £40,000.

The minutes of the Weekly Board of 1829 records having decided that the wards to be opened after the first phase of Wilkins' hospital was opened 'should be named *Cambridge, Egremont, Fitzwilliam, Fuller, Grosvenor, Harris, Hope, King's, Newcastle, Oxford, Radcliffe, Winchester and York.* The Chaplain was requested to see the above names painted on the doors or over the entrances to the wards'. Obviously things were refreshingly different and much less complicated in those days! One may be sure that the Chaplain, unhampered by reams of forms from Works and Estates Officers would have carried out this work with alacrity! The wards opened in the second and third phases of Wilkin's new hospital were named *Apreece, Brodie, Burton, Cholmondely, Crayle, Drummond, Holland, Hudson, Prince's, Queen's, Rosebery, Wellington and Wright.*

Thus many of the existing ward names were transferred to the new hospital, but some were dropped in favour of the names of more recent benefactors, or new patrons. Nevertheless, despite the additional wards and some renaming, it was becoming increasingly difficult to include all the new names. A solution to this potential diplomatic minefield came about because Wilkin's new long wards were divided into two by a central kitchen, which gave an opportunity to give a name to each half of the ward; thus *Oxford* was paired with *Newcastle*, *Kings* with *Cambridge*, *Fitzwilliam* with *Egremont*, *Wellington* with *Talbot*, *Queen's* with *Pepys*, and *Prince's* with *Kent*.

A Sub-Committee of the Board of Governors was appointed in 1876 "to take into consideration the mode in which the wards have been named, and whether any alterations might be made with advantage to the Hospital".

The Sub-committee reported back

> that after investigating as well as the materials at their command enabled them, beg to report, that at the completion of the present Hospital the wards were named, most of the names in the old hospital being retained. There are now twenty-nine wards for the sick and two day wards, and they appear to have been named on the following plan, viz. : *Kings, Queens, Princes, Kent, York, Cambridge,* after the Royal Family, who have so materially aided the Governors in carrying on the affairs of the Hospital, by affording their patronage from the foundation to the present time. *Winchester, Oxford, Grosvenor, Newcastle, Fitzwilliam, Egremont, Cholmondely, Talbot, Wellington, Rosebery, Belgrave, Pepys, Burton, Drummond, Hope, and Fuller,* being named after Governors who from time to time have taken considerable part in the management of the Hospital, some of them having been Vice-Presidents, but none of these names appear in the list of those who have bequeathed money to the Hospital. *Winchester* was probably after Dr. Richard Willes, Bishop of Winchester, who was the first President, and died soon after he was appointed in 1734. *Oxford* from the second Earl of Oxford, the first Trustee. *Grosvenor* and *Belgrave* from the family to whom all are so much indebted for their liberality by leasing to the Governors a large portion of the land on which the Hospital stands at a nominal rent, the first lease dating back from 1767. *Burton* from Mr. Francis Burton, Treasurer from 1786 to 1806, and who gave £500 towards building the new Hospital. *Fuller,* from Mr. H.P. Fuller, many years a Visiting Apothecary to the Hospital, and to whose exertion the building of the new Hospital was in a great measure due. *Ratcliffe* probably from the Ratcliffe Trustees, who gave £1,000 towards building the new Hospital. Only two wards have been named after any of the Medical Staff of the Hospital and that not until 1870, viz., To Mr.*Hunter* in the new Wing, and *Brodie* a day ward. *Harris, Crayle, Wright, Holland, Hudson and Williams,*

from individuals who bequeathed money to the Hospital, in the aggregate to upwards of £160,000.

A day ward was named after Sir Thomas *Apreece*, whose bequest (after litigation and compromise) exceeded £120,000, the largest legacy as yet received.

Under these circumstances the Committee cannot recommend that any of the present names of wards should be altered, for even indeed if any of the present names were removed to make room for the names of those who may have recently left money to the Hospital, there would be seven individuals who have bequeathed (in sums not less than £5,000), £65,000, who have not as yet had their names connected with any ward. Since the Committee was appointed notice has been received of a legacy of £10,000.

The Committee are of the opinion that where a considerable sum is bequeathed, say from £1,000 and upwards, that a more lasting memorial than is the custom at present should be made of benefactors by having the name placed in some part of the Hospital, and as it would be from want of space manifestly impossible to place such a list in the Board Room, the Committee suggest that such notification should be placed in the corridor at the entrance to the Chapel.

It is pure chance that such a similar position was chosen in the new St. George's Hospital at Tooting to display the old endowment and legacy plaques from Hyde Park Corner. Of all the names on the list it is interesting to note that only two members of the medical staff, both surgeons, were deemed to have made sufficient contribution to the hospital to justify a ward being named after them; although by 1876 no less that ten St. George's surgeons had been Sergeant Surgeons, and both physicians and surgeons had been giving their services on an honorary basis, but their professional eminence and service to the hospital was ignored.

Eventually the second name of the double wards was dropped so Newcastle, Cambridge, Egremont, Talbot, Pepys, and Kent disappeared, and after 1876 only minor changes were made to the ward names at St. George's Hospital at Hyde Park Corner. In 1885 Kings ward was renamed *William King* ward in response to the terms of the will of William King, who bequeathed the hospital £100,000, and in 1889 York ward was renamed *McCalmont*, after Hugh McCalmont of 9 Grosvenor Place, Hyde Park who also left the hospital a legacy of £100,000. In 1901, out of respect to the life and reign of Queen Victoria,

Queens formerly Queens and Pepys was renamed *Queen Victoria*. After Mrs M. A. Curwen left £40,000 to St. George's in 1923 on condition that 'it be used for the maintenance of a ward to be known as *Ewing*, 'Princes' ward was renamed to meet Mrs Curwen's wishes; and in 1935 *Marie Tempest* replaced the name Belgrave, to mark the generous donation received from this popular actress.

The closure of the day wards led to the disappearance of the name 'Apreece', one of the hospital's greatest benefactors, and 'Brodie', after the surgeon, whose name was eventually transferred to the Atkinson Morley's Hospital along with the name 'Kent'. The name of Brodie is used in the new St. George's Hospital. Burton and Cholmondely wards were later converted into the X-Ray department and the North Operating Theatre. The paediatric beds were transferred to the Victoria Hospital for Children in the late forties, but the name Rosebery was retained for the clinical classroom which then occupied the ward area. Otherwise the names of the hospital remained unchanged until the hospital closed in 1980.

The designation of the Grove Fever Hospital in Tooting to St. George's Hospital in 1953, five years after the introduction of the National Health Service, gave the medical staff an opportunity to influence the choice of names for the newly acquired wards as the Board of Governors had now assumed different responsibilities and objectives. A few old names were reintroduced: such as *Caroline,* after the old Queen's ward, *Rosebery,* and *Belgrave.* Apart from *Lanesborough,* after the name of the house in which St. George's Hospital was first founded and *Princess Louise,* after HRH Princess Louise, the ever helpful Patroness of the Victoria Children's Hospital, the names chosen were those of former distinguished members of the medical staff. These included *Allbutt, Allingham, Amyand, Bence Jones, Bromfield, Buckland, Cheselden, Gray, Gunning, Hewitt, Jenner, Keate, Ogle and Edward Wilson.* The dental ward was named after Sir John *Tomes,* (1815-1895) the dental pioneer and one of the first people to master the art of administering ether anaesthesia, who had no connection with either St. George's or the Royal Dental Hospital. Apart from Tomes the only other name not to be carried forward into the new buildings at Tooting was that of poor William Bromfield, who was a Surgeon to St. George's from 1744 until 1780, and whose son, Charles was Assistant Surgeon from 1778 until 1780. Bromfield had been a much respected surgeon who was also elected to the distinguished post of Anatomical Demonstrator to the Company of Surgeons in 1744, when Cheselden was its Warden. It is recorded that Bromfield covered the complete course of anatomy and surgery in just thirty-six lectures, and these were delivered to a full house, unlike William Hunter's lectures. The latter found to his chagrin that he was unable to compete with David Garrick's performance in another type of theatre, and, as a result, was forced to alter the time of his presentations to the afternoon, so he did not clash with the great actor! This suggests that the students were gaining a wide exposure to the humanities. Bromfield was one of the great teachers of his day, and his omission from the list of ward names at the present St. George's Hospital serves to demonstrate the vagaries of fashion and fortune in the selection of names. Some individuals in the present crop of names would have difficulty in being classed in the same rank, let alone be able to bear comparison with many of their predecessors and contemporaries whose names have been forgotten. Present and future generations should be aware that St. George's Hospital and its Medical School owe just as much, if not more, to those unsung heroes whose names have been omitted as to those now in vogue.

As the new St. George's Hospital contains so many new names we feel that short guide outlining the connections may prove both instructive and interesting for those curious enough to wonder who was thus commemorated,

As a matter of interest only three names survived the entire period that the hospital was situated at Hyde Park Corner, and these were: Oxford, Winchester and Ratcliffe. The only names which had been used at sometime in the old hospital to transfer to Tooting were: McCalmont, Harris, Drummond and Wright. Purists will say that there was a Hope ward in both establishments; in fact this is true, although two different Hopes were involved. The one at Hyde Park Corner was named in 1829 after a governor of the hospital and not James Hope, the cardiologist, who was not appointed to St. George's Hospital until 1834 but whose name is now given to one of the cardiac wards at Tooting.

3

The Present and Recent Names of the Wards and Buildings of St. George's Hospital

ADDISON WARD

Thomas Addison, MD

Thomas Addison, whose name will always be associated with the destructive disease of the adrenal gland which he described in 1855, never actually worked at St. George's Hospital, but was registered as a pupil for one year under Sir Everard Home, John Hunter's brother in law.

Addison was born in 1793 at Long Benton near Newcastle where his father was a grocer and flour dealer. He received his early education at a small school run by John Rutter, a parish clerk, who later taught the son of George Stephenson. Addison then attended a grammar school in Newcastle before entering Edinburgh University where he studied medicine, and from this school he obtained his Doctorate in Medicine in 1815. Soon after he qualified he moved to London and enrolled as a pupil at St. George's but shortly afterwards he was appointed house surgeon to the Lock Hospital in Southwark. This was one of several Lock hospitals which were originally established to care for cases of leprosy.

As the incidence of leprosy gradually declined, the Lock hospitals were used to treat the increasing number of cases of venereal disease – it was thought that the name 'Lock' originated probably from the fact that outside the hospitals were baskets of rags for the lepers to wipe their filthy sores. The rags were originally called *les locques* (French for 'rags') but this was changed to *les locks* and later the word was used for the buildings themselves. Less likely is that the hospitals were all situated outside the boundaries or turnpikes leading into the towns, hence the patients were in a sense 'locked out'. Leper hospitals were also sometimes known as Lazar Houses because many of them were founded and administered by the Order of St. Lazurus of Jerusalem, which was a branch of the Knights of St. John of Jerusalem. The Order's main house was at Burton Lazars in Leicestershire. A Lock Hospital was founded in 1746 close to St. George's Hospital at the junction of Chapel Street and Grosvenor Place. Whilst he was working at the Lock Hospital, Addison enrolled under Dr. Bateman at the Public Infirmary, where he was taught the diagnosis and treatment of skin diseases, some of which he described for the first time and which bear his name.

In 1819 Addison became a Licentiate of the Royal College of Physicians, from which college he received a Fellowship in 1838. Armed with his licentiate Addison entered Guy's Hospital in 1820 as a pupil, and for the rest of his life he was associated with the hospital as a physician.

His successive appointments included: Assistant Physician in 1824, Lecturer in Materia Medica at the Aldersgate School of Medicine in 1827, and then full Physician in 1837, and thereafter he worked in association with Dr. Richard Bright (1789-1858), also of renal fame who described chronic nephritis which became known as Bright's disease, for almost twenty years. The pair of them ran a lecture course in medicine which became internationally famous. Addison was a brilliant diagnostician, but his reputation suffered by being considered brusque with patients and apparently unconcerned with the niceties of treatment; for the latter, in retrospect, we may judge him less harshly, given its unpalatable nature and frightful results. Thomas Addison was also Consulting Physician to the South London Dispensary and President of the Royal Medical and Chirurgical Society. His career was dogged by recurring attacks of severe depression which he feared dreadfully, and it was these that eventually forced him to retire. It was during one of these attacks that he jumped out of a window in Brighton, and sustained head injuries which led to his death in 1860. He was buried in Lanercost Abbey, near Brampton, Cumbria alongside close members of his family.

Addison's eponymous association with suprarenal disease has insured that his name lives on as the founding father of modern endocrinology. It was not all plain sailing, however, and his ideas cut little ice with the British medical establishment initially. It took a Frenchman, Trousseau, to recognise the significance of the discovery and give it Addison's name. Many other substantial contributions to medicine and medical education were made by Addison, as he wrote widely on subjects as diverse as the anatomy of the lung and the role of the airsacs in pneumonia, poisons, female disorders, and dermatological conditions.

Not only Guy's Hospital and Medical School are conscious of the debt they owe to the talents and industry of Thomas Addison, but also the wider world of medicine in general has benefitted from his contributions, so it is entirely appropriate that the Renal Medicine Unit at St. George's Hospital should bear the name of one of the hospital's most illustrious former pupils.

ALLINGHAM WARD

Herbert William Allingham, FRCS
1904 was a very sad year for St. George's Hospital, as two of its most promising young consultants: Herbert Allingham, the surgeon and Lee Dickinson, the physician, both died in tragic circumstances at the early age of 42.

Herbert William Allingham was the eldest son of William Allingham. The latter had qualified and practised as an architect before entering St. Thomas's Hospital as a student. After qualifying in 1855 William volunteered for service as a surgeon in the Crimea, where he was present at the siege of Sebastopol, before being posted to Scutari, where he worked in several hospitals. After returning to England he worked for a short period as a surgical registrar at St. Thomas's Hospital, before first setting up in practice in Finsbury Square, and then in Grosvenor Street. Herbert William was born in 1862. William specialised in diseases of the large bowel, and although he never worked at a teaching hospital, he was on the staff of the Great Northern & Central and St. Mark's Hospitals, and wrote *Diseases of the Rectum* which was in its day regarded as the definitive work on this subject.

Herbert William was educated at Chatham House, Ramsgate, and University College School in London, where he did not distinguish himself, but nevertheless he was determined to follow in his father's footsteps and train to become a surgeon. Allingham entered St. George's Hospital as a student in 1879 where he was taught by Pickering Pick, Timothy Holmes, Thomas Whipham and William Howship Dickinson. The young Allingham was quickly recognised as an outstanding medical student, so that after qualification in 1883 he had no difficulty in being appointed to the post of house surgeon. In the following year he was made a surgical registrar, and became the demonstrator in anatomy. Having obtained his Fellowship of the Royal College of Surgeons, he was appointed Assistant Surgeon to St. Mark's Hospital in 1885, and then Surgeon to the Great Northern Hospital (now the Royal Northern) in 1887, both of which were appointments which his father had held some years earlier. Herbert Allingham was then elected Assistant Surgeon to St. George's Hospital in 1894, and took rooms in Grosvenor Street where he consulted in private practice.

Allingham's skill as a surgeon became increasingly recognised, so much so that he was appointed Surgeon to the Household of King Edward VII, and then Surgeon in Ordinary to the Prince of Wales, who later became King George V. Sir Humphry Rolleston one of his colleagues remarked 'This success only made Allingham more generous to his juniors'. It seemed that Herbert Allingham was destined to reach the very pinnacle of his profession but, alas, this was not to be.

In 1903 whilst operating on a syphilitic patient Allingham cut himself, and he in turn became inoculated with the dread disease. He became extremely sick and was away from the hospital for over a year, during the course of which he suffered another crushing blow when his German wife, to whom he was devoted, died. As a result poor Allingham developed a severe depressive illness, it was thought that a convalescent holiday in Egypt would restore him to full health, but, unfortunately, whilst in Marseilles awaiting a passage across the Mediterranean he died from an overdose of morphine. St. George's was robbed of one of its brightest stars.

William Lee Dickinson died at his father's home in Tintagel, Cornwall in the same year at the same age of 42 from a catastrophic haemoptysis caused by pulmonary tuberculosis; and to give some support to the belief that 'misfortune always comes in threes', two years later Mr A Marmaduke Shield, another surgeon, cut himself whilst operating on a syphilitic patient, as a consequence of which he suffered such serious damage to his hand that he was obliged to take early retirement.

AMYAND WARD

Claudius Amyand

Of French origins, Claudius Amyand was the second son of Isaac Amyand of Marnac, Xaintonge, and was born in Paris sometime between 1681 and 1686. Although it is known that he was naturalised as a British citizen in London in 1700, nothing is known of Amyand's medical education, although it is possible that because of his strong friendship with Ambrose Dickins he was apprenticed to Claude Bernard. Ambrose Dickins had been born in 1687, and in 1702 was apprenticed to Sergeant-Surgeon Claude Bernard for seven years. So keen an apprentice was he that he married Bernard's daughter in 1710, and on the death of Bernard later in the year he succeeded him as Sergeant-Surgeon to Queen Anne. Dickins was Warden of the Barber Surgeons in 1728, their Master in 1729, and in 1745 when the surgeons cut the suture which bound them to the barbers he was made assistant of the new Surgeons' Company and one of their Examiners. He was Sergeant-Surgeon to Queen Anne, George I and George II until he died in 1747.

Amyand's apprenticeship did not follow the traditional pattern: he fought in the Battle of Blenheim, and, possibly, in the Battle of Oudenarde. In 1715, Amyand was commissioned as Surgeon of Lumley's Horse, the Dragoon Guards, and his commission continued until 1739.

Amyand was elected Fellow of the Royal Society in 1716. During the 1720's Claudius Amyand inoculated the Princesses Caroline and

Amelia against smallpox under the watchful eye of Sir Hans Sloane, the Royal Physician, after Lady Mary Wortley Montagu, a globe-trotting noblewoman had introduced smallpox vaccination to England from Constantinople in 1717. Lady Mary's beauty had been previously marred by the dreaded disease and her nephew and only brother had died from it. Lady Montagu's son and daughter were inoculated in Turkey and she returned to England determined to persuade the medical profession of the benefits.

Claudius Amyand and Ambrose Dickins were appointed Sergeant Surgeons to King George II, but strangely Amyand, despite this appointment, did not become a member of the Barber Surgeons until 1728. Why this delay?. Could this have been due to prejudice against his French ancestry?. If this were the case it seems strange that he held a post in the Royal Household, and had been also a senior surgeon of several years standing at one of the few metropolitan hospitals. It seems more likely that he had fallen foul of a single individual who was for a while able to obstruct his advancement, because once admitted to this body his popularity became evident and progress through the official hierarchy was rapid, as very quickly he became first Warden, and then Master of the Company.

Amyand's career moved in a series of fits and starts, for, before he became a member of the Company of Barber Surgeons, he was appointed as the first Principal Surgeon at the Westminster Infirmary in 1721, where he was later joined by Dickins and Cheselden, and it was these three who performed the majority of the surgery undertaken in that institution.

Claudius Amyand joined the committee set up by the Westminster Infirmary with the remit to choose new premises to replace the Chapel Street building, which was in a dreadful state of repair. Amyand sided with the minority, which included Dickins, Tessier and all the other doctors in suggesting Lanesborough House as being the ideal building for the new hospital. When the Westminster Directors turned down this suggestion, Amyand and all his colleagues resigned, although Amyand and Dickins agreed to continue to attend to patients for a period of time without charge. This did not imply any weakening of their resolve to move, and they continued their alliance with the determined minority who remained united in their desire to occupy the more commodious accommodation available at Lanesborough House, and very soon the lease was signed which led to the creation of a new hospital: St. George's. Amyand and Dickins were two of the original six lessees of Lanesborough House.

Amyand and Dickins were appointed Principal Surgeons to the newly founded St. George's Hospital in 1733, and Cheselden, their colleague from the Westminster, joined them a short time later. The Hospital opened in January 1734, and Amyand, Dickins and Cheselden were quick to establish the good principles and high standards of surgical practice which are maintained to this day at St. George's.

In 1735 Amyand described the first successful appendicectomy which he undertook on a boy named Hanvil Anderson, who was aged 11 at the time. Amyand recorded 'Tis easy to conceive that this operation was as painful to the patient as laborious to me'. The operation lasted half an hour, and however laborious it might have been to Amyand, it must have been a colossal ordeal to poor Hanvil, especially when one realises that the age of general anaesthetics was still over a century away. This operation should have perpetuated Amyand's name in medical history, but, however much it may be regretted, Mestivier in France has been credited by history for the first appendectomy, although Amyand's operation was performed some 22 years earlier.

Claudius Amyand wrote extensively on the surgical cases he treated, and a number of his papers appear in the Transactions of the Royal Society. He was happily married to his wife, Mary, who brought up their nine children: three sons and six daughters. Prosperity attended his successful career, so much so that he acquired a large house in Castle Street and several country estates, but sadly he did not live to a great age to derive maximum enjoyment from them, as he died suddenly at the age of 55, following a fall in Greenwich Park.

BAILLIE WARD

Matthew Baillie, MD, FRS
Matthew Baillie was yet another doctor associated with St. George's Hospital who left his native Scotland to find fame and fortune in London.

Matthew Baillie was the son of James Baillie, a parish minister, who became Professor of Divinity in Glasgow, and Dorothea, the sister of William and John Hunter. James and Dorothea had a daughter, Joanna, who became a poetess, whereas Matthew followed a more conventional path in the steps of his uncles to a career in London medicine. Baillie was born in Shots, Lanarkshire in 1761, and was educated in Hamilton, first at the English School, then from the age of seven he attended the Latin School under Mr. Whale. At the age of thirteen Baillie entered Glasgow University where he read Greek and Latin. Aged eighteen Baillie was persuaded by William Hunter to leave Glasgow and come south to study medicine. He entered Balliol College, Oxford, and continued reading the classics and mathematics but it was natural that during his vacations he stayed with his uncle, William, at his Anatomy School in Windmill Street, where he attended lectures as well as being the recipient of private tutorials.

Matthew was the apple of William's eye, and every moment they spent together was used by the older man to impart his knowledge and love of medicine to his nephew. After William Hunter's death in 1783 Baillie, having obtained his BA at Oxford, enrolled as a perpetual student at St. George's where he was a pupil of his uncle John for one year. When William Hunter died, he had left Matthew as his sole heir. Matthew's inheritance included William's house and School of Anatomy in Windmill Street, the family estate in Long Calderwood, Scotland, and five thousand pounds. Matthew felt that John Hunter was entitled to the family estate, and made it over to him, but he retained the Windmill Street property, and began to lecture there shortly after William Hunter's death sometime before he had qualified. Baillie shared the lecturing with William Cruickshank FRS (1745-1800)[1] with whom

---

[1] William Cumberland Cruickshank was born in Edinburgh in 1745 and educated at both Edinburgh and Glasgow Universities obtaining an MA in Glasgow before coming to London to assist William Hunter in Windmill Street. Cruickshank was highly thought of as a lecturer in anatomy and as a surgeon. Living at 40 Leicester Square, he was a Member of the Corporation of Surgeons, a Fellow of the Royal Society and attended Samuel Johnson in his last illness. His old University later conferred upon him an honorary MD, but sadly he died of apoplexy in 1800 at the relatively early age of 55.

he also shared the profits which amounted to a little over £750 in the first year. Baillie continued at the School of Anatomy until 1799.

In 1786 Baillie passed his BM and was appointed Physician to St. George's Hospital. In 1789 he was awarded his MD and in the following year he became a Fellow of the Royal College of Physicians in 1790, and a Fellow of the Royal Society in 1792. Fortune smiled on Matthew Baillie throughout his medical career. William Hunter's patronage had given his career a flying start, and, after his marriage to Sophia, the sister of Lord Denman, the Lord Chief Justice, and youngest daughter of Dr. Thomas Denman (1733-1815), the Obstetrician to the Middlesex Hospital, he was referred many patients by his father-in-law, which enabled him to build up a large and prosperous practice. To cap it all Baillie, in 1798, took over the practice of Dr. David Pitcairn MD FRCP FRS (1749-1809), his close friend who was a Physician to St. Bartholomew's Hospital.

On October 23rd 1793 Matthew Baillie was present at that fateful meeting in the St. George's Boardroom when John Hunter in arguing with John Gunning, William Walker and Robert Keate, suffered a fatal coronary thrombosis. The delightful water colour painted by Arthur David McCormick in 1901 for Clinton Dent, the surgeon, which hangs in the Boardroom of the present hospital, shows Matthew Baillie and James Robertson Barclay MD FRCP (1756-1817) standing on the hospital steps watching the sedan chair bearing Hunter's Body being carried to the coach, where Everard Home, Hunter's brother in law, directs the coachman to Hunter's house at 28 Leicester Square.

By 1800 he was so busy in practice that he was obliged to resign his post at St. George's Hospital. He was one of the leading physicians in London, and it is reputed that he sometimes made as much as ten thousand pounds a year, which would at just 1.5% inflation be worth over £185,000 today. Baillie's reputation as physician was such that he was appointed Physician Extraordinary to King George III, and, together with Heberden and Halford, he tried, but unfortunately failed, to wrest the management of the King's recurring illness from Dr. Willis and place it on a more humane basis. He was, like Heberden, offered a baronetcy but he refused to accept it. Later Baillie was appointed physician to Princess Charlotte, but he also attended other members of the Royal Family including HRH Caroline, the Princess of Wales and HRH Princess Sophia. Other patients who sought Baillie's opinion included Lord Byron, William Pitt, Sir Walter Scott and Richard Brinsley Sheridan.

One of the lessons this book illustrates over and over again is that a great reputation and an income to match may be achieved only at a formidably high price. Those who spend their time restoring it ignore the frailty of the human frame at their peril. Baillie worked tremendously long hours, sometimes as many as sixteen a day, and, as a consequence his health suffered. He eventually fell victim to tuberculosis and spent more time at his country house in Duntisburne where he enjoyed the company of Edward Jenner. Baillie never recovered from the tuberculosis and died in 1823, at his country house, and was buried in the parish of Duntisburne Abbots, Gloucestershire. He is commemorated in Westminster Abbey along with his uncles William and John Hunter, and Thomas Young.

Matthew Baillie in some ways was like his uncle John, and could be fiery and irascible, but differed from him in that he turned his back on scientific and academic research, despite having the intellectual equipment with which to conduct it, in favour of making a fortune. He will be remembered by posterity for his *Morbid Anatomy of some of the most important Parts of the Human Body* which was published in 1795, just a year before he was appointed to St. George's Hospital. It was the first book to treat morbid anatomy as a separate subject. The majority of the anatomical descriptions in the book were an account of his own dissections, but a few may be attributed to Morgagni and the Hunter brothers. A major omission was any account of diseases of muscles, the central nervous system and the skeleton. Nevertheless, he was the first to define cirrhosis of the liver, distinguish between infective and other cysts of the liver, and to describe the appearances of a gastric ulcer. Baillie's book was a huge success, and it was translated into most European languages. Five editions were published during the course of Baillie's lifetime; and the book still remains a classic for the accurate depiction of morbid pathological change. In 1822 he published a short paper on *Observations on Paraplegia* which gave some account of the effect of disease on the nervous system, but it was not in any way as detailed as

33

his earlier book, which, as a matter of interest, he had dedicated to Dr. David Pitcairn, whose practice he was to take over. He also wrote a short essay on *Pulsation of the Aorta in the Epigastrium*, and showed that it was rarely associated with any internal structural change.

Matthew Baillie left his collection of specimens, books and drawings to the Royal College of Physicians. The famous gold-headed cane that had previously belonged to John Radcliffe, and which had been passed down through Drs. Mead, Askew and William Pitcairn, who handed it on to David Pitcairn, who left it in turn to Baillie, was given to the College by his widow, Sophia.

Dr. Alastair Hunter (1909-1987), physician to St. George's (1947-1974) and Dean of the Medical School (1956-1971) was a direct descendant of Matthew Baillie. A portrait of Matthew Baillie from the school of John Edmund Hoppner RA (1758-1810) hangs in the hospital at Tooting.

BARNES WARD

Robert Barnes, MD, FRCP, FRCS (Hon)

Robert Barnes was born in Norwich in 1817, and educated partly at home, and partly in Bruges. His father was an architect and one of the founding members of the Royal Botanical Society, as well as being the founder of the Botanic Garden in Regent's Park.

At the age of fifteen Robert Barnes was articled to Dr. Richard Griffin, a Norwich practitioner, but when the family moved to London he came with them and continued his medical studies in the capital; attending first University College Hospital and then the Great Windmill Street School before he entered St. George's Hospital. He qualified MRCS in 1842 and then spent a year in Paris before settling down in practice in Notting Hill. Whilst working in Notting Hill Barnes became a lecturer in Forensic Medicine at Dermott's, one of the many private medical schools. He was awarded his MD in 1848 and elected a Fellow of the Royal College of Physicians in 1857. Soon, he was appointed Obstetric Physician at the London Hospital, and then to a similar post at St. Thomas' Hospital. In 1874 he was elected Obstetric Physician at St. George's Hospital.

Although Robert Barnes was a leader in the field of gynaecology he did not possess the Fellowship of the Royal College of Surgeons, nevertheless the Governors of St. George's allowed him to operate at the hospital, and he became a great exponent of ovariotomy which was regarded as a complicated technical procedure. Barnes was given his own small operating theatre, which was in a side room off Apreece ward. It is not clear at this remove whether this arrangement was dictated by a sense of decency, or whether, lacking a Fellowship, he was considered unfit to play in the major league. Whatever the reason this curious precedent rapidly became enshrined in tradition, and gynaecology retained its own small operating theatre at St. George's up to the time of the Second World War. Barnes was a prolific writer of articles on obstetrics and gynaecology, and his abilities as an operator came to be recognised by the Royal College of Surgeon, who awarded him an Honorary Fellowship in 1883. Robert Barnes was not always infallible as a diagnostician. On one occasion he sent a young lady for two to three weeks convalescence at the Atkinson Morley's Hospital, where, on arrival, she promptly gave birth to a baby. The Governors immediately required Barnes to give an explanation as to why a pregnant woman was sent for convalescence. His answer was that at the time she was seen he did not know whether her distended abdomen was due to a tumour or mere pregnancy and he thought a short period of convalescence would help to decide matters one way or the other, which certainly turned out to be true. This pragmatic approach did not save Barnes from getting a stern rebuke from the Governors.

Barnes retired from St. George's in 1883 but maintained his interest in the hospital. In 1905, the Centenary Year of the Royal Medical and Chirurgical Society, he was elected an Honorary Fellow. In retirement he lived in Eastbourne where in his words he was able 'never to lose an opportunity to take a dip' in the sea, as he explained: 'some of his most pleasant memories were associated with water'; and after swimming he loved the 'rubbing and drying with a coarse towel' as he felt 'the friction was equivalent to a massage'. It would appear that he genuinely enjoyed bathing. He wrote on one occasion 'At Eastbourne some swimmers dive off the end of the pier; on coming out they receive a shower bath of fresh water. I have no direct experience of this practice and give no opinion about it. At the bathing places on the French coast it is customary to supply a bucket of warm fresh water for the feet . This is certainly a luxury by restoring warmth after the chill resulting from the long paddling prevalent in these places'. And, one would have thought, a certain recipe for chilblains in those disposed to this condition. Swimming was one of his great pastimes and Robert Barnes was obviously a close observer of other swimmers and their foibles.

In recognition of Barnes' services to St. George's a Robert Barnes Laboratory of Pathology was opened at the hospital, at the time of his death in 1907. When St. George's moved to Tooting the name Barnes disappeared for a while, but fortunately it was re-introduced a few years ago when another obstetric ward was opened, so it is now associated with the speciality of which he was one of the great pioneers.

BELGRAVE WARD

Belgrave
When Sir Richard Grosvenor who had been created Earl of Grosvenor by William Pitt in 1754 was given a Viscountcy only a few weeks later, he chose the title of Viscount Belgrave, after the name of a hamlet near his country seat, Eaton, in Cheshire. Henry Lupus Grosvenor, the fourth Viscount, who was to be elevated to the Dukedom of Westminster by Queen Victoria, served as the Treasurer of St. George's Hospital from 1873 to 1899, and it was through his good offices that the Board of Governors were able to lease another strip of land from the Grosvenor Estates, to build an additional wing to create the extra space between the patients' beds as requested by Florence Nightingale, who had been made an Honorary Governor of St. George's in recognition of her pioneering work in the Crimean War.

The Duke of Westminster's generosity was acknowledged when one of the three wards in the new block was named Belgrave when it was opened in 1867.

Nearly seventy years later, in 1935 Dame Marie Tempest (1864-1942) who was born Mary Etherington and acknowledged as one of the greatest stars of the stage in her day offered to put on a matinee performance at the Theatre Royal, Drury Lane, to mark her fifty years as an actress and singer, with the aim of raising money to fund a Marie Tempest ward for actors and actresses at St. George's Hospital. With no hesitation the Board of Governors gratefully accepted the wonderful offer, and, in the presence of King George V and Queen Mary, Dame Marie Tempest in the company of a galaxy of West End stars which included John Gielgud, Yvonne Arnaud, Gladys Cooper, Robert Donat, Gladys Cooper, Hermione Baddeley, Markova, Ivor Novello, Mary Ellis, Evelyn Laye and George Robey put on a sparkling performance to raise over £5000 to found the ward. Lords Greville and Winchilsea, the treasurers of the hospital accepted the proceeds of the matinee from Dame Marie Tempest, and, in return, gave her the deeds of the ward at the end of the performance.

Lord Greville whose name has been sadly forgotten at St. George's served the hospital loyally and with distinction for over forty years having been appointed Chairman of the Board of Governors in 1914 and relinquished the office on the introduction of the National Health Service in 1948. Charles Beresford Fulke Greville, the third baron, the second son of the second Lord Greville of Clonyn and Violet, the second daughter of the fourth Duke of Montrose was born in 1871. From 1892 until 1893 he served as ADC to the Lord Lieutenant of Ireland before becoming a Captain in the 7th. Hussars from 1898 to 1905 during which time he was ADC to the Governor General of Bombay from 1900 to 1904 and then ADC to Lord Northcote, the Governor of Australia from 1904 until 1908. In 1901 he succeeded to the title of Baron Greville, as his elder brother had died following an operation for cancer of the throat, and in 1909 he married Olive, the widow of Henry Kerr of New York, and daughter of J. W. Grace of Leybourne, Kent, at St. Paul's, Knightsbridge. Soon after being elected Chairman of the Board of Governors, Greville took temporary leave of absence to serve first as a major in the Lovat Scouts, when he was mentioned in despatches, next in the Reserve Cavalry, and finally in the General Staff Office. In 1919 he returned to St. George's where he skilfully guided the further development of St. George's at Hyde Park Corner, and was most influential in gaining unanimous agreement for the rebuilding of the hospital in outer London. Once again St. George's has ignored the achievements of one of its outstanding servants. Lord Greville died in 1952.

The Earl of Winchilsea and Nottingham (14 th. Earl of Winchilsea and 9th Earl of Nottingham) was another loyal supporter of St. George's who gave his time and energy freely for the benefit of patients and staff from the time he was elected Treasurer in 1922, when he was then Viscount Maidstone, until his death in 1939. Guy Montague George Finch-Hatton was born in 1885, and educated at Eton and Magdalen College, Oxford, and became Viscount Maidstone in 1898. In 1908 he was commissioned as a Lieutenant in the Royal East Kent Yeomanry. After marrying Margaretta Armstrong, the daughter of Anthony Drexel of Grosvenor Square, and Baltimore, USA, in 1910, Maidstone served in Flanders and France in the first World War, firstly as a Lieutenant Commander in the RNVR in charge of the siege guns, and then as a Lieutenant Colonel in the Royal Flying Corps, thus achieving the distinction of serving in all three of the armed services. He was awarded the Distinguished Service Cross, the Croix de Guerre and the OBE. After the Great War he became a member of the stock exchange before being elected Treasurer to St. George's Hospital in 1922. Winchilsea, who was the hereditary lord of the Royal Manor of Wye, was the great grandson of 12th Earl who in 1829 disagreed ferociously with the Duke of Wellington, then Prime Minister, and Robert Peel, over their proposed emancipation of Ireland in an attempt to avert civil war. Winchilsea accused the duke of introducing 'popery into every department of the state'. The 'Iron Duke' challenged Winchilsea to a duel in Battersea Fields. The challenge was accepted but when the two met, the Duke fired wide and Winchilsea fired into the air and promptly apologised for his intemperate language. Philip Guedalla in his biography of the Duke of Wellington described the 12th. Earl of Winchilsea as 'an unimportant peer distinguished by a loud voice, a mannerism of flourishing a large white handkerchief when making speeches and the *abandon* of his Protestant invective'. Winchilsea's great grandson was the complete opposite: quiet, unassuming, patient, courteous, sympathetic and kind to the staff of St. George's, and always striving to do his best for the hospital. Sadly, he died in 1939 at the relatively early age of 53.

After Marie Tempest's magnificent performance which raised over £6,000 Greville and Winchilsea persuaded the Board of Governors to rename Belgrave ward as the Marie Tempest ward for actors and actresses. The small cost of refurbishing the ward was more than handsomely covered by the matinee proceeds, so the remainder of the donation was placed in the Dame Marie Tempest Endowment Fund, which was to be used for the upkeep of the ward. The ward was not used to full effect by the theatrical fraternity, so, with Marie Tempest's permission, when beds were not required for their intended purpose, they could be used by private patients. Naturally the medical staff were delighted and made full use of the ward. Regrettably, on one occasion Marie Tempest wished for an actress friend of hers to be admitted, but no bed was available – they were all occupied by private patients! The governors resolved that in future at least one bed must always be kept vacant, to avoid a repetition of this embarrassing situation.

Herbert Wilcox, the film producer and wife of Dame Anna Neagle, the actress hoped to raise sufficient funds to provide a room for use by members of the film business. A premiere performance of his film *Our Fighting Navy* starring Robert Douglas was held at 'The Plaza', Haymarket, and the proceeds were given to the hospital but proved insufficient to endow a bed. Later a concert was held at St. Martin's in the Fields to raise money to endow a bed for musicians, in memory of Harry Plunkett Greene, a singer and son-in-law of Sir Hubert Parry. The Plunkett Greene Fund was supported by Sir Adrian Boult, Sir Henry Walford Davies and the Archbishop of Canterbury. Over £2,000 was raised and it was agreed that if the hospital was rebuilt there would be a Harry Plunkett Greene bed, but of course, the subsequent introduction of the National Health Service changed everything.

Interestingly, the Marie Tempest ward was used as a recording studio in 1938 when Turner Layton, the music hall artist, formerly of Layton and Johnstone lying in bed with a broken leg recorded *Thanks for the Memory* and *Tears in my Heart* for Columbia Records. St. George's were given a special royalty for the records sold. In the same year, a Christmas Party on the Children's ward was televised. This was the first time that a TV programme was beamed by the BBC from a hospital. Several well known names took part including Freddie Grisewood, Margaretta Scott and Derek McCulloch (Uncle Mac), but to the delight of the children the star attraction were the seven clowns from Bertram Mills's circus who performed acrobatics in the small ward.

In 1948, the Dame Marie Tempest Endowment Fund, along with the Atkinson Morley and the Samaritan Funds, were amalgamated in the general endowment fund by the new Board of Governors appointed by Aneurin Bevan, the Minister of Health. The Marie Tempest ward continued to be used by private patients at Hyde Park Corner until the closure of the hospital in 1980.

In 1953, Belgrave was one of the very first names chosen by the Board of Governors of St. George's for a ward in the recently designated Grove Fever Hospital.

BENCE JONES WARD

Henry Bence Jones, MA, MD, FRCP, FRS
The name Bence Jones, associated with the word 'protein' became one of the most familiar eponyms to generations of medical students, and many may have thought with some justification that his reputation rested solely on this discovery. In fact Bence Jones was so little impressed with the discovery of the protein that he did not bother to mention it even in his autobiography, nor was it referred to in the *Lancet*, or the *Medical Times and Gazette*, when he died. Such an omission might well have been deliberate as Bence Jones should be remembered as one of the leading physicians and celebrated chemists of his generation. Indeed Florence Nightingale described Henry Bence Jones as the 'best chemical doctor in London'.

Bence Jones was born in 1814 at Thorington Hall in Suffolk, the son of William Jones, a Lieutenant Colonel in the 5th. Dragoon Guards, and Matilda, the daughter of Bence Bence, the rector of Beccles. Henry Jones took his second forename from his mother's family (who seemed keen to use it), and, in time, plain Henry Jones became better known as the rather more distinguished Henry Bence Jones. He was educated at Harrow, and Trinity College, Cambridge, where he rowed for the college eight. He entered St. George's in 1836, first as an apprentice to the Apothecary, then as a medical pupil. All pupils in those days had to attend private schools for their anatomy teaching, and the Royal Institution for chemistry lectures. At the Royal Institution Bence Jones was given lectures by Michael Faraday (1791-1867), who had been appointed Professor of Chemistry there in 1833, in succession to Sir Humphry Davy. Bence Jones was to write a biography of Faraday in 1870. Bence Jones also enrolled at University College to work in the laboratory of Thomas Graham (1805-1869), the Professor of Chemistry, who was one of the founders of physical chemistry, and it was from him that Bence Jones learned his colloid chemistry. In 1841 Bence Jones travelled to Giessen in Germany where he worked for several months with Baron Justus von Liebig (1803-1873), the Professor of Chemistry, and one of the most illustrious chemists of his generation. On returning to England, Bence Jones obtained a Licentiate of the Royal College of Surgeons in 1842, and became a Bachelor of Medicine in 1845.

In 1845 Bence Jones was appointed Assistant Physician to St. George's Hospital. In the same year because of his reputation as an outstanding chemist he was asked by Drs. MacIntyre and Watson to help them in the diagnosis of a 45 year old man who was suffering from bone pains. On heat testing the urine he observed a strange phenomenon, with this Bence Jones had identified the myeloma protein which he was to describe later, thus he was credited with the discovery of the definitive test for the diagnosis of the newly recognised disease, myeloma.

Henry Bence Jones was appointed Physician to St. George's Hospital in 1846, and was awarded his MD in 1849. His reputation as a physician grew rapidly with the publication of some thirty scientific papers including *Animal Chemistry in its Application to Stomach and Renal Diseases* (1850), *Gravel, Calculus and Gout* (1842), *The Chemistry of Urine* (1857) and *Lectures on the Application of Chemistry and Mechanics to Pathology and Therapeutics* (1870). Bence Jones was elected to the a Fellowship of the Royal College of Physicians and to the Fellowship of the Royal Society in 1845. Soon Bence Jones had established through his boundless energy and enthusiasm, a large private practice and a wide circle of illustrious friends which included: Charles Darwin, Thomas Huxley the biologist and physician, John Tyndall the Irish physicist, Benjamin Disraeli, Prince Albert and Hermann von Helmholtz the physiologist and physicist. Bence Jones was not always popular with his colleagues because of his strong determination, his hastiness and his unwillingness to concede when he was wrong. Nevertheless he was one of St. George's finest physicians – a gifted clinician and eminent scientist, who was one of the founders of true scientific medicine.

Bence Jones became Secretary of the Royal Society, and the Royal Institution, a Censor of the Royal College of Physicians, and served on the Royal Commission set up to investigate the cattle plague of 1865. He was a great supporter of the Hospital for Sick Children, Great Ormond Street, and campaigned for the foundation of a College of Chemistry.

Henry Bence Jones retired as a Physician to St. George's in 1862, but was appointed Consulting Physician to the hospital in 1868, a post he occupied until his death in Brook Street, London in 1873.

BISHOP WARD

Isabella Russell Bishop, MB, ChB, FRCOG
Isabella Bishop was born in Scotland in 1912 and qualified from Edinburgh University Medical School in 1937. After appointments at Redlands and the Elsie Inglis hospitals, Miss Bishop decided that she wished to specialise in obstetrics and gynaecology, so she took up an appointment at St. Chad's in Birmingham in 1939. In 1940 she migrated even further south to occupy firstly, a junior appointment at Ilford Maternity Hospital, and then a registrar post at the Samaritan Hospital for Women in central London.

In 1943 Isabella Bishop anxious to gain further experience applied for, and was appointed to, a registrar post at St. James' Hospital, Balham, thus beginning a lifelong association with that hospital. Miss Bishop, as she was always addressed by her colleagues but popularly known as 'Izzy', was appointed Consultant in Obstetrics and Gynaecology to St. James' Hospital and the Weir Maternity Hospital in 1948. After the closure of the Weir Hospital Miss Bishop continued her consultancy at St. James' until her retirement in 1977.

Miss Bishop did not seek the limelight and she was content not to strive for national or international honours, but she was deeply respected in her time and place. As an index of this regard she was an examiner for the Diploma and the Membership examinations of the Royal College of Obstetricians and Gynaecologists, as well as for the Central Midwives' Board. She was a popular member of the Medical Women's Federation and the Women's Gynaecological Visiting Club. 'Izzy' Bishop was a good teacher who expected others to share her enthusiasm for providing a service of the highest standard. She found laziness or incompetence intolerable, and the guilty came in for very sharp rebukes from her.

Outside medicine Miss Bishop had a serious interest in the countryside, and was an extremely active member of the Royal Horticultural Society, the National Trust in Scotland and the Royal Society for the Protection of Birds. She also shared a deep love of classical Greece and Rome with Mr. Jeremiah Burke, her surgical colleague and long-time friend at St. James' Hospital. The two enjoyed many holidays exploring Italy, Greece, Spain and France together.

BRODIE WARD

Sir Benjamin Collins Brodie, Bart. PRCS, FRS
Brodie was born in 1783 in Winterslow, Wiltshire, the son of Peter Brodie, the local rector, and Sarah, whose father, Benjamin Collins, was a banker and printer in Milford, close to Salisbury, and (sensibly) was given his maternal grandfather's names. The Brodies, who hailed from Scotland, were related by marriage to Thomas Denman, the obstetrician, and Matthew Baillie, the St. George's physician and nephew of William and John Hunter.

Benjamin Brodie was privately educated by his father, and at the age of eighteen he travelled to London to study medicine. From 1801 to 1802 he attended the anatomy lectures at Great Windmill Street given by James Arthur Wilson, who was nicknamed 'Maxilla' on account of his initials, with whom Brodie later quarrelled. In 1803 Brodie became a pupil of Sir Everard Home at St. George's Hospital, and qualified as a member of the College of Surgeons in 1805. He was then appointed a house surgeon, and demonstrator in the Anatomy School. He combined these posts with assisting Sir Everard Home in private practice, as well as helping him at the College Museum. In 1808, and not quite twenty five years of age, Brodie was appointed Assistant Surgeon to St. George's Hospital, but he did not forsake his interest in anatomical dissection, and continued to demonstrate and lecture with 'Maxilla' Wilson at Great Windmill Street until 1812.

In 1810 Brodie was elected a Fellow of the Royal Society, where he soon gave two papers: *On the Influence of the Brain on the Action of the Heart and the Generation of Animal Heat*; and *On the Effects produced by certain Vegetable Poisons (Alcohol, Tobacco, Woorara)* which earned him the Copley Medal in 1811, an honour never before awarded to one so young. The world was at Brodie's feet; in 1819 he was appointed Professor of Anatomy, Physiology and Surgery at the Royal College of Surgeons, and in 1822 he was elected Surgeon to St. George's, by which time he was having a profound influence on the development of surgery and medical education.

At St. George's Hospital Brodie used his influence to direct events to his own advantage. By this time Brodie and James Wilson, who was now a physician at Hyde Park Corner, disliked each other intensely, the reason behind this was rumoured to have arisen from some pecuniary dispute between Brodie and Wilson's father. Their animosity for each other came to a head in 1834 when a vacancy occurred for the post of a second Assistant Surgeon. James Wilson supported Samuel Armstrong Lane for the post. Lane had trained at St. George's and was running a private anatomy school in Grosvenor Place called 'The School of Anatomy and Medicine adjoining St. George's Hospital' but was ambitious to become a surgeon at St. George's. Lane was an admirable candidate for the vacancy, but because he was supported by Wilson, Brodie decided that he could not vote for him, and would back Edward Cutler instead, a less impressive candidate. Brodie canvassed the medical staff and the Governors to vote for Cutler and at the election Cutler won by 178 votes to 99. Poor Lane was the victim of a campaign of vilification which does much to sully Brodie's reputation: to favour indifferent candidates in an attempt to settle personal scores brings nothing but discord to the institution concerned. Predictably the matter was not closed, and there was more to come in this case as some of the Governors had seen through Brodie's pettiness, and got their revenge in 1843, when Charles Hawkins, an assistant and friend of Brodie's was put forward as a candidate for the vacancy of Assistant Surgeon, they turned the tables on Brodie and elected Henry Charles Johnson, an inferior candidate, for fear that they would be accused of being under Brodie's thumb. Thus one dishonourable action breeds another, and all suffer.

Benjamin Brodie was by now intent on establishing St. George's own medical school, and again displayed a degree of arrogance by purchasing a house for these purposes in Kinnerton Street in 1836, and then later requesting that the hospital should pay him £275 a year rent for the use of his premises – a quite intolerable misuse of his position! For a number of years Lane's and St. George's School led an uneasy co-existence, until Lane was appointed to St. Mary's in 1845, leading to the closure of his school in 1863. Five years later premises were found for the St. George's Medical School near to the hospital in Knightsbridge. Brodie may have behaved badly, but at least he was a prime mover in St. George's having its own school. In 1840 Brodie resigned his position at St. George's to concentrate on his practice and the College of Surgeons but remained a Governor up to the time of his death.

At the College of Surgeons, Brodie became a member of the Council in 1829 and became vice president in 1842 and 1843, by which time he was working tirelessly for a Royal Charter for the College, which was granted in 1843. Benjamin Brodie was one of the three hundred original fellows of the new Royal College of Surgeons, and became its first President in 1844, he was mainly responsible for introducing the fellowship examination in an effort to improve professional standards. He continued as a member of the Council of the College up to the time of his death in 1862. Brodie had previously been President of the Royal Medical and Chirurgical Society in 1839.

Benjamin Brodie assisted to Sir Astley Cooper at the operation to remove a sebaceous cyst from the head of George IV. The King was impressed with Brodie and made him one of his Surgeons He then became Surgeon to William IV and was made a baronet, and elevated to Sergeant-Surgeon in 1834. Brodie's other patients included Robert Peel (1788-1850) whom Brodie treated when the former Prime Minister fell off his horse in Rotten Row, on 29th. June 1850, and injured his shoulder, but despite Brodie's care he succumbed three days later; and Sir Isambard Kingdom Brunel (1806-1859), the engineer and inventor, who inhaled a half-sovereign whilst performing a conjuring trick at a children's' party. Brodie performed a tracheotomy on Brunel, and having modified a pair of forceps he stood the patient on his head and extracted the half-sovereign. For many years the forceps and the coin were in the possession of St. George's, but the temptation of owning these historic items proved to be too much for someone, and sadly they have disappeared. Brodie was mainly interested in diseases of the joints, and the urinary system.

In 1853 Benjamin Brodie was elected President of the Ethnological Society, and this honour was followed by other presidencies, including those of the Section of Social Economy for the National Association for the Promotion of Social Science (1857), the first one of the General Medical Council (1858-1860) and the Royal Society (1858-1861).

Sir Benjamin Brodie suffered from failing vision in his later years, and after undergoing an operation for the removal of his cataracts by Sir William Bowman at his home, Broome Park, Betchworth, Surrey, he died on October 21st. 1862. Timothy Holmes suggested that Brodie's death was caused by a malignant tumour of the shoulder, and it was ironic that it should happen to someone who had spent a lifetime treating diseases of the joints.

Brodie's nephew, George Bernard Brodie MD FRCP, Obstetric Physician to Queen Charlotte's Lying-In Hospital in the latter half of the nineteenth century was a student at St. George's Hospital in 1859.

BUCKLAND WARD

Francis Buckland
Two St. George's Hospital pupils shared the name of Francis Buckland, both achieved fame and distinction, but neither held a consultant post at the hospital. They were possibly related, but living in different centuries, and it is now conjecture as to which of the two Bucklands is remembered at the hospital today.

The first, Francis Trevelyan, the son of William Buckland who became Dean of Westminster, was born at Christ Church, Oxford, in 1826. Francis was educated at Cotterstock, Laleham, Winchester, and Christ Church, Oxford, where he obtained a BA in 1848. Buckland entered St. George's Hospital as a pupil in 1848, and became a house surgeon in 1852. In 1854 Francis Buckland was appointed Assistant Surgeon to the Life Guards. It was sometime during this period that he decided to turn his back on medicine, and devote his time, interest, and considerable talents to a study of natural history, particularly fauna. This decision was not altogether surprising because, since childhood, Buckland had exhibited a passionate interest in animals, keeping both monkeys and bears as pets. He appeared to have an uncanny affinity for all kinds of animals, and was skilled at training them. When young he had an unenviable reputation for annoying his elders by playing practical jokes on them, which often involved the participation of his current pet.

On leaving the army, Francis Buckland began to study seriously and systematically the habitat and habits of animals, fish and birds. His observations were published in his four volumed 'Curiosities of Natural History'. Then, in 1859 for some reason which remains totally inexplicable Buckland suddenly became possessed of the idea that the church of St. Martin's in the Fields was an inappropriate resting place for John Hunter's body, so he spent sixteen days searching the vaults of St. Martin's, until he found Hunter's coffin, and then arranged for it to be reinterred in the North Aisle of Westminster Abbey. There were no further such aberrations, and Buckland devoted the remainder of his life to Natural History. When *The Field* was first published in 1856, Buckland joined its staff and wrote regular articles until 1865, when he launched his own weekly natural history journal entitled *Land and Water*.

By now Buckland's main interest had gradually shifted from mammals to fish. He was a keen salmon fisherman, and undertook detailed research into the behaviour of this mysterious fish. His accumulated scientific knowledge on this arcane topic made him a natural candidate for appointment as the Inspector of Salmon Fisheries in 1867, and in this post he produced a number of excellent reports, which led, over time, to an improvement in salmon breeding and protection. Buckland was an avid collector of specimens, and he assembled a natural history museum in his own home. Dr. Francis Trevelyan Buckland died at the early age of 54 in 1880 following an operation, and was buried at Brompton Cemetery.

Many of the records relating to how ward names came to be chosen at St. George's Hospital have been lost, and there is no information to help with the name 'Buckland', but it was first used as a ward name in 1953, when all the wards of the Grove Fever Hospital were given names soon after its designation to St. George's Hospital. As the first Buckland ward was a fever ward, and a number of his contemporaries held senior posts at St. George's, it is perhaps more than likely that it was named after the other Buckland: Brigadier Francis Edward.

Francis Edward Buckland was born in 1905 at Sunbury, Middlesex, and educated at Winchester, Oriel College, Oxford, and St. George's Hospital, where he qualified in 1932. After his house appointments Buckland joined the Royal Army Medical Corps, and was posted to India, where he served in a number of military hospitals. Whilst in the subcontinent he prepared a thesis on Typhus, for which he was subsequently awarded an MD in 1940.

On returning to England in 1940, Francis Buckland developed his interest in pathology, and in 1943 was recognised as a specialist by the Army, by which time he was working at the Army Emergency Vaccine Laboratory, East Everleigh, where he helped to produce anti-scrub typhus vaccine.

When peace was declared in 1945, Frank Buckland was promoted Acting Lieutenant Colonel, and posted as Assistant Director of Pathology to Germany with the British Army occupying the Rhine. By now he was a much respected pathologist, and had written many papers on penicillin and leptospirosis. On completion of his tour in Germany he was seconded to the Microbiological Research Department at Porton Down, before being posted as Assistant Director of Pathology in the Far East. From 1950 until 1952 Buckland was a member of the Congo, Kenya and Tanganyika Expedition.

In 1952 Frank Buckland was promoted to the rank of Brigadier and returned to Porton Down. Before leaving the army, in 1956, he had held further senior posts in both London, and overseas in the Middle East. Buckland retired from the Army in 1957 and joined the Medical Research Council Common Cold Research Unit in Salisbury, where he remained until his sudden death in 1965.

CAROLINE WARD

Caroline
Caroline was one of the names used for a ward at the Grove Fever

Hospital soon after it was designated to St. George's. The name Caroline had never been used previously at Hyde Park Corner, although a ward had been named 'Princesses' in 1736, after Isaac Ware had completed the first phase of his extension to the original Lanesborough House, and was chosen to acknowledge the generous donations given by their Royal Highnesses Princesses Anne, Amelia and Caroline, daughters of King George II and Queen Caroline. The princesses were probably encouraged to support the hospital by their brother, Frederick, the Prince of Wales, who patronised St. George's from its very beginning, and who was President from 1734 until his death in 1751 from an abscess which was caused by a blow from a cricket ball. A more noble end than that of his father who succumbed when he fell off a toilet! One of the first four wards opened in Lanesborough House had been named 'Prince's' after Prince Frederick. When St. George's was rebuilt by William Wilkins in the nineteenth century the ward name 'Princesses' was dropped. 'Prince's' survived longer and was not dropped as a ward name until 1923, when it was renamed 'Ewing' following receipt of Mrs. M. A. Curwen's bequest .

As soon as Isaac Ware had completed the second phase of his extension to Lanesborough House, in 1738, an additional five wards were opened, and it was one of these that was given the name of 'Queen's' to mark the generous support that St. George's had received from Queen Caroline when the Westminster Hospital refused to hand over any of the funds which the Governors of the newly established hospital at Hyde Park Corner had previously contributed to its treasury.

Caroline of Ansbach (1683-1737) was the daughter of John Frederick, Margrave of Brandenburg-Ansbach. Cultured, intelligent and deter-mined, she was in every way the antithesis of her husband, the future George II (1683-1760) who was humourless, choleric, and boorish, whom she married in 1705. Short in stature, scarlet of complexion with bulging eyes, the future George II had little in his favour, other than he was devoted to his wife and he attempted to learn to speak some English unlike his father George I (1660-1727), the first Hanoverian King of Great Britain and Ireland, and elector of Hanover, who was most unpopular, as he preferred to spend his time in Germany in the company of his mistresses. The King's absence allowed Sir Robert Walpole, the

Whig leader the freedom to establish supremacy and chair, on the King's behalf, a small group of ministers which was really the forerunner of the present-day cabinet and as such he was our first 'prime minister'. Many generations of St. George's students have reason to be grateful to Queen Caroline for it was her idea to dam the River Westbourne in Hyde Park so allowing the formation of the Serpentine so allowing many to enjoy rowing there in the summer months whilst a hardy few ventured there to swim in the winter.

When George I died in his carriage whilst being driven to Hanover in 1727, George II succeeded to the throne as King of Great Britain and Ireland, and elector of Hanover. George II who had disliked his father intensely, immediately sought to dispose of Robert Walpole, the First Lord of the Treasury, and his father's minister; but Queen Caroline, who had the intelligence to appreciate Walpole's abilities in managing the House of Commons, intervened and stopped the sacking of the Whig leader. It would have been difficult to find another leader who commanded so many votes due mainly to his clever manipulation of patronage, and undoubtedly an election would have returned him in an even stronger position. Caroline liked Walpole and took every opportunity to escape from her husband and discuss politics with her favourite politician. She also cultivated friendships with Alexander Pope and John Gay. It was the latter who wrote the political satire *The Beggar's Opera* which publicly expressed criticism of the early troubled years of George II's reign, with its outbreaks of smallpox and influenza-like illnesses, and financial turmoil which culminated in the bursting of the South Sea Bubble. George was shrewd enough to listen to his wife, as well as heeding the advice of his ministers. When George was overseas, Caroline acted as Regent, and in that capacity was able to aid Walpole's success in stabilising the turbulent political scene which marked Walpole's emergence as the first Prime Minister of this country.

Queen Caroline died in 1737 but by this time George II was beginning to win a grudging degree of popularity, which culminated in widespread admiration when he courageously led his army and won the Battle of Dettingen in 1743. He was the last British monarch to go into battle. He temporarily lost favour when he subordinated British interests to Austria, but as the years rolled on and with a string of victories to the national credit, such as the victory at Culloden which suppressed the Jacobite uprising led by the Young Pretender, Clive's victory at Plassey, the capture of Quebec by Wolfe and the successful prosecution of the Seven Years War, George II ended his long reign in 1760 in modest triumph. Queen Caroline was the dominating influence in the early years in conjunction with Walpole, and later Henry Pelham and William Pitt strove to ameliorate the public dislike for the second Hanoverian monarch.

As a fitting memorial to Caroline's popularity *Queen's* ward survived at St. George's through the re-building of the hospital in the 1830s, but in 1901 it was decided to rename the ward after Queen Victoria to mark her long and successful reign, as one of the country's greatest monarchs, despite her curious preferences for oddities such as John Brown, the gillie from Balmoral, and exotics like Benjamin Disraeli, her prime minister. Interestingly, the newly named ward remained generally known as *Queen's* until the hospital's closure at Hyde Park Corner in 1980.

The name *Caroline* was one of only five non-medical names out of the twenty ward names given to the Grove Fever Hospital wards in 1954.

It is difficult to understand now why the name *King's* was chosen to name a ward at St. George's after the unpopular George II. It was not until 1885 that *King's* ward was renamed *William King* to mark his bequest of £100,000 to the hospital.

EDITH CAVELL WARD

Edith Cavell

Edith Cavell's association with St. George's Hospital is somewhat tenuous as it came about by way of the Fountain's Fever Hospital, which was built in 1901 and was after a very short while renamed the Grove Fever Hospital on which the St. James and Knightsbridge Wings now stand. The Fountain name was used again for an emergency hospital, erected in 1912 opposite the Grove Fever Hospital, which latterly was used for children with learning difficulties, and stood where the present Lanesborough Wing is now situated. The name of Cavell was first used at St. George's for one of the nurses' homes which now forms part of Clare House.

Edith Cavell was born in Swardeston, Norfolk in 1865, and educated at Lane, Somerset, and Brussels. At the age of thirteen she began to wonder whether to take up a career in nursing, and as a means of gaining some practical experience to find out if its appeal would last, she applied to become an assistant nurse at the Fountain's Fever Hospital. How she managed to obtain parental approval for such a radical move at this age remains a mystery, and the fact that she came from a respectable background – her father was a Vicar – at a time when nursing was not a regarded with the same reverence that it commands today, only serves to deepen the mystery. She was quite dishonest in her application in failing to reveal her real age, nevertheless she was accepted and began to work at Tooting. In less than three months she had made up her mind that a career in nursing was the one that she wished to pursue, but her entry into nursing was delayed because having a small legacy she travelled on the continent; and, with a strange irony in the light of what was to come, in Bavaria she endowed a 'free' hospital with a fund to purchase instruments.

Cavell entered the London Hospital in 1895 where she completed her training in two years, after which she moved to Maidstone where she took charge of a typhoid hospital. Her stay at Maidstone was short, and she returned to the London Hospital, where she worked as a staff nurse, before working in poor law institutions in Highgate and Shoreditch.

Edith Cavell then decided to return to Belgium, which she had enjoyed as a schoolgirl, and it was here that she was to remain for the rest of her life. Her first appointment in her adopted country was in Brussels where she joined Dr. Depage in 1906 to help him establish a training school for nurses. He was so impressed by Edith Cavell's enthusiasm, energy and administrative skills that a year later he invited her to become the first matron of his Clinic, the Berkendael Medical Institute, as well as taking charge of the nursing side of the hospital of St. Gilles.

On the outbreak of the First World War in 1914 Edith Cavell refused the opportunity to return to the comparative safety of England, preferring to remain in Brussels, where she felt she would be able to offer practical help to the victims of the looming hostilities. The Germans granted her permission to stay, and to use the Berkendael Institute as a Red Cross Hospital, where she and her staff would treat both the Allied and German soldiers who were wounded in the course of battle.

Edith Cavell and her nurses set about the daunting task of caring for troops who had sustained some of the most horrific injuries of modern warfare. Her example and supervision of her dedicated staff ensured that many of those who were at first thought to be beyond recovery, against all the odds began to pull through. It was at this point that Edith Cavell recognised the enormous dilemma she faced. She realised that once the Allied soldiers had recovered, they would be arrested and taken prisoners of war, only to face great hardships in captivity. Edith Cavell's solution was simple, she joined an escape network where she and others helped more than 600 Allied troops to cross the Belgian border into neutral Holland and so step into freedom.

The Germans became suspicious when the numbers of troops admitted to Edith Cavell's hospital did not tally with the number of deaths and discharges. As a result in August 1915, she was arrested and imprisoned by the Germans. In October of this year Edith Cavell was brought to trial. On being denied a proper defence she was found guilty of 'conducting soldiers to the enemy' and sentenced to death by execution. No appeal was allowed and four days later, on October 12 Edith Cavell was brought before the firing squad, she turned and said to the chaplain 'Standing, as I do, in the view of God and eternity, I realise that patriotism is not enough. I must have no hatred or bitterness towards anyone'. As the sun began to rise Edith Cavell was shot. She was aged 50. At the end of the end of the war in 1919 Edith Cavell's body was brought back to England and was reinterred in Norwich Cathedral. The marble statue of Edith Cavell by Sir George James Frampton (1860 – 1928) which stands in St. Martin's Place, close to Trafalgar Square, was unveiled in 1920. The statue, which stands in front of a twenty foot high granite background, is rather grotesque and is inscribed with the words 'Patriotism is not enough'. It is said that when it was unveiled a high ranking soldier turned to Lady Margot Asquith and whispered 'The Germans will blush when they see this'. She answered with a gentle rebuke in the form of a question 'Won't the British?'. Frampton's other works include *Peter Pan* in Kensington Gardens.

CHADBURN WARD

Maud Mary Chadburn, CBE, MD, BS

Maud Mary Chadburn was a pioneer and, during her professional career, one of the most prominent women in medicine. She worked selflessly throughout her long life for the advancement of women in medicine.

Maud Chadburn was born in Middlesborough in 1868, and educated in Crawley and at University College, London, before proceeding to the Royal Free Hospital Medical School which was then known as the London School of Medicine for Women. After qualifying in 1893, she took up appointments as resident anaesthetist and curator of the museum at the Royal Free Hospital, during which period she was awarded her Doctorate of Medicine. To gain more experience Chadburn then took a post at the Clapham Maternity Hospital, which had been founded in 1889 by Dr. Annie McCall and Miss Marion Ritchie as the first maternity hospital where women were only treated by female doctors, and where midwives, maternity nurses and female medical students were trained entirely by women. Her next appointment was at the New Hospital for Women, which later became known as the Elizabeth Garrett Anderson Hospital, before she returned to the Royal Free Hospital in a curious combination of roles: as Assistant Physician and Surgical Registrar.

After her appointment as Surgeon to the Women's Settlement Hospital at Canning Town in 1898, Maud Chadburn devoted herself almost entirely to the cause which was closest to her heart: the advancement of women to a position of parity in medicine. She felt that the best way to secure a recognised place for women in medicine was to establish hospitals like the Clapham Maternity Hospital where women would be treated only by women doctors. The first hospital which she opened was the South London Hospital for Women, built in South Clapham in 1912 at a cost of £35,000, which was raised by public subscription. Chadburn's second hospital, which was also built entirely from voluntary subscription, the Marie Curie Hospital in Hampstead, was opened in 1928. One does not have to subscribe to the Politically Correct agenda which embraces mixed wards, and other examples of equality taken to the point of embarrassment, to feel that Chadburn and her supporters were

54

ultrafeminist to an almost ridiculous degree in their rigid separation of the sexes. As there is no evidence that the innermost thoughts on their sexuality were any different to ours, there is thus no reason to think that they acted as they did out of a misplaced sense of prudish delicacy; the fact is that they felt impelled to proceed in this way to break through the barriers erected by male dominance of the profession, and the lay prejudice of both sexes against women in medicine, pockets of which, grumbling darkly in corners, linger on into present times - both within and without the hospital environment.

Maud Chadburn became the Senior Surgeon to the South London Hospital in 1912, and served as its Vice Chairman until the introduction of the National Health Service in 1948 when this post was abolished, although she continued to serve as Senior Surgeon until her retirement in 1951.

Miss Chadburn's other appointments included the Chairmanship of the Marie Curie Hospital from 1928-1934, the Chairmanship of the Marie Curie Cancer Research Committee from 1928 to 1952, and the Presidency of the London Association of the Medical Women's Federation from 1926 to 1927. For 63 years she was a member of the British Medical Association and in recognition of her services for the advancement of women in medicine Miss Chadburn was made a Commander of the British Empire in 1934.

Maud Chadburn died in 1957 at the grand old age of 89 years. Her hospital, the South London Hospital for Women, was closed in 1985 as part of a rationalisation programme of hospital services carried out by the Wandsworth Health Authority in order to centralise beds on the St. George's Hospital site. Fortunately, Maud Chadburn's unique contribution to the history of medicine in the first half of the 20th century is remembered still at St. George's.

CHAMPNEYS WARD

Sir Francis Henry Champneys, Bt, MA, DM, FRCP
Sir Francis Champneys, who was born in London in 1848, was the fourth son of the Very Reverend William Weldon Champneys, DD, the rector of St. Mary's, Whitechapel, later the Vicar of St. Pancras, Canon of St.

Paul's Cathedral and finally, Dean of Lichfield.

Champneys was educated at Winchester, and Brasenose College, Oxford, where he was captain of Boats. In the Steward's Cup at Henley he led his boat without a cox, and won the race – but was disqualified. The incident provoked such interest that soon afterwards the coxless fours was introduced into rowing events.

In 1870 he gained a first class honours in Natural Sciences, and was awarded a Radcliffe Travelling Fellowship which enabled him to spend eighteen months studying in Vienna, Leipzig and Dresden. During one of his long vacations he stayed up at Oxford to dissect a chimpanzee, and subsequently wrote his first medical publication *On the Muscles and Nerves of the Chimpanzee and Anubis*. He entered St. Bartholomew's Hospital in 1872, and qualified as a Bachelor of Medicine and a Member of the Royal College of Surgeons in 1875. After qualification he became a medical registrar and casualty physician, and was a colleague of Robert Seymour Bridges (1844 – 1930), who studied medicine at St. Bartholomew's Hospital, and practised until 1881 before he turned to poetry. Surprisingly he was appointed Poet Laureate in 1913. Champneys and Bridges remained on friendly terms for the rest of their lives. A year after qualification Champneys was admitted as a Member of the Royal College of Physicians and married Virginia, the daughter of Sir John Warrender Dalrymple.

In 1880, having been influenced towards a career in obstetrics by Matthews Duncan, the physician accoucher, he was elected assistant obstetric physician to Robert Barnes at St. George's Hospital, and obstetric physician to the General Lying-in Hospital. In the election at St. George's Hospital he achieved an overwhelming majority over Barnes' own son, Fancourt, who only managed to attract one vote – presumably that of his father. It was remarked that 'the father was inclined to cut up rough!', but there is no evidence to suggest that he did so on this occasion. In 1885 following Barnes' retirement Champneys was elected obstetric physician to St. George's, and having proceeded to Doctor of Medicine in 1888 he remained until 1891 when he was invited, following Matthews Duncan's death, to return to St. Bartholomew's Hospital as Physician Accoucher and Lecturer in Midwifery and Diseases of Women and Children, where he remained until his retirement in 1913.

56

Champneys was succeeded at St. George's Hospital by W. Radford Dakin.

Champneys was a leader in his chosen speciality, and was responsible for introducing many innovations including with Sir John Williams the Listerian principles of antisepsis into obstetric practice at the General Lying-In Hospital, in an attempt to eradicate puerpual infection.

Sir Francis was a member, before becoming chairman, and finally president (1912-1914) of the Obstetrical Society of London. The Midwives Act of 1902 provided for the creation of the Central Midwives Board, and in 1903 Champneys became its first chairman, an office he held for the next twenty seven years. From 1911 to 1926 he was the Crown nominee of the General Medical Council. Champneys was President of the Royal Society of Medicine (1912-1914), and in 1913 he became President of the Section of Obstetrics and Gynaecology at the International Congress of Medicine held in London.

Following Champneys retirement to Nutley, Sussex, he continued to maintain his interest in the development of obstetrics, and at the age of 81 he was one of the founders of the British College of Obstetricians and Gynaecologists, of which he was vice-patron and councillor at the time of his death. Champneys' record of public service was rewarded when he was made a Baronet in 1910. Sir Francis Champneys was a very accomplished amateur musician, who composed anthems, as well as conducting a private choir, which he often accompanied on an organ which he had installed in his own home. Champneys died in Sussex in 1930.

CHESELDEN WARD

William Cheselden
William Cheselden was born in 1688 at Burrough in Leicestershire, and became an apprentice of William Cowper, the anatomist, in London in 1703. Later he became apprenticed to Mr. Ferne, the surgeon, at St. Thomas' Hospital. By 1711, Cheselden is listed as a lecturer in anatomy, but he suffered a public slap in the face in 1714 when the Company of Barber Surgeons fined him £10 for dissecting bodies in his own house, which contravened their Bye-Law of 1588, which forbade anatomical

dissection outside the Barber-Surgeons Hall. Cheselden never forgave the Barber Surgeons for this reprimand, and was even more irritated by the long standing association of the surgeons with the barbers, which he felt the current status of the surgical arts had rather outgrown. With great energy he canvassed his colleagues to follow the example set previously by the surgeons of Paris who founded their own company. After a long struggle Cheselden finally achieved his aim in 1745 when the Company of Surgeons was founded.

Cheselden was appointed Assistant Surgeon to St. Thomas' Hospital in 1718, and a year later he became a full Surgeon. He was a man of great ability and drive, and a surgeon and teacher with extensive interests who had published papers on topics as diverse as *Cutting for Stone* and *An Account of Human Bones found in a Roman Urn at St. Albans* which he presented to the Royal Society, to which he had been elected a Fellow at the incredibly young age of 24 in 1712. Like many surgeons Cheselden was both industrious and ambitious and readily accepted an additional appointment as Surgeon to the recently founded Westminster Infirmary in 1724. He resigned his post at this institution in 1733 at the time of the dispute over its future location, which left him free to accept the post of Surgeon to the newly opened St. George's Hospital at Hyde Park Corner.

At St. George's, Cheselden undertook all the operations for renal and bladder stones until his retirement in 1737. After he retired from St. Thomas' Hospital in 1738 he concentrated on his very large private practice, and also acted as Surgeon to the Chelsea Hospital, a post to which he was elected in 1737.

William Cheselden was Surgeon to Queen Caroline, and his extensive practice included such illustrious patients as Sir Isaac Newton, and he was a friend of Sir Hans Sloane (1660–1753), the physician and naturalist, Richard Mead (1673–1745), the successful physician who followed John Radcliffe as leader of his profession and Alexander Pope (1688–1744), who immortalised him in the line ' I'll do what Mead and Cheselden advise'. Pope was friendly with Thomas Addison and Lady Mary Wortley Montagu with whom he later quarrelled.

Cheselden died in Bath in 1752 and a notice in the April edition of the *Gentleman's Magazine* stated 'William Cheselden, Esq.; an eminent anatomist, lithotomist, and surgeon to the Royal Hospital, Chelsea; at Bath; he had drank ale after eating hot buns, upon which being very uneasy, he sent for a physician who advised vomiting immediately, which advice, had he taken it might, it is tho't, have saved his life'. Cheselden was buried in Chelsea Hospital. His portrait by Jonathan Richardson the younger (1694-1771) hangs in the Royal College of Surgeons.

THE PHILIP CONSTABLE BOARDROOM

Philip Herbert Charles Constable, OBE, MA

Philip Constable was arguably the most able administrator who has ever been in the service of St. George's Hospital. Constable supervised and facilitated the many changes that became necessary in 1948, when St. George's lost its voluntary status and was drawn into state control on the introduction of the National Health Service. He ensured through polite yet skilful diplomacy that the hospital, its medical staff and the medical school, developed close and harmonious working relationships with those who chatted in the corridors of power, in order that negotiations with the Ministry of Health and the University of London worked to the advantage of everyone at Hyde Park Corner.

Philip Constable was born in Oakley Park in 1898, and attended Cambridge Grammar School until the age of sixteen. By then the First World War had just been declared, and the young Constable was anxious to fulfil his patriotic duty to serve his country, so, concealing his real age from the recruitment officer, he was enlisted into the Worcester regiment. Philip Constable's outstanding leadership qualities soon singled him out, and he was commissioned as a first lieutenant. He fought in Flanders and was wounded in 1917.

As soon as the Armistice was signed Philip Constable returned to England to resume his studies. He entered Fitzwilliam College, Cambridge, in 1921, and went on to gain a BA degree in history, Constable then secured a post as Charity Organiser for the YMCA in India, where he clearly made a reputation for himself for, on his return to the United Kingdom, he was asked to help raise the funds necessary for the building of Southend General Hospital. As soon as the hospital was completed Philip Constable was asked to stay on in the capacity of Hospital Secretary. This was to be his first experience of hospital administration.

St. George's Hospital was facing difficulties in 1944. Mr. Ewart Mitchell, who had been appointed Hospital Secretary the previous year promptly resigned when he ran into a dispute with Sir George Cory, the deputy Chairman, over the range of his responsibilities. Cory, who had supervised most of the day to day workings of the hospital during the war, was reluctant to step aside and allow Mitchell to have a free rein. This irked Mitchell to the point where he felt that he had no alternative other than to resign. It transpired that Sir George Cory had been paid £450 per annum for his services during the war, and being a Governor and Trustee of the hospital, this emolument seemed to be contrary to the laws of the charity. There was a great deal of sympathy amongst the medical staff for Ewart Mitchell, who wanted the House Committee to refuse to accept his resignation, and this may have prompted an anonymous complaint that was made to the Charity Commissioners concerning this matter. In the event the Commissioners, after due consideration, were unable to come to a decision and suggested that the matter should be taken up with the Attorney General.

The Governors decided against this course of action and matters were allowed to come to rest but it was decided that the House Committee should set up a sub-committee to review the management of the hospital and the medical school. The medical staff objected to the composition of the sub-committee, as well as its terms of reference. This opposition forced the House Committee to invite the Medical School Committee to consider what alterations to the rules were going to be necessary to bring the medical school and the hospital into a closer and happier working relationship; whilst it confined itself to the question of the replacement of the Hospital Secretary, and how best it could ensure that the rules and regulations were amended so that the new Secretary would have the same powers as the Secretaries and House Governors of the other London Teaching Hospitals. The King Edward's Hospital Fund for London was invited to give advice on the appointment of the Secretary, and, after visiting St. George's, they were extremely critical of the arrangements that were in existence, whereby the hospital secretary was little more than a clerk who prepared the minutes and kept the accounts, whilst the day to day management of the hospital was in the hands of a Governor, usually the deputy Chairman of the Board. The King's Fund advised that an experienced administrator should be appointed at a salary of £1500 per annum as House Governor, with responsibility for the management of the hospital, and general superintendence over all resident and non resident medical, nursing and lay staff, except in professional medical and nursing matters.

In 1945 Philip Constable was appointed House Governor at a salary of £1500-£2000 per annum. Southend in general and especially the Chamber of Trade, the British Legion, the War Efforts Committee, the Rotary Club, the Carnival Association but especially the staff of Southend General Hospital were sorry at his departing. It was said that he gave his 'heart and soul and the hospital is richer for his services'. A reporter for the 'Southend Observer' wrote 'I do not know what the organisers of fetes, sporting events, gymkhanas etc., will do when Mr. Constable leaves Southend'. It was said that he could do a job any day as a BBC commentator as he had an especial ability for this type of work and possessed a fine microphone voice. It was very much Southend's loss but St. George's gain as working at great speed Philip Constable familiarised himself with all the details of St. George's Hospital's activities, and the people who were responsible for them, and in doing so he was able to bring into his own hands the reins of power. He was to prove himself an outstanding administrator, who was universally liked by the staff, who held him and his opinions in the greatest of respect.

Constable served as House Governor until his retirement in 1962, when he was replaced by Richard Ellis. In retirement Philip Constable took charge of the Hospital Centre of the King Edward's Hospital Fund for London. For his services to hospital management, and for his leadership in establishing the Administrative Staff College for the training of young administrators, he was awarded the OBE. Philip Constable died in 1978 at the age of eighty.

DAKIN WARD

William Radford Dakin, MD, FRCP

William Radford Dakin was born in Cheshire in 1860, the son of John Dakin JP, and educated at Macclesfield Grammar School, and Owens College, Manchester, (which later became the University of Manchester) before entering Guy's Hospital to study medicine. After qualifying in 1883 Dakin decided to specialise in obstetrics and gynaecology, and was appointed resident obstetrician to his own teaching hospital. Soon he was appointed Physician to the General Lying-in Hospital, and then, in 1891, and at the relatively early age of thirty one, he was elected Obstetric Physician and Lecturer in Midwifery to St. George's in succession to Sir Francis Champneys.

It is recorded in the Medical School Gazette that 'When Dakin came to us it was a recent innovation for obstetric specialists to perform any except vaginal operations, and surgeons looked with sceptical eyes on the abdominal adventures of the gynaecologist'. This attitude quickly changed when Dakin, quietly confident, showed that he was a highly skilled surgeon, with a wide and firmly based knowledge of his chosen subject. Almost immediately Dakin was welcomed by his surgical colleagues, who valued and respected his opinion, and he was highly esteemed outside St. George's. Nevertheless, the Board of Governors, recognising that Dakin's successors might not be so gifted and talented, resolved that all future senior obstetric and gynaecological appointments must possess the Fellowship of the Royal College of Surgeons.

Dakin's services were sought after by other London hospitals, and he held appointments at the Royal Hospital for Women and Children, and the Great Northern Hospital. At various times he was an Examiner in obstetrics and gynaecology for the Royal Colleges, and the University of Oxford. Dakin published a number of papers as well as writing several chapters on gynaecological procedures for Jacobson's *Operative Surgery*, and his eminence as a gynaecologist and obstetrician led to his election firstly to the Vice Presidency, and then to the Chairmanship of the Midwives Board of the Obstetricians' Society,

Radford Dakin was an accomplished artist which enabled him to illustrate the excellent handbook he wrote on midwifery which became the 'bible' for students at that time. At St. George's he took an active interest in the Graphic Society, and was the President for some years, frequently taking care to exhibit his paintings at the Society's exhibitions. These exhibitions must have been superb with the talents of Dakin, Clinton Dent, the surgeon, and the young student, Edward Wilson, on display. Dakin was also an expert fly-fisherman – a sport he often pursued with the highly entertaining neurologist, James Collier (1870-1935) who was a physician at St. George's from 1903 until 1935, and Dakin often entertained colleagues and students at his house in Grosvenor Street for games of billiards.

Radford Dakin retired from St. George's in 1912 at the very early age of fifty-two in order to devote more time to his main interest: art; but as soon as the First World War began in 1914 he offered his services to the Red Cross. He served for a time on the Italian front before being appointed surgeon to the English Hospital at Haute Marne. Later Dakin served the French Army as Chirurgien de Secteur, running the hospital at Villeneuve-sur-Lot where his second in command was Professor Tonks who had been head of the Slade School. In recognition of his distinguished war service he was made a Chevalier of the Legion d'Honneur as well as receiving the Croix de Guerre.

After peace was declared Radford Dakin returned to retirement at his home which overlooked Bradford-on-Avon, where he had laid out beautiful rock gardens stocked with rare alpine plants, and had built a small studio in which he spent many happy hours at the easel. Radford Dakin died in his seventy-sixth year.

DALBY WARD

Sir William Bartlett Dalby, MA, MB, FRCS
Sir William Bartlett Dalby was Aural Surgeon to St. George's Hospital from 1872 until 1892, when he pioneered a number of operative procedures on the auditory meatus and the mastoid bone.

Dalby was born in Ashby-de-la-Zouch in 1840, his university education took place at Sidney Sussex College, Cambridge, before he entered St. George's as a medical student in 1863. During this phase of his life he had the rare distinction of occupying rooms in the grand Constitution

Arch, which had been erected in the 1820's by Decimus Burton, which were probably extremely uncomfortable and lacked many amenities; but these meagre facilities were offset by its close proximity to the hospital. After qualifying in 1866, William Dalby became a general practitioner in Chester, but he quickly became disenchanted with the slow pace of life in the provinces and longed to return to metropolitan conviviality. He was fortunate in being able to indulge himself in these whims, and therefore he abandoned Chester for a more congenial existence in London, where he began studying diseases of the ear.

Dalby passed the fellowship examination of the Royal College of Surgeons in 1870, and thereafter became assistant to James Hinton (1822-1875), an 'aurist', and author of *Mystery of Pain* (1866). Otology gained clinical respectability through the efforts of Joseph Toynbee (1815-1886)[1] who was appointed to St. Mary's Hospital in 1852. From 1850 Toynbee practised at 18 Savile Row, a road in which both Benjamin Brodie and Richard Bright also practised. James Hinton was appointed to Guys Hospital in 1863, and took over Toynbee's practice in 1866. Under Hinton's skilful tuition William Dalby became knowledge-able and experienced in the diagnosis and treatment of diseases of the ear,

---

[1] Joseph Toynbee was a most eminent Ear, Nose and Throat surgeon. He entered St. George's as a student in 1834 and at the same time enrolled at University College. He passed his MRCS in 1838 and was one of the original three hundred Fellows of the Royal College of Surgeons elected in 1844. Toynbee was also elected FRS before being appointed to St. Mary's Hospital. At St. Mary's, Toynbee's practice flourished and he published his book *Diseases of the Ear* but tragedy struck in 1888 when he was experimenting for a cure for tinnitus. He inhaled a mixture of chloroform and hydrocyanic acid, then held a rag over his mouth and nose performed a Valsalva manoeuvre and died. As the Pupil's Register records at St. George's 'at least that is supposed to be how his death occurred, for he was found dead in his consulting rooms by his butler'. Toynbee was just over 50 years of age. Outside medicine Joseph Toynbee had a number of interests. For many years he was the Treasurer to the Royal Medical Benevolent Fund which supports members of the medical profession and their families who have fallen on hard times. The members of St. George's Hospital branch of the Royal Medical Benevolent Fund are amongst the most successful fund raisers for the organisation nationally. Toynbee founded the Village Club in Wimbledon. In 1868 a drinking fountain was erected at the top of Wimbledon Hill in memory of Joseph Toynbee.

so that when St. George's Hospital decided to appoint an aural surgeon for the first time in 1872, he was the natural candidate for appointment. Three years later, on Hinton's death, Dalby took over the practice in Savile Row, and when Dalby retired the practice was handed on to Arthur Cheatle. Humphry Rolleston remarked that 'for nearly eighty years Number 18 Savile Row has been the Mecca for the Deaf'.

Dalby was particularly interested in overcoming the problems associated with the education of the deaf and dumb, and he advocated the use of lip reading and articulation. He wrote extensively on this subject, as well as publishing a number of papers including *Contributions to Aural Surgery*, *Diseases of the Mastoid*, *Foreign Bodies and Osseous Growths in the External Auditory Canal* and with a fascinating title: *Strange Incidents in Practice*. For his pioneering work on the educational treatment of incurably deaf children he received a Knighthood in 1886.

In his practice at St. George's, William Dalby did not perform a complete mastoid operation, (drainage only without attempting to remove the air cells), but he was the first to remove exostoses from the external auditory canal using a dental drill operated by a foot pedal. Dalby was quick to condemn any type of treatment or practice which could not be fully justified; and it is recalled that once when lecturing to the students on a certain operation, which he did not perform, he began 'You make a small incision – about a foot long and let out a little pus – about a pint!'.

Sir William Dalby was very fashionable, smartly dressed and in appearance resembled a retired colonel. He was fond of society, clubs, literature and the arts. He retired from practice in 1892 soon after he had reached his sixtieth birthday. In retirement he wrote a novel and published *Dr. Chesterfield's Letters to his son on Medicine as a Career*, as well as pursuing his many interests outside medicine, which not only included literature and the theatre, but also riding, shooting and fishing. He emerged from his retirement briefly in 1894 when he was elected President of the Medical Society of London, and the first President of the Otological Society. Sadly his retirement was marred by the tragic loss of his eldest son in a boating accident at Sandhurst, and the serious injuries suffered by his second son whilst serving in the army during the Great War.

Sir William Dalby died at his home in Montague Place, London in 1918.

DRUMMOND WARD

Lieutenant-Colonel William Charles Drummond

Charles Drummond was the second child of the two sons and two daughters born to Andrew-Berkeley Drummond and his wife, Lady Mary Percival, the daughter of the second Earl of Egmont. Andrew-Berkeley was the son of Robert Drummond, an eminent banker, whose father was the fourth Viscount Strathallan and the great-grandson of the Duke of Rutland.

Charles was born in Cadlands, Hampshire, on 4 July 1796. Unlike his father he shunned a career in banking and followed a number of his cousins into the Army, where he attained the rank of Lieutenant-Colonel by the age of twenty nine. It is possible that as a young subaltern he was involved in the defeat of Napoleon at Laon, and the occupation of Bordeaux by the Duke of Wellington in 1814. Drummond would certainly have celebrated the defeat of Napoleon by the 'Iron Duke' at the Battle of Waterloo in 1815, and his subsequent banishment into exile on St. Helena. Moving from the European theatre Drummond served next in India. After the defeat of the Gurkha tribesmen in 1816, and the crushing of the Marathas with the annexation of their empire to British India in 1818, life in the Army must have seemed rather dull to Charles Drummond as he left the Army in 1824, and in 1825 he put his name forward for election as a Governor of St. George's Hospital. His name was tabled in the Boardroom for the statutory four weeks and then in June 1825 he was elected a Governor.

Charles Drummond was clearly keen to be involved intimately in the affairs of the hospital, because in less than two years he succeeded another army officer, Colonel Harnage, as one of the two Treasurers to St. George's Hospital. Drummond's co-Treasurer was Henry Holland who was elected in 1824. Drummond and Holland shared the onerous responsibility of the Treasurership in the critical phase which led up to the signing of the contract for the rebuilding of St. George's Hospital. Even after that it would not be all plain sailing, as they had to strike a

66

delicate balance between making sure that finances were available for the continued running of the existing hospital, while at the same time being able to convinced their colleagues that St. George's would not be plunged into bankruptcy bearing the costs of the new building. Henry Holland lost his nerve at this juncture thinking that the hospital would be made bankrupt, and decided that he must resign as Treasurer in 1829, just a matter of weeks before the contracts were due to be signed. Having faced the ferocious Marathas, Drummond was made of sterner stuff and continued at his post single handed until Sir George Duckett, Bart was appointed as second Treasurer. Drummond and Duckett recommended to the Board that the rebuilding programme could be financed, and the two of them were signatories to the Articles of Agreement, with William Wilkins, William Brown, Francis Read and Zachariah Bowden, for the new St. George's Hospital at Hyde Park Corner.

As a reward for keeping his nerve during this time of suspense, a ward in the second phase of Wilkins' building was named after Charles Drummond, and it is appropriate that a ward in the present St. George's Hospital bears his name, to record his courage and conviction. What is more surprising is to find that Henry Holland lent his name to a ward in the second phase of the new hospital which was opened in 1831.

Charles Drummond continued to serve as Treasurer to St. George's Hospital until 1855 when he was duly thanked for his services before retiring to his house in Charing Cross.

DUKE-ELDER WARD

Sir William Stewart Duke-Elder, FRS, GCVO, MD, DSc, LLD, MA, ChB, FRCS, FRCP, Ph.D, Hon.FRCS Ed, Hon.FRACS, Hon.FACS, Hon.DSc (Northwest, McGill), Hon. MD (Utrecht, Strasbourg, Ghent), Hon.MD (Dublin), Meikle Fellowship, Toronto (1959), Bowman Medal (1957), Lister Medal (1956), Gonin Medal (1954), Gullstrand Medal (1952), Proctor Lectureship (1951), Doyne Medal (1948), Research Medal of the American Medical Association (1947), Donders Medal (1947), Howe Medal (1946), Nettleship Medal (1933) Fothergillian Medal (1962), and the Lang Medal (1965)

An extremely impressive list of honours! It has proved impossible to identify any other St. George's Hospital Surgeon or Physician who received as many accolades as Sir Stewart Duke-Elder. Duke-Elder, or 'The Duke' as he was popularly known, was undoubtedly one of the most eminent of St. George's adopted sons – and a great man of scientific medicine.

Duke-Elder was born in Tealing, near Dundee, in 1898, the son of a minister, and from the time he entered the Gordon Academy his outstanding scholastic ability became evident. Stewart Duke-Elder entered the University of St. Andrews in 1915 and qualified in 1923, having already obtained a First Class Honours degree in Natural Science and a BSc. in Physiology, as well as picking up a number of prizes *en route*. A year after qualification he obtained his Fellowship of the Royal College of Surgeons, and barely eleven months later he was awarded his Doctorate of Medicine for his thesis entitled 'Reaction of the eye to changes in osmotic pressure of the blood'. A year later his thesis on 'The nature of intraocular fluids and the pressure equilibrium in the eye' brought him a well deserved D.Sc.

Duke-Elder then came to London where he was appointed clinical assistant to the Ophthalmic Department at St. George's Hospital, and so began an association which lasted over fifty years. At this time he also worked with Professor Starling and Dr. Drummond at University College on the mechanism of raised intraocular pressure. In 1926 he was appointed Assistant Ophthalmic Surgeon to St. George's Hospital, and in 1931 he was elected full Ophthalmic Surgeon. His appointments at St. George's were mirrored by similar ones at Moorfields Eye Hospital, but unfortunately he was forced to resign from the latter on medical advice in 1936.

By 1932 Duke-Elder had published the first volume of his *Textbook of Ophthalmology* and he was from then on recognised as being one of the world's leading ophthalmologists. His *Textbook of Ophthalmology* ran to seven volumes and was completed by 1954. It has been described as the greatest work of any kind whatsoever produced by a single author. About this time Duke-Elder recognised that his work required updating, so he embarked on his fifteen volumed *System of Ophthalmology*. For this monumental effort he enlisted the help of some of his colleagues, but he remained largely responsible for the overall content of work, which was completed in 1976. Duke-Elder also wrote a number of other textbooks, and he made a phenomenal number of contributions to scientific journals.

After his appointment as Ophthalmic Surgeon to St. George's Hospital at the age of 33, he was soon called upon to operate on Ramsey Macdonald, the Prime Minister. Shortly afterwards he was appointed to be the Surgeon Oculist to King Edward VIII, and, at the age of 35, absurdly young for a doctor, he received his knighthood. Sir Stewart Duke-Elder's subsequent royal appointments to both King George VI and Queen Elizabeth II brought him a KCVO in 1946 and GCVO in 1958.

During the Second World War Duke-Elder joined the Royal Army Medical Corps as a Lieutenant, but promotion was astronomically rapid, and by 1940 he was promoted to Brigadier, and Consultant Ophthalmic Surgeon to the Army.

Duke-Elder served his chosen speciality with great distinction, but his international pre-eminence made growing demands on his time to the point where he was able to devote only a minimal amount of his energies to St. George's. He played leading roles in creating the Institute of Ophthalmology in London, and the national Faculty of Ophthalmologists. His outstanding contribution to ophthalmology was marked by his election as President of the International Council of Ophthalmology in 1950, a position he held for 12 years, until he was made an Honorary Life President.

Sir Stewart Duke-Elder retired from St. George's Hospital in 1963, but he continued to take an active interest in its affairs until his death in 1978 at the age of 79. It was his great misfortune to suffer from severe emphysema during the last three years of his life. His wife Phyllis, whom he married in 1928, was also a doctor, and she helped both with his clinical practice and his research.

FRANKAU WARD

Sir Claude Howard Stanley Frankau, Kt., DSO, CBE, MS, FRCS
Claude Frankau, the youngest son of Frederick Frankau, a well known barrister, was born in 1883, and educated at Rugby, before entering St.

George's Hospital in 1901. After passing the conjoint examination in 1907, Frankau immediately proceeded to sit, and pass, the Fellowship examination of the Royal College of Surgeons at the minimum permitted age of twenty five in 1908. He then took the MB BS finals in 1909, before undertaking his house officer posts. After holding a number of junior posts including that of Resident Obstetric Assistant, Claude Frankau was appointed Surgical Registrar in 1910, and elevated to Assistant Surgeon in 1912 when he was barely twenty nine years of age.

On the outbreak of the Great War Claude Frankau joined the Royal Army Medical Corps, and took charge of a forward clearing station in France. His surgical ability, initiative and outstanding administrative skills were quickly recognised, and brought him rapid promotion to the rank of Colonel in the post of Surgeon to the Fifth Army. Frankau's war record was impressive, his courageous and distinguished service led to three mentions in despatches, the award of the Distinguished Service Order, and a Commandership of the Order of the British Empire.

After demobilisation Claude Frankau returned to St. George's, where he took the Mastership of Surgery with a gold medal in 1921, and was appointed Consultant Surgeon in charge of the Genito-Urinary department in 1926. Later the Fracture Department came under his wing. Claude Frankau, tall, good looking, capable, witty, but cool and somewhat aloof, was popular with the students as a teacher, and highly regarded by his colleagues. He was clearly a born leader, who took an active role in hospital politics, and his opinion was canvassed on every matter. Unlike a number of surgeons in the history of St. George's the anaesthetists found working with Claude Frankau a positive pleasure. George Edwards said of him 'he was the soul of punctuality; straight-forward and simple in his methods; and he was unfailingly polite to everybody'.

Outside St. George's Frankau examined for the University of London, and was a Member of the Court of Examiners of the Royal College of Surgeons from 1926 to 1934. He became President of the Association of Surgeons in 1937-38, and President of the Section of Surgery in the Royal Society of Medicine from 1938-39.

It was with a sad inevitability that Frankau was caught up in the toils of the Second World War, for as soon as it was declared he was chosen

70

as Director of the Emergency Medical Service for London and the Home Counties. The Directorship was a post of immense responsibility, with the ultimate authority to ensure the provision of treatment for civilian casualties, as well as making the necessary arrangements for the care of servicemen transferred back to the UK after injury during 'Operation Overlord'. These arrangements included the organisation of port, transit and home base hospitals; the equipping and supply of thirty six operating theatres; teams of doctors and nurses for the landing craft; and the safe distribution of service casualties by ambulance trains. Claude Frankau was in his element and as a result of his superb organisation and the hard work and dedication of his staff that of the 166,000 casualties which occurred between D-Day and VE-Day less than one percent died as a result of their injuries. Frankau richly deserved the knighthood conferred on him in 1945.

At the end of the hostilities Sir Claude returned to St. George's where he remained until his retirement in 1948. He retired to his home, Ickleton Grange near Saffron Walden where he farmed and kept a herd of Jersey cows. In retirement Frankau paid frequent visits to St. George's staying in London at the Athenaeum Club, of which he was a popular member. Sir Claude Frankau died at Ickleton Grange in 1967 aged eighty four.

Frankau married twice, his first wife Edith died in 1934, and his second wife, Isabella, whom he married in 1935, was a well known psychiatrist.

FULLER WARD

The Fullers Family

For over 150 years from 1766 there was an almost continuous connection between the Fuller family and St. George's Hospital. *Fuller* ward is actually named after Henry Peter Fuller, the son of John Fuller, who came from Dorking, and having trained at St. George's Hospital in the late 1770s, set up a famous apothecaries' practice in Piccadilly. One of John's ancestors was Thomas Fuller (1654–1734) who had no connection with St. George's but was a well respected and leading apothecary in his day. In his 'Pharmacopoeia Extemporary' he advocated

71

the use of horse dung, live woodlice, earthworms and human urine for many common disorders.

John Fuller's elder son, John, who was born in 1782, entered St. George's in 1803 and was a house surgeon from November 1805 until June 1806. Sadly, the young man died in 1807 from a fever said to have been brought on 'through overdoing himself' in a cricket match; but his younger brother, Henry Peter, who was born in 1785, carried on the family tradition and entered St. George's as a student under Everard Home in 1811. Henry Peter obtained his MRCS in 1813, and then joined the family practice in Piccadilly. It is said that he had a very large practice amongst the middle classes, and is described as having 'great faith in drugs which he ordered in large quantities and peculiar combinations'. Throughout his professional career, Henry Peter remained a staunch supporter of St. George's, although after his training he held no appointment other than as a visiting apothecary and a governor for many years.

Henry Peter Fuller was himself a great benefactor and as a member of the Rebuilding Committee he sought the necessary funds by persuading a number of his wealthy patients to subscribe to the building of the new St. George's Hospital in 1832. It was for his considerable unwavering support that the Hospital decided to name a ward after him. Henry Peter Fuller retired in 1862 and died in Stoke Poges at the age of 81 in 1866.

Henry Peter Fuller's two sons both trained at St. George's Hospital. The elder, Henry William became a physician (1857-1873) to the hospital. Henry William was born in London in 1820 and educated at Rugby under Dr. Arnold and King's College, Cambridge before entering St. George's Hospital. Qualifying MB in 1843 he was appointed assistant physician in 1848. On Dr. Robert Nairne's retirement in 1857 Henry William Fuller was appointed physician to St. George's, an appointment he held until his death in 1873. H.W. Fuller held a similar appointment at the North London Hospital for Consumption and the School for the Indigent Blind. Fuller was described as a sound and hard working doctor although by no means brilliant. Nevertheless, he enjoyed a large private practice and was respected enough by his colleagues to be appointed Censor of the Royal College of Physicians in 1866. It is probable that Henry William would have received even greater recognition for his

72

contributions to the medical literature, if he had not succumbed to abscesses of the lung and brain in 1873 at the relatively early age of fifty three. Fuller's treatises *On Rheumatism, Rheumatic Gout and Sciatica* (1852) *On Diseases of the Chest* (1862) and *On Diseases of the Heart and Great Vessels* (1865) were regarded as classics in their day.

Henry William's younger brother William after qualifying at St. George's carried on the family's practice in Piccadilly. William's son, Henry Roxburgh was a pupil at St. George's Hospital from 1876-1880 and after undertaking a resident surgeon's and obstetric assistant's post, he took over the established practice in Piccadilly. So ended the long association of the Fuller family with St. Georges.

GRAY WARD

Henry Gray, FRS, FRCS

Henry Gray's name is synonymous with a textbook which is recognised throughout the world. Gray's *Anatomy* has been sold in countless thousands, yet it is difficult to appreciate that the original of this vast tome, with its seven hundred and eighty two pages of text, and its three hundred and sixty three illustrations by Dr. Henry Vandyke Carter,[1] a demonstrator in anatomy to St. George's, was completed in less than the five years before Gray's untimely death at the early age of thirty five.

Gray was one of four children born to Ann and William Thomas Gray,

---

[1] Henry Vandyke Carter was born in 1831, the son of Henry Barlow Carter, an artist. Henry was educated at Hull before entering St. George's Hospital as a student in 1849. After qualifying in 1852 Carter was appointed Demonstrator of Anatomy at St. George's and in 1856 he was awarded his MD. It was during his time in the Anatomy department at St. George's that he became friends with Henry Gray and collaborated with him in the production of one of the most famous books of all time – *Gray's Anatomy*. Gray's lucid descriptions of the human anatomy were enhanced by the excellence of Henry Vandyke Carter's illustrations which have been described as the best that have ever accompanied a book of anatomy. In 1856 Carter left St. George's to become Assistant Surgeon to the Indian Medical Service but soon returned to his love for anatomy as the professor of this subject in Bombay. Carter retired from the Army in 1888 as Deputy Surgeon General and Honorary Surgeon to Queen Victoria. He died in 1897.

a messenger to King George IV,[1] and later to King William IV, in Wilton Street, Belgrave Square, in 1827. Henry had two brothers, one, Thomas who became a barrister at Her Majesty's Court of the Queen's Bench, Belgrave, and the other, Robert, a naval surgeon who was lost at sea aged twenty two. Henry's sister Marian died at an early age. Henry Gray enrolled as a perpetual student at St. George's Hospital in 1845.

As a student Gray won the triennial prize of the Royal College of Surgeons, in 1848, for his essay on the origin, connections and distribution of the nerves of the human eye. He qualified as a member of the Royal College of Surgeons in 1848 and was appointed house surgeon at St. George's. He worked under Robert Keate, Caesar Hawkins, Edward Cutler and Thomas Tatum. At the very early age of twenty five, Gray became a Fellow of the Royal Society and one year later, in 1853, he was appointed Lecturer in Anatomy to St. George's Hospital Medical School, in Kinnerton Street, which was only in its' infancy as it had been established in 1849. At the same time Gray acted as Surgical Curator to the Pathological Museum.

Between the years 1852 and 1858, in addition to his *Anatomy* treatise, Gray published a number of papers including *On the Structure and Use of the Spleen* for which he won the Astley Cooper prize (1853); *On myeloid and myelo-cystic tumours of the bone; their structure, pathology, and mode of diagnosis* (1856); *An Account of a dissection of an Ovarian Cyst which contained brain* (1853) and *On the Development of the Ductless Glands in the Chick* (1852).

---

[1] King's Messengers were first appointed in 1199 by King John to carry mail to fellow monarchs but during the reign of Henry VIII the Messengers took on the role of a private police force and helped in the dissolution of the monasteries. In 1547 the forty gentlemen were formed into the Corps of King's Messengers. The messengers were loyal to the Crown throughout the Civil War and in 1660 they were given an official badge of office – a silver greyhound embroidered on their tunics which was replaced in 1714 by a metal badge. In 1824 George IV lent the Messengers to the Foreign Office and since then they have carried messages to and from embassies although their first responsibilty is to the Crown although one or two still run messages between the Queen and the Prime Minister during Royal tours. Today their number totals only twenty five but a Queen's Messenger is still recognised by his distinctive badge of office - the silver greyhound which is now displayed on his tie.

Gray became a Fellow of the Royal College of Surgeons in 1860, and his future seemed secure when Caesar Hawkins and Edward Cutler retired as surgeons from St. George's Hospital in 1861 and were replaced by the assistant surgeons, Prescott Hewett and George Pollock, as Gray was a favoured candidate for one of their vacant posts. Tragedy struck two weeks before the election was due to take place, when Gray became infected with small pox, caught from a nephew, and died within a very few days. It is a telling commentary on the state of medicine at the time to realise that this occurred sixty odd years after Edward Jenner vaccinated James Phipps with some of the 'matter' from the cow-maid, Sarah Nelmes' cowpox pustules, and that even medical men with strong connections to Jenner's old teaching hospital disregarded the benefits of routine vaccination at their peril.

Gray never married, but perhaps in view of his surgical expectations, at the time of his death he was engaged to a Miss Winter. He lived throughout his life at 8 Wilton Street, which now bears a blue commemoration plaque, and was buried in Highgate Cemetery alongside other notable St. George's men such as: Robert Lee MD, the obstetric physician (1835-1866), James Hope, the cardiologist (1801-1841) and Atkinson Morley, the governor and benefactor (1781-1758).

GROSVENOR WARD

Grosvenor

The name of Grosvenor is almost synonymous with that of St. George's, but it would have been very different if the first Lord Berkeley had not reneged on an agreement he had made with the widow of one Alexander Davies, because his name may well have figured more prominently in the annals of St. George's Hospital.

Alexander Davies, a London scrivener, who had inherited land including the large Manor of Ebury on the death of his uncle, Hugh Awdeley (Audley) at the age of 85 in 1662, died in the Great Plague of 1665 leaving a widow and a six month old daughter, Mary. Awdeley who was a lawyer, had amassed his riches through his dealings in the pre-Civil War Court of Wards which apportioned lands forfeited to the Crown. Under the terms of Alexander Davies' will all of his estate which included,

100 acres of land between Oxford Street and Piccadilly (Mayfair) and 480 acres between Hyde Park and the Thames (Belgravia and Pimlico) yielding an income of £1300 a year, passed to Mary, leaving his widow, who promptly remarried to become the wife of John Tregonwell, with the daunting task of sorting out his affairs in addition to being held responsible for his debts. It is interesting to note that Alexander Davies' estate included the marsh and meadowlands of the manor of Ebury which had been farmed by the Monks of Westminster Abbey before the Reformation. When King Henry VIII dissolved the monasteries he sold most of its land, keeping Hyde Park for his own use, thus leaving Westminster Abbey with only a small remnant of the land it once owned. It was on some of the land which the Abbey still retained that James Lane built his Lanesborough House in 1719, and eventually the Dean and Chapter of Westminster sold the freehold, as well as two adjoining houses, to the newly established St. George's Hospital in 1735 for £500.

The land which Alexander Davies had purchased was considered to be of poor quality, and therefore of little value until London began to expand in the middle of the seventeenth century. Faced with the burden of an increasing mountain of debt brought about by her late husband's improvident and highly speculative adventures, Mary Davies' mother thought that she had no alternative than to put her seven year old daughter and the manor of Ebury up for auction, and the highest bidder was the Lord Lieutenant of Ireland, Lord Berkeley of Stratton, who, seeing this purchase as a way to secure land for himself, and a potentially wealthy wife for his ten year old son, Charles, offered £5000 for this bizarre job lot of girl and land. Berkeley had previously built himself a large house in Piccadilly, and was now busy acquiring the land around it, which included what is now known as Berkeley Square and Stratton Street, when he recognised this transaction as being a marvellous opportunity to extend his land holdings to include the ownership of a potentially valuable estate beyond the turnpike at the western end of Piccadilly, or Hyde Park Corner as it was later known.

As part of the agreement with Mary Tregonwell, Lord Berkeley had agreed to pay her £5000 immediately and a further £3000 in land settled on his and the young Mary Davies as part of the marriage contract.

Berkeley paid over the £5000 but later he denied that he had ever made an offer of a further £3000 when he could not raise the sum, so the agreement fell through, and Mary's mother was left to start again the search for another prospective suitor who could put forward a sufficiently large sum of money to win the hand of her rather unattractive daughter, and her much more attractive inheritance.

Sir Thomas Grosvenor, the third Baronet, of Eaton, a title which had been purchased by the first Baronet in the 1620's from the unscrupulous Duke of Buckingham, seeing his chance to acquire an estate with possible untold potential, moved at great speed to repay Berkeley's £5000, and quickly married Mary Davies on her twelfth birthday on 10th October 1677 at St. Clement Danes. Sir Thomas, just twenty-one years of age, yet possessing a degree of financial shrewdness well beyond his years, immediately put down a further £1000 to purchase a reversionary interest so that if Mary died before she reached her twenty-first birthday her inherited land would be passed on to him.

As she grew older Mary Davies began to intensely dislike the arrangement she had been forced into by the desperate straits facing her mother, and campaigned vigorously to regain her land from the Grosvenor family. After Sir Thomas died in 1700, Mary Davies converted to Roman Catholicism and married Edward Fenton. The newly wedded Mr. and Mrs. Fenton soon hoped that they would enjoy a part of their inheritance, but the Grosvenors were quite shameless in the lengths to which they were prepared to go in order to protect their newly acquired wealth. They first sought to exploit Mary's conversion to Rome, which would be highly unpopular at that time, thus gaining the support of the Protestant ascendancy; and then to destroy her credibility completely they had her declared insane. And, as if wish were father to the deed, it is sad to record that Mary did die of insanity in 1730.

Sir Richard Grosvenor, the son of the unhappy misalliance between Mary Davies and Sir Thomas, who succeeded to the baronetcy on his father's death, immediately set about developing the land. By 1720 he had laid out Grosvenor Square, and, like his father before him, he demonstrated an unusual degree of business acumen. Grosvenor spent little of his own money, preferring to lease his land for a ninety-nine year period, which he had introduced to the builders, and then he insisted that the design and architecture of their buildings strictly adhered to the rigid rules that he had laid down. It appears that in his own person he was one of the forerunners of the now ubiquitous Planning Authorities, but happily he had a consistent and coherent vision of what he wanted. The only latitude that was allowed was in the interior layout of the buildings. After the expiry of the lease Sir Thomas Grosvenor proposed that the property would be sold again on the basis of a new ninety-nine years lease. This arrangement enabled the future Grosvenors to create a self-perpetuating property empire from which they were to amass fortunes.

After St. George's Hospital was established in Lanesborough House in 1733 the Board of Governors set about developing the hospital, and having purchased the freehold of Lanesborough House from Westminster Abbey, they were anxious to acquire additional land on which they could extend the already overcrowded buildings. The Governors approached the fourth baronet, Sir Richard Grosvenor in 1735 hoping that he would sell two acres of land on the south side of Lanesborough House to them. Grosvenor refused at first, but after protracted negotiations which lasted until 1767, he at last relented and agreed to lease the ground to the Governors for ninety eight years at a peppercorn rent, 'so long as the premises should be occupied as a public hospital'. The eastern half of the William Wilkins' new St. George's Hospital was built on this land eventually.

Sir Richard Grosvenor, the seventh baronet, was created Baron Grosvenor in 1761, and in 1784 he was elevated to the Earldom of Grosvenor and the Viscountcy of Belgravia by William Pitt the Younger, who was of the view that 'Anyone worth £10,000 a year is worth a peerage'.

In 1831, the then Earl of Grosvenor was created Marquis of Westminster, and his grandson, Hugh Lupus Grosvenor, was given the Dukedom of Westminster by Queen Victoria in 1874, at which time Hugh Lupus with an income of over £250,000 a year was far wealthier than Her Majesty. Hugh Lupus added to the family fortunes by his first marriage to Constance Leveson-Gower, the daughter of the Duke of Sutherland, who owned most of the county of Sutherland, as well as a number of properties including Cliveden, the Palladian Mansion

78

overlooking the Thames, which Hugh Lupus inherited, and in which he entertained Queen Victoria during Ascot week. When Hugh Lupus sold Cliveden to the Astors he incurred the monarch's displeasure, but the Queen acknowledged his lifelong generous service to so many public causes on his death, when she added a hand-written note to her wreath as 'A mark of sincere respect and regard and esteem from Victoria RI'.

Hugh Lupus Grosvenor was, like so many other members of his family, a member of the Board of Governors of St. George's, and from 1873 to 1899 he served as treasurer. It was through him that the hospital obtained the lease of another plot of land on which to extend the Wilkin's building, in order to satisfy the need for more space between the beds demanded by Florence Nightingale, who had been made an honorary member of the Board in recognition of her services to nursing. Belgrave, Williams and Hunter Wards were added to the end of the southern wing extending down Grosvenor Crescent, but the total number of beds in the hospital was only increased by one! The land was generously leased at a pepper-corn rent with the proviso that if the building ever ceased to be used as a hospital the leasehold would revert back to the Grosvenor Estate, for the price that St. George's had paid for the leasehold. At that time no one contemplated that St. George's would ever cease to exist at Hyde Park Corner, but there was considerable public indignation in 1980, when St. George's transferred to Tooting, and the Grosvenor Estates handed over a paltry sum of less than £30,000 in return for their land. Public opinion was ignorant of the background to the arrangements, and, worse still, failed to recognise the generosity which the Grosvenors had displayed in sparing the hospital large rental charges for so many years. In effect the hospital had paid nothing in rents. With the return of the land, the Grosvenor Estates now owned part of the vacated hospital building so the Department of Health, blissfully free of ideas as to what to do with their part, had little option but to allow them to purchase the remainder of the building, which has been transformed into the Lanesborough Hotel,

Grosvenor was introduced as a ward name at Hyde Park Corner in 1830 on the completion of the first phase – the east wing – of William Wilkins new St. George's Hospital. It is only proper that the multiple benefactions in the name of Grosvenor should continue to be remembered in the new St. George's Hospital at Tooting.

GUNNING WARD

John Gunning

Two Gunnings, both bearing the first name of John, have been surgeons to St. George's Hospital; but the ward is named after the elder of the two, who was in fact the uncle of the second John Gunning.

John Gunning, the nephew, was elected Surgeon in 1800, and although his appointment continued until 1823 it was largely nominal, as he spent the whole period away from the hospital, most of the time serving as Surgeon in Chief to the Army. He was present at every action throughout the Peninsular War. Gunning chose to remain in the army as he preferred the excitement of the battlefield to civilian practice. His last major engagement was at the battle of Waterloo under Wellington, but as soon as peace was declared in 1815 he settled in Paris, where he lived until his death at the age of 90.

The elder John Gunning was born at Swainswick in Gloucestershire in 1734, and was educated at Westminster School. He then entered St. George's Hospital as an assistant to Mr. Caesar Hawkins, with whom he worked for five years, before being elected Assistant Surgeon to the hospital in 1760, at the age of twenty six. Gunning succeeded David Middleton as Surgeon in 1765, and continued in this appointment until his death in 1798.

In 1773 he was elected Steward of Anatomy at the Surgeons Hall, but for some reason (probably to do with money) he declined to take up this post, preferring to pay a fine in mitigation for his refusal. This strange behaviour did not prevent his advancement because from 1784 until 1798 he was a member of the Court of Assistants and Examiners of the Corporation of Surgeons. He became Master of the Corporation in 1789 and at the end of his year in office he delivered a blistering critique of the corporation which was exposed as having an empty library, no lectures, and cursed by poor management. In 1790 he was elected as the first Professor of Surgery to the Corporation but soon resigned on the grounds that the post was too time consuming. This was inconsistency of an exceptional degree, and suggests either that he was markedly hypocritical, or that he conducted his public affairs on the basis of 'do as I say , and not do as I do'. This approach is not entirely foreign to a certain type of surgical mentality, which can spot problems a mile away, but appears disinclined to translate this fortunate gift into preventative action. Not surprisingly its motto is 'I told you so'.

Gunning disliked his colleague John Hunter, whom he regarded as being overbearing, selfish, and far too readily inclined to put his research interests ahead of his obligations and responsibilities as a surgeon. Their differences became even more acute when Keate was elected to succeed Charles Hawkins, in preference to Hunter's prodigy and brother-in-law, Everard Home. Hunter then recommended the admission of two pupils who were not supported by Gunning or his allies. A bitter altercation followed at the Weekly Board Meeting on 16th October 1793, which led to Hunter's apoplexy and much publicised sudden death in the hospital.

Ironically, Gunning succeeded Hunter as Surgeon General to the Army on the latter's death. Gunning also became Senior Surgeon Extraordinary to the King. John Gunning died in Bath in 1798 leaving his wife, Dorothy, who was the sister of Dr. Richard Warren of St. George's, four daughters, and one son, who was expelled from Westminster School in 1793 for rebellion. Joseph Gunning who was John's brother was both the secretary and solicitor to St. George's Hospital for more than fifty years.

GWILLIM WARD

Calvert Merton Gwillim, MD, FRCP, FRCS, FRCOG, DPH
Calvert Gwillim, 'Gwilly' as he was known by both colleagues and students, or 'David' by his closest friends, was born in Ceylon in 1899, and then educated at Swansea and St. Bartholomew's Hospital. After qualification in 1921 he became a house surgeon at Leicester Royal Infirmary, where he obtained a Diploma in Public Health in 1923, and a year later a Doctorate of Medicine in Obstetrics.

Gwillim was then appointed as Gynaecological Tutor and Assistant Medical Registrar to St. George's Hospital, where, from his earliest days, he showed a steely determination to become as highly qualified as possible, and reach the pinnacle of his chosen speciality as both a practitioner and teacher. By 1927 Calvert Gwillim was a Fellow of the Royal College of Surgeons, and in 1936 he was appointed Assistant Obstetric Surgeon to St. George's Hospital. His other appointments included Obstetric

81

Physician and Gynaecologist to the Samaritan Hospital, Maidenhead and Bexley Hospitals, as well as The Weir Maternity Hospital in Balham, which was later to become closely affiliated to St. George's Hospital.

Calvert Gwillim was a brilliant teacher and an extremely competent and gifted surgeon, who paid the greatest attention to detail, and woe betide the student who had not been aware that it was four sutures and not three he had recorded that had been inserted into the hidden depths of a wound. No concession was ever given to the fact that the only person who could have possibly seen this was Gwillim himself. Students were invariably left standing on a stool holding on to a retractor where the only view they had was of 'Gwilly's forehead as he operated away buried between the legs of the patient.

Gwillim's great talents were widely recognised, and he was made a Fellow of the Royal College of Physicians in 1940, and received the Fellowship of the newly founded Royal College of Obstetricians and Gynaecologists in 1942, but despite such national recognition, much to his credit he preferred to devote his time and energies to his patients and students at St. George's Hospital, where he was deeply interested in the affairs of the Medical School, and at one time was President of the Rugby Football Club. Gwillim turned his back on medical politics, and only rarely supported the Royal Colleges that had honoured him. He was not a frequent or loquacious 'contributor' at conferences, or to the medical press, although for a short period he did relent and served as President of the Section of Gynaecology and Obstetrics of the Royal Society of Medicine. However, his outstanding and lasting contribution to the development of gynaecology was his teaching, and his brilliant editorship of *Operative Surgery* or *Ten Teachers* as it was popularly known. Gwillim's chapters on vaginal hysterectomy and uterine prolapses remain classical masterpieces, and his reputation as a teacher and world-wide authority on his chosen speciality assured that his services were sought after as an examiner by both the Royal College of Obstetricians and Gynaecologists and the Universities; and although he never relished the thought of being away from Hyde Park Corner, he did occasionally relent, and was acknowledged as a searching but extremely fair examiner in gynaecology in both Oxford and Ceylon.

During the Second World War as a member of the Emergency Medical

Service Gwillim spent a short time at St. Stephen's Hospital, before returning to St. George's Hospital, where he lived in, and acted as a general and casualty surgeon. It fell to his responsibility to evacuate the hospital when a 500 pound bomb fell into the Medical School library but failed to explode.

Although Calvert Gwillim, who was short in stature and had a tic around his left eye, did appear on first acquaintance to be somewhat morose and severe, he was, by all accounts, far and away the most learned of his colleagues as a teacher, as well as being more skilful and accomplished as a surgeon than either of the other two gynaecologists: Harold Kirwan Taylor, who was a tall, charming, elegant, slightly foppish, latter day Beau Brummel, and the popular, rugged, good looking, sporty yet sleepy eyed Anthony Charles. All who broke through the barrier found Gwillim to be an intensely likeable and loyal friend. 'Gwilly' was renowned for his biting sense of humour, and his throwaway one liners usually made the rounds – and the pages of the Medical School Gazette. Many of his quips could not be repeated in these pages but always elicited guffaws of laughter from his students, and he was never averse to telling stories against himself. On one occasion he recalled that he asked a patient why she had come to see him and she replied ' Well, I had to consult you because you have such a funny name!'

Calvert Gwillim, who had few interests outside of medicine apart from bridge, collecting oriental ceramics and walking in his beloved Gower Peninsula, retired from practice in 1966, and died in Reading in 1972 at the age of 72.

HARRIS WARD

Harris

Harris was the name chosen for the second floor, easterly facing central ward, in the first phase of Wilkin's new St. George's Hospital when it was completed in 1829. The name was transferred to Tooting in the early 1990s, in response to further developments in the cardiac department. Its adoption at Tooting was only because 'Harris' had been a ward name used at Hyde Park Corner, where it was used mainly for ophthalmic, and ear, nose and throat surgery under the care of specialists such as

Brudenell-Carter, R.R. James, Duke-Elder, Bridgeman, Miller, Catford, Dalby, Jory, Peacock and Periera; although Harris Ward was directly above Fuller Ward which had housed the beds used by Alastair Hunter and Aubrey Leatham for cardiological patients.

The identity of Harris remains, like Wright (see later), a mystery. The minutes of the Weekly Board make very few references to anyone of the name Harris, save recording the payment of their annual subscriptions. Unfortunately there is no longer in existence a record of the many people who were cajoled into parting with their money by Dr. Fuller, to defray the costs of rebuilding St. George's Hospital at Hyde Park Corner, in the nineteenth century. If such a record was still extant it may have proved helpful in identifying the equally elusive figures of Harris and Wright

Lists of the Governors of St. George's Hospital appeared in the Annual Reports dating from 1822 which are preserved. Another document in the archives of the hospital lists the Governors in the year 1807. In this document the names of James and Quarles Harris are listed as Life Governors, so both of them subscribed £100 each to secure this distinction. James Harris is listed as a life Governor up to 1833, and Quarles Harris does not cease to be a life Governor until 1843. It is likely that either one or even both of them made a substantial contribution towards the rebuilding programme, but regrettably it is impossible at this distance to determine who it was donated the money, and it is probably of little consequence as one hundred and sixty years have passed since their surname was taken to grace a ward at St. George's. The preservation of the name *Harris* at Tooting serves to remind us of the loyalty and long service to St. George's which was shown by so many supporters whose names are now sadly forgotten, when it was a voluntary hospital.

HAWKINS WARD

The Hawkins Family

For many years Hawkins was used as the name for a ward at both St. George's and the Atkinson Morley's Hospital, and both acknowledged the contributions made by members of the Hawkins family to the hospitals concerned. It is only recently that it was decided without any good or sufficient reason to prefix Hawkins with Caesar, thus ignoring the inestimable debt that St. George's owes to the second Charles Hawkins. According to Burke, the Hawkins family can trace their descent from Colonel Caesar Hawkins, who commanded a troop of horse for the King Charles I during the Civil War, and who is chiefly to be remembered for his defence of Greenland House.

Caesar Hawkins the Elder was born in Ludlow in 1711, the son of a surgeon of the town, and great grandson of the Colonel. In 1735 Hawkins, who had studied under his father and another surgeon, Mr. Ranby, was admitted to the Company of Surgeons, and in the same year he was elected Surgeon to St. George's Hospital at the ridiculously early age of 24, just two years after the hospital was founded, where he joined Dickins, Amyand and Cheselden. In the year following Hawkins was appointed Surgeon to Frederick Louis, Prince of Wales, whose bitter hatred of his parents was equalled only by the savage abhorrence with which they (especially his mother) regarded him, and therefore it comes as no surprise to learn that the political classes exploited this antipathy, so that Frederick became the focus of opposition to the government. The vicious infighting which swirled around this desperately dysfunctional family did not prevent Hawkins' preferment, which is the highest testament to his personality and his professional abilities; and his standing in royal circles reached its peak in 1747 when he became Sergeant Surgeon to Frederick's father King George II. Frederick died in 1751, predeceasing his father. His son, George then aged twelve took over both his father's title and his surgeon, and he retained the latter when he in turn came to the throne as King George III on the death of his grandfather. Hawkins retired from St. George's Hospital in 1774, at the same time as Ambrose Dickins following their altercation with the Board, and was created a Baronet in 1778. Sir Caesar Hawkins died in 1786. It is said that he was a very dextrous surgeon who attracted a large surgical practice when he was still very young. Reputedly, he made over one thousand guineas a year from bleeding alone, which represents a sum considerably in excess of what practitioners might earn today. Hawkins wrote little, but invented a cutting gorget which he wielded with great speed and skill on patients, long before general or local anaesthetics were discovered.

Caesar Hawkins' brother Pennell became Master of the Surgeons' Company, and was also a Sergeant Surgeon. Sir Caesar's portrait by Hogarth hangs in the Royal College of Surgeons, and a poor copy, which was given by his grandson, Caesar H Hawkins, in 1852, hangs in the Interview Room in Grosvenor Wing, St. George's Hospital.

Charles Hawkins, eldest son of Sir Caesar Hawkins, also studied medicine, and followed in his father's footsteps by being appointed Assistant Surgeon to St. George's Hospital in 1773, a year later he was elected Surgeon, a post he occupied until he resigned for reasons unknown in 1792. However, he applied to be re-elected in 1798 and was successful again in being appointed Surgeon and served in this post until 1800. Charles, like his father before him, was Sergeant Surgeon to King George III, and in 1800 he became the first Master of the College of Surgeons. Charles Hawkins did not make any contribution to surgical literature. It was said that his working life was fully occupied looking after the huge private practice he inherited from his father.

Charles' cousin, George Hawkins, son of Pennell Hawkins, was elected Surgeon to St. George's Hospital in 1780, but resigned this post after only three years service. The next member of the Hawkins' family to serve St. George's was Caesar Henry, the son of the Reverend Edward Hawkins, and grandson of Sir Caesar. Caesar Henry was born in Bisley, Gloucestershire in 1798, and was educated at Christ's Hospital before serving as a pupil to a Mr. Sheppard. In 1818 young Hawkins entered St. George's as a student of John Hunter's brother in law, Sir Everard Home, and Benjamin Brodie. He became a member of the Royal College of Surgeons in 1821, and was elected Assistant Surgeon in 1829, gaining rapid promotion to Surgeon later in that year with the resignation of Thomas Rose. Caesar Hawkins, nicknamed 'The Emperor', was another remarkably able man: he became President of the Royal College of Surgeons in 1852, and again in 1861, he was a College examiner for a number of years, and gave the Hunterian Oration at the College in 1849. In 1862 he was appointed Sergeant Surgeon to Queen Victoria, and a few years later he was elected a trustee of the Hunterian Museum, and a Fellow of the Royal Society.

Caesar Henry Hawkins was said to have been a superb surgeon, and was credited with being the first to successfully perform an ovariotomy,

86

he also pioneered the operation of colotomy. However, he was a strong advocate of conservative management, and it was said of him that 'he was always more anxious to teach his pupils how to save a limb than how to remove it'. Hawkins made a considerable contribution to medical literature, and he was a respected teacher, who was always willing to give his colleagues the benefit of his great experience. In 1861 he retired from St. George's Hospital, but remained a Consulting Surgeon until his death in 1884. During his retirement he was often seen in the Hospital, giving his much sought after opinion on difficult cases at the request of his younger colleagues.

Another Hawkins who served St. George's Hospital in the last century was Charles Hawkins. Although it appears unlikely that he was closely related to the members of the other Hawkins family, he was a greater servant of the Hospital than the others who bore his surname, despite the fact that his ambition to become a Surgeon to St. George's was unfulfilled due to the vagaries of the voting system employed by the Board of Governors at that time. Charles Hawkins was born in 1812, the son of Anthony Montonnier Hawkins MD of London and educated at Charterhouse and St. Mary's Oscott, a Roman Catholic college outside Birmingham before entering St. George's as a student in 1831. He qualified as a member of the Royal College of Surgeons in 1836, and immediately became assistant to Benjamin Brodie. By 1843 his abilities as a surgeon were widely recognised, and on the election of Thomas Tatum to Surgeon, Charles Hawkins was the popular choice to replace him, he had found favour with Benjamin Brodie and the remainder of the medical staff, and was the outstanding candidate. In those days election to the medical staff was by vote of the full membership of the Board of Governors; on this occasion, despite being made aware of the very definite views of the medical staff, the wayward Governors voted for a much less impressive candidate: Henry Charles Johnson. Although Hawkins was presumably deeply hurt by this cavalier rejection, he never allowed it to show, and he devoted the rest of his life to his beloved St. George's. Timothy Holmes, a fellow surgeon said 'It is much to the credit of Mr. Hawkins that a repulse so mortifying as this did not act against his interest in St. George's nor make him slacken in using all his energies in its service'. He continued to be active in that service up to the close of his long life, and he was for a very long period the pre-eminent figure on the Board of Governors. He served as Treasurer to the Board from 1865 to 1870. During this time his proposal to place elections in the hands of a small (and presumably better informed) sub-committee, rather than the whole Board of Governors, was accepted, and became the standard practice for all future appoinments.

Charles Hawkins was a friend of Atkinson Morley, a wealthy hotelier and member of the Board of Governors, and he upheld and reinforced the latter's support for the novel concept of convalescence as a means of hastening a favourable outcome after illness. It is suggested that he influenced Morley to leave the major share of his fortune to St. George's Hospital for the express purpose of building a convalescent hospital. After Morley's death Charles Hawkins played a major role in the successful establishment of the Atkinson Morley's Hospital in Wimbledon. Throughout his life he was a great benefactor, and he presented the hospital with a number of valuable items including the copy of Richard Wilson's 'View of St. George's Hospital' (Richard Wilson who lived between 1713 and 1882, a Welshman, inspired by Claude, Cuyp and Gaspar Poussin was a prolific painter of landscapes and portraits) which now hangs in the Boardroom. Later Hawkins presented a much more valuable painting to St. George's Hospital. It was of Count Soliraul's (Soleirol or Solaire) horse and his dog, Rose, and the painting was originally by John Sartorius (1755-1828). Count Soliraul, a French Protestant refugee, was the proprietor of the Cocoa Tree Club,[1] a meeting place for both the Tories and the Spectator Club, and when he retired the membership, anxious to commemorate the event, gave sixty guineas to William Hogarth (1697-1764) in order that he should add the Count to the painting sitting astride his horse.

---

[1] The Cocoa Tree opened in the late 17th century as The Cocoa Tree Chocolate House in Pall Mall. The Cocoa Tree was used as a sign for chocolate after it was first brought to England in 1652. In 1657 Roger North (1653-1734), the lawyer and writer claimed that 'the use of coffee houses seems newly improved by a new invention called chocolate houses'. The Cocoa Tree Chocolate House was used as the headquarters of the Jacobites in 1745 but a year later it was converted into a private club which had a reputation as one of the most notorious gambling centres in London. The Club closed at the end of the nineteenth century.

At a later date either Hogarth, or even a third artist, painted St. George's Hospital in the background.

When Count Soleirol died his two daughters went to live with Hogarth. On their death the composite painting passed to Maria Burke, Hogarth's grand-daughter. She married a James O'Brien and their eldest daughter, Elizabeth Helen, who had married a Mr. Campbell eventually acquired the painting. Elizabeth Campbell had the misfortune to fall from a tree in Hyde Park, though why this strange accident occurred is unknown as this was not the period when mature women were accustomed to climb trees! She was treated by Robert Keate of St. George's, who saw the painting on one of his visits; he offered twenty pounds for the painting as he wished to present it to his hospital. The offer was refused at that stage, but on Mrs. Campbell's death the painting was passed on to her son, Mr. Robert F. D. Campbell, a sanitary engineer and surveyor living at Lancaster Gate, with specific instructions to sell the painting. Robert Campbell wrote to Charles Hawkins offering him the first refusal. Hawkins purchased the painting, and presented it to St. George's Hospital where it remained until the late 1920s. It was at this time that the hospital architect, Mr. H. Percy Adams offered 200 guineas for the painting, and despite protestations from Sir George Turner, the Surgeon, the Board of Governors sold the painting to Adams. It is impossible to feel other than sorry for poor Charles Hawkins, as once again the Board of Governors (albeit a different one) had treated him shabbily. Perhaps fortunately, Charles Hawkins was not alive to witness this second episode of casual indifference. He had died in 1892. Obviously selling the family silver is not a new phenomenon!

Despite the fact that Charles Hawkins did not obtain a consultant appointment at St. George's, he was highly respected in medical circles, and he became the Inspector of Anatomy, Vice President of the Medico-Chirurgical Society and a Member of the Council of the Royal College of Surgeons (1866-1873). Hawkins also collected together Benjamin Brodie's scientific papers and published them in three volumes.

Some may wish to argue which of the many Hawkins made the most significant contribution to St. George's, but it is difficult not to entertain the greatest admiration for the last Charles, who in spite of the cruel blow to his career prospects delivered by the Governors in 1843, apparently bore no grudge and spent the next fifty years in the service of the hospital and its Board of Governors. This reveals a nobility and generosity of spirit rarely seen in any walk of life. On his death the Weekly Board minuted that it 'desires to place on record its deep sense of loss sustained by the Hospital in the death of Mr. Charles Hawkins who throughout a long, useful and honourable life devoted his time, his energies and his thoughts to the best interests of the Hospital and contributed in so many and varied ways to its well being'.

HEBERDEN WARD

William Heberden, MA, MD, FRCP, FRS
William Heberden was the second son of William Heberden, MD, FRS, (1710-1801), a renowned physician, who practised in Cambridge and London, and was also a lecturer in Materia Medica and a classical scholar who wrote *Commentarii de Morborum Historia et Curatione* (Commentaries on the History and Cure of Diseases), which was published posthumously, had been described by Dr. Samuel Johnson as 'ultimus Romanarum' – the last of our learned physicians; and Dr. W. C. Wells remarked that 'No other person, either in this or any other century, has ever exercised the art of medicine with the same signity, or contributed so much to raise it in the estimation of mankind'.

A father with a reputation of this order set extremely high standards and needed some living up to, but William Heberden the younger had the mettle for the task, as well as the name. He was born in 1767, and educated at Charterhouse, and St. John's College, Cambridge, where he passed his BA in 1788, proceeding to his MA in 1791, at Christchurch, Oxford. It strains credulity to believe that only a year after qualifying MB in 1792, he was appointed Physician to St. George's Hospital. In what appears to have been a positive frenzy of achievement over the next few years he had obtained his MD (1795), been made a Fellow of the Royal Society (1796), been admitted as a Candidate of the College of Physicians (1795), and was made a Fellow of that College in 1796. He was to become Censor of the College of Physicians in 1799 and 1808.

With the same frantic speed that he had attained his academic distinctions, William Heberden established his practice and reputation.

90

He wrote his *Observations on the Increase and Decrease of different Diseases , particularly the Plague* in 1801, and, a year later, his translation of his father's renowned work was published. In 1795 he was appointed Physician Extraordinary to Queen Charlotte, and became her Physician in Ordinary in 1806. He resigned his post at St. George's in 1803 after a tenure of only 11 years, and in 1805 he was appointed Physician Extraordinary to King George III, and Physician in Ordinary in 1809. So popular was Heberden with the King that he was offered a baronetcy and a pension on more than one occasion, but Heberden always declined this honour. By all accounts it appears that Heberden's practice was considerable, but, to its detriment, he became pre-occupied in attempting to secure proper medical treatment for King George III, whose putative porphyria led to frequent episodes of insanity which were being treated by Dr. Francis Willis, a director of a lunatic asylum, who, understandably, favoured restraint as the best treatment for the King's uncontrollable outbursts. Heberden, Halford and Matthew Baillie attempted to persuade Spencer Perceval, Henry Addington, and other senior members of the Queen's Council to hand the treatment of the sick King over to them. Unfortunately for His Majesty the Queen's Council disagreed, and Willis remained responsible for King George III's welfare, although Heberden continued to visit the King until the latter died in 1820.

William Heberden's wife, Elizabeth, to whom he was devoted, bore him nine children, but it was her lot to predecease him in 1812 shortly after their seventeenth wedding anniversary. Heberden was devastated at the tragic loss of his wife. Immediately he gave up his practice and settled in Datchet, near Windsor, where he brought up his young family. Occasionally he paid a professional visit to Windsor, but when not tending to his family's needs Heberden occupied himself by translating into English Plutarch's *Brotherly Love* and Cicero's *Letters to Atticus*. He also wrote a short dialogue on general education. In 1826 he returned to London but, shortly after his return, his son Henry, a medical student at St. George's, died of sepsis, in 1828, from a wound incurred whilst he was dissecting, and this sad event was quickly foreshadowed by the death of another son and his eldest daughter. In his grief Heberden sought consolation in Christianity, and soon he became engrossed in biblical exegesis. In

1830 he published his *Reflections on the Gospel of St. John*, and, in 1839, he translated the *Catholic Epistles*. By their encouragement his friends prevailed upon him to translate the complete *Apostolic Epistles*, and the *Book of Revelations* which was published in 1839. His preoccupation with religious studies continued until his death in 1845 at his home in Cumberland Street, London.

William Heberden was buried in the family vault at Windsor. After the brilliant start to his career, the melancholy and unfulfilled mature years were probably influenced greatly by his deep solicitude for his King and his family; and attempts to emulate his father would doubtless seem rather trivial when set against these enduring concerns.

FREDERICK HEWITT WARD

Sir Frederick William Hewitt, KCVO, MVO, MA, MD
Frederick William Hewitt was born in London in 1857, the eldest son of an agricultural chemist. Hewitt was educated at Merchant Taylor's School, and the Royal School of Mines, before he read Natural Science at Christ's College, Cambridge. He entered St. George's Hospital as a student in 1880, and qualified MRCS, LRCP in 1882, MB in 1883, and then proceeded to his Doctorate of Medicine in 1886.

Unfortunately Frederick Hewitt suffered from poor eyesight which forced him to change his career in mid-course, discarding a career in clinical medicine he turned his attention to the developing field of anaesthesia, and became one of the most prominent and influential figures in this developing speciality.

Doctors at St. George's were slow to recognise the importance of anaesthesia, although Dr. John Snow had given them an early lead in being the anaesthetist to the Outpatient Department in the middle of the nineteenth century, a curious anomaly, as well as administering anaesthesia to some of the in-patients, and the Queen, the importance of skilled anaesthetists remained unrecognised at St. George's. After Snow's departure the responsibility for giving the anaesthetics rested with the apothecary who had had no formal training. In 1879 W. H. Bennett later to become Sir William Bennett, the surgeon was appointed 'chloroformist' at a salary of twenty pounds a year. Hewitt recognising that there was no future for him as an anaesthetist at his own teaching hospital was forced to look elsewhere for an opportunity to practise his chosen speciality. He was appointed Anaesthetist to Charing Cross Hospital in 1884, and then gained similar appointments at the National Dental Hospital in 1885, and the London Hospital in 1886. By the turn of the century, Frederick Hewitt was generally recognised as one of this country's leading anaesthetists, and was appointed as anaesthetist to King Edward VII. Hewitt was called upon, in 1902, to anaesthetize the uncrowned king for his appendectomy, the illness which delayed his coronation. Hewitt was made a Member of the Royal Victorian Order in recognition of his services. When George V succeeded his father as sovereign in 1910 Hewitt was asked to continue as the royal anaesthetist.

By 1897 St. George's Hospital, had recognised the importance of skilled anaesthetists and appointed Henry Menzies and Joseph Blomfield (Blumfeld) but neither were given the status of consultants. Two years later Llewelyn Powell was appointed to another anaesthetic post and in 1902 accepting Hewitt's pre-eminence in the field, he was offered the unique appointment of Physician Anaesthetist, and he remained in this post until shortly before his death in 1916. Hewitt's great contributions to anaesthetic practice included his research into safer mixtures of nitrous oxide and oxygen, the dangers of chloroform during the induction of anaesthesia, the development of a number of pieces of equipment including: the dental prop, his modification of Junker's chloroform bottle, and his redesign of Thomas Clover's inhaler. Frederick Hewitt's book *Anaesthetics and their Administration* was first published in 1893, and reached its fifth edition six years after his death, was very popular and regarded as a reading 'must' amongst students of the discipline.

However, by far his greatest contribution to the speciality of anaesthesia was his campaign to improve the training, education and standing of the anaesthetist. In 1909, at the Medico-Legal Society's meeting, he proposed that anaesthetic instruction must be compulsory for all medical students, and the giving of anaesthetics, except by qualified medical men, should be a penal offence. Both proposals were accepted, and led to the drafting of the Anaesthetics Bill, which due to other business was unfortunately never passed by Parliament. For his invaluable contribution to the standing of anaesthetics in Great Britain, Hewitt was awarded a Knighthood.

Sir Frederick Hewitt was a superb clinical anaesthetist and teacher, and his appointment to St. George's Hospital in 1902 laid the foundations for the development of a first class department of anaesthesia which is now one if not the largest and busiest departments in London.

Hewitt died of a carcinoma of the stomach in 1916 in Brighton where he was buried. Sir Frederick Hewitt's name is not only remembered at St. George's, but at the Royal College of Anaesthetists, where there is an annual Hewitt Lecture.

HOLDSWORTH WARD

Sir Frank Holdsworth, ChM, FRCS

Although Frank Holdsworth was a major figure in orthopaedic surgery in his time, his enduring claim to fame today is for his signal contribution to postgraduate medical training. He was born in Bradford in 1904, and educated at Bradford Grammar School before attending Downing College, Cambridge; his medical studies were undertaken at St. George's Hospital: he gained his Fellowship of the Royal College of Surgeons in 1930, and his Masters degree in Surgery (Ch.M.) in 1935. For a short time he held junior surgical posts at St. George's prior to becoming a surgical registrar at the Royal Infirmary in Sheffield, where he worked for the rest of his life. Large conurbations based on heavy industry have a disproportionate share of major trauma, and this frequently involves orthopaedic injury. Sheffield was no exception in having plenty of the latter, nor was it unusual in those days for not having a dedicated department to deal with it. Holdsworth was invited to take over orthopaedic and trauma cases, bringing them together into a new department, and he became the first orthopaedic specialist in the city in 1937. As a corollary to this he was quick to see the enormous potential of rehabilitation, and he was a major influence in creating one of the first Spinal Injury Centres in the country at Lodge Moor Hospital, which has an international reputation.

When Holdsworth was a young consultant continued medical training after graduation was very much a hit and miss affair, and usually geared to passing the professional diploma examinations of the Royal Colleges in one's chosen speciality, and as such it was very much the responsibility of the individual trainee to organise periods of relevant study within the limits imposed by the post; this was long before the concept of regulated hours, overtime, and study leave. In fact the system was derived from the old apprenticeship scheme of things. Consultants spent less time in the public hospitals, and pre-NHS many were not paid (hence the term 'Honorary Consultant'), so they had to make a living in private practice, and for all practical purposes the majority took little or no interest in the formal training of their juniors. There were, of course, exceptions to this rule, but they were sufficiently thin on the ground to merit widespread renown, their posts were keenly sought after, but they were often scorned by their less sympathetic colleagues. In London there were one or two private courses run by individuals which acted as a type of crammer, and which were in fact lineal descendants of the old Anatomy Schools; but they did not exist in the provinces. Most of the teaching was of an ad hoc type provided by the goodwill of well disposed registrars, who had themselves only recently been mauled during their rites of passage, and could still remember what the examiners were wanting. In short there was no commitment to organised training.

Holdsworth made a visit to the USA before the formation of the National Health Service, and came into contact with the American system, where the training of Residents was for a fixed period, and senior staff were involved throughout this time with the preparation of these juniors for specialist status. He became familiar with the custom of Staff Conferences which were attended by the whole department, and indeed were open to all, to which the participants would bring their problem cases to be discussed in front of the group. These sessions were, and continue to be, extremely valuable as a means of exploring a topic by shedding light on it from all manner of different angles, it stretches the mind much more and demonstrates the depth and subtlety of clinical problems and how individuals approach them, it is thus generally more stimulating than the didactic approach which springs from the formal lecture. It certainly made a huge impression on Holdsworth, who adopted it on his return to England: his rendering of the concept was that all comments would be given with equal weight, and to avoid sycophancy the juniors were asked to give their views first, this was a novel way of teaching, a sort of medical free-for-all, with no 'flannel'. It was frowned upon if an individual did not enter the spirit of the gathering, and if a person's words continued longer than there were ideas to support them. In this way Holdsworth began his crusade to establish postgraduate training, for many years his was a voice in the wilderness. He encountered a degree of hostility from his colleagues, who felt that he was distracting their juniors from their real task in hand by his emphasis on education. He gradually built up a large and first class unit, which was known nationally and internationally as being justly famous for its training methods as well as for the high quality of its' clinical work. The rotating registrar scheme was developed by Holdsworth, so that trainees could see across the whole range of the speciality in the region: the different approaches to common conditions, and the more esoteric disorders dealt with by surgeons who had developed a special interest in them. It was said that only one trainee failed to get his Fellowship during the rotation, in all the years that it was in operation. Never afraid of controversy, as a surgeon he was well known for promoting internal fixation as the best means of dealing with fractures, a position vigorously challenged by more conservative colleagues.

For many years his views on postgraduate training were lost on his colleagues, who had a deeply ingrained aversion to change, but this did not deter him from the struggle to be heard, indeed as a proud Yorkshireman it probably made him knock even louder on the closed doors of medical prejudice, until first he managed to get a toe in the door, and ultimately was able to push it open; by which time his reputation was secure as the single most important national figure in the fight for junior doctors to be given proper training. And with recognition came reward: he had been an examiner for the Royal College of Surgeons, in 1958 he was elected on to the Council of the College, and at the time of his death he was Senior Vice-President. of the College. He had served as the President of the British Orthopaedic Association, and was an Honorary Fellow of the American College of Surgeons, the American Academy of Orthopaedic Surgery, and the South African Orthopaedic Association.

As a person he was an archetypal Yorkshireman, intensely proud of his

96

birthright, blunt, honest, and warm, who did not suffer fools gladly, but whose friendship once given was a guarantee of unconditional loyalty. As pastimes he enjoyed fishing, travelling, the study of history, good food and good company. He was a member of the conspiracy of Northerners to keep secret the natural beauty and the many advantages of life in the North to prevent mass migration from the South. Shortly before his death in 1969, after a long and painful illness which he did not allow to interfere with his work or his extracurricular campaigns, he received a well deserved knighthood, and an Honorary Chair in the University of Sheffield, which gave him great pleasure. Generations of junior doctors should revere the name of this doughty figure who fought so single-mindedly for their access to postgraduate education.

HOPE WARD

James Hope, MD, FRCP, FRS

There are two men with the name of James Hope who have special links with St. George's Hospital. The first of these was a benefactor whose name was apportioned to a ward at the original hospital at Hyde Park Corner, but the more significant Hope, who is dealt with here, was one of the most important of the early cardiologists working in the first part of the 19th century, and it is his name that now adorns one of the cardiac wards in the new hospital at Tooting.

The family from which he sprang had their proud roots in Scotland, but were now living in Stockport where Mr. Hope senior was a successful merchant, presumably in the cotton trade which was already flourishing in Manchester and its locality. He retired at the age of 44 with an income of £4,000 a year, to Prestbury, in Cheshire, to enjoy the fruits of his mercantile prowess by pursuing the life of a country gentleman and cultural dilettante. James born in 1801, was the 10th of 12 children. Separated by some years from his elder siblings, and held in awe by his younger ones, he was rather an isolated little boy, a prodigious reader, who also had the run of the countryside, where he appears to have been a largely self-taught fly fisherman, who perforce had to make his own rods, lines and flies. He was educated locally, and then by his own tutor, before attending Macclesfield Grammar School where he proved to be an apt and very gifted pupil. It was his ambition at that stage to study the law and become a barrister like one of his elder brothers, his father would have preferred him to go into business and did not enter the boy for Oxford. James spent an indecisive and unprofitable year at home before his father decided he should study medicine; this proposal met with opposition from the boy, but he was cajoled into accepting his father's views by a senior physician from Manchester who was visiting one of his relatives. He was sent to Oxford, where he remained for about 18 months, this seems a time of little formal activity because he never registered with the university authorities. His father recalled him, and packed him off to Edinburgh in 1820. There was a well known aphorism of the day which claimed that apropos of medicine: 'London for practice, Edinburgh for theory' Stangely enough, James, with a prescience beyond his years, made his father promise that if he went north to study his father would raise no objection to a London career after he qualified!

With his future settled James went off to attend to the present. He hated dissection, and always wore gloves and used forceps to avoid physical contact with the specimens, but as the clinical part of the course developed James began to shine, and he became a successful student. It is said that he was somewhat shy and reserved, but he forced himself to take part in debates and clinical disputes, with such skill that in 1823 he was elected to be one of the four presidents of the Royal Medical – Surgical Society of Edinburgh, though he was disappointed to come second in the election. Early in 1824 he qualified and became first a House Physician, and then a House Surgeon, where he found to his suprise that intimacy with visible disease helped prepare him for his medical studies; this approach to pathology he recommended to his students in turn. It was at this time that he began a life-long habit of drawing diseased structures, which proved to be of enormous benefit when he came to write his treatises. After his junior posts in his alma mater, he came to London and found work in surgery at St. Bartholomew's, during this time he sat the membership examination of the College of Surgeons, where he was told by Mr. Cline, after being questioned for 17 minutes: 'You know your profession, sir, there is no need to detain you'. Like all young men of education and private means he embarked on a tour of Europe, but was so impressed by the standard of medical education in Paris, which, like the country, had been shaken up by the revolution, that he decided to stay. A knowledge of French would facilitate his studies, so for a month of 12 hour days he did nothing but speak and read the language, becoming sufficiently fluent that he could understand and contribute with ease. He was attached to Professor Chomel at La Charité as a clinical clerk for a year which was a tribute to his linguistic skills. At the conclusion of his time in Paris he toured Germany, Switzerland, Italy, where he refused the offer of a lucrative practice in Florence, before making his way home to begin the serious business of making a name for himself.

There can be few who have subjected the prospects to such a careful forensic study as Hope. He had learned that the 20 most famous physicians in London together earned about £80,000 per year, and he reckoned that it would take him about 5 years to reach this point, when in fact it took him 12 years. This of course was a huge sum of money in those days. He was prepared to walk, do without servants, remain a bachelor, anything to achieve his ambition. Another major difficulty lay in his path: he had not trained in the capital and therefore lacked that network of connections which could be used to advance his practice, finally he had no patron who could be relied upon to apply leverage in those elevated circles where appointments were made. Hope realised, with that cold logic which informed all his decisions, that if he wished to prosper it had to be by his own efforts, and that to attain his goal of being the foremost London physician of his day he had to make a reputation. He started a private practice in Lower Seymour Street, which he learned to his chagrin was not the most fashionable area; in his first year he earned £200, and his income stayed in that range for several years to come. Gradually things picked up, and he saw no reason to move.

Hope knew that in his circumstances his salvation would only come through publishing, and his practice would take off once he became known as a leading figure in medical science. He had continued to draw pathology throughout his early training, and he began to prepare the ground for his two major books: one on Morbid Anatomy and the other on Heart Disease illustrated by his own plates suitably coloured. He allotted seven years for this project. To keep abreast of medicine he became a senior student at St. George's Hospital, he made meticulous notes of cases, even of conversations and arguments, so he was always prepared to act as a reference library; at the same time he urged the hospital to appoint Clinical Clerks to make notes, the scheme found favour and appropriately enough he was made the first of this new breed.

Laennec had introduced the art of auscultation less than a decade before Hope visited Paris, and he had the novel opportunity of learning from the master himself. Blessed with excellent and delicate hearing Hope found no difficulty in acquiring familiarity with the technique, and returned to England as something of a pioneer in this subject, which was held in low esteem by British doctors, because practitioners who used the technique felt that it was so far superior to anything else that they could rely implicitly on their findings. This was not the case in practice, and Hope's method of combining it with the general signs of the patient's condition was in the event much more accurate. He insisted that his comments and diagnosis were read out before the post-mortem examination, and he was rarely in error. He would invite critics along to read their views at the same time. Few came, and then never twice!

To determine the cause of the normal heart sounds Hope experimented with donkeys. A sharp blow to the head to render them senseless was followed by a rudimentary tracheotomy and ventilation with a pair of bellows, while Hope opened the left side of the chest with a saw. Simultaneous observation and auscultation gave the answer, and he demonstrated his findings to others, one of whom later was to claim that he had performed the crucial test, because Hope, bogged down by work, was delayed in publication. This attempt at plagiary by someone he considered a friend failed, but only after a long battle. Hope's other experiments, which were conducted with woorara (curare) rather than concussion confirmed the definitive explanation of the heart sounds, and this led to his election to the Royal Society.

Hope abandoned at least one of his resolutions and married Anne Fulton in 1831, by all accounts they were very happy together, and had a son who became Sir Theophilus Hope. One of the penalties of marriage was that he had to stop reading at meals, but there were compensations: he could dictate to his wife whilst he was eating, and for a year they slaved to complete the book on heart disease which ran to 600 pages. It was a work involving colossal industry, but worth it in terms of

100

recognition. The book was well received in North America where Hope has always been recognised as a seminal figure in cardiology, although largely forgotten in his own land. Translated into German and Italian, the popularity of the book was very gratifying to its author, and went through three editions during the last 8 years of his life, including a major revision with much additional new work in 1839.

In 1834 Hope's mentor at St. George's Hospital, Dr Chambers fell ill, and the Board decided to appoint an Assistant Physician to cope with the Outpatient load. The post went to Hope who resigned from Marylebone Hospital to devote all his time to this new post, which involved seeing approximately 4000 new cases each year. His health was suffering from the way he pushed himself, and only two weeks after he been appointed a full Physician in 1839, he coughed up some blood, a tragic irony for this rising man who had at last achieved all his professional objectives. As the tuberculosis took hold he rapidly went downhill, but had the satisfaction of being made a Fellow of the Royal College of Physicians in the last year of his life, a rare honour for those not trained in London, but which he could only regard as something of a consolation prize for losing life itself.

Strong as ever in his Anglican faith, in which he had campaigned to have the first chaplain elected to the hospital, he resigned from the staff and spent his last days with his beloved wife and child. He died in May 1841.

As a man he was driven by a fierce ambition, he calculated his ascent with precision, and drove himself with a remorseless determination to attain the outward trappings of success. Having done so much to acquire them he was spared pitifully little time to enjoy them, and there is a lesson here for those who wish to learn about Life. He was happily married, but does not appear to have had the comfort and consolation of many close personal friends. In his day one imagines he was more admired than liked by his contemporaries, and regarded as worthy but somewhat distant and intimidating because of his prodigious industry; that his name fell into oblivion in his own country may in part be due to his untimely death before he had taught that accumulating dynasty of young men who interweave anecdote and reminiscence to embellish a well-worn persona that may be then handed on to posterity.

THE TREVOR HOWELL UNIT

Trevor Henry Howell, MRCS, LRCP, FRCPE

Trevor Howell was the son of a Barnsley surgeon and a nurse. He was said to have experienced an unhappy childhood, yet grew up to have an infectious sense of humour. Howell was educated at Bradfield College, and St. John's College, Cambridge, and St. Bartholomew's Hospital, London, where he qualified in 1934. He then worked with Paul Wood in Edinburgh, and proceeded to pass the membership examination of the Royal College of Physicians of Edinburgh in 1937. Howell then became a research assistant at the Post-Graduate Medical School, Hammersmith, before entering general practice in Worthing, West Sussex.

During the second World War Trevor Howell joined the Royal Army Medical Corps. Serendipity, which does not normally play a major role in Army postings, saw to it that he was posted to the Royal Hospital, Chelsea, where he immediately developed what was to become his lifelong interest: the care and welfare of the elderly. Later in the war he was less fortunate in being transferred overseas to Burma and India. He returned to England in 1946 still intent on making his career in the care of the elderly, he took a research fellowship at St. John's Hospital, Battersea, and within a very short while he had established a research unit in geriatric medicine. As soon as the National Health Service was introduced in 1948 Trevor Howell was appointed a consultant physician, with a special interest in geriatrics, at St. John's Hospital, and later he became Physician Superintendent at Queen's Hospital, Croydon.

In 1947, with the assistance of seven other geriatricians, Lord Amulree, Marjory Warren, Lawrence Sturdee, Lionel Cosin, Eric Brooke, Tom Wilson and Alfred Mitchell, Howell formed the 'Medical Society for the Care of the Elderly'. The society flourished and eventually changed its title to the 'British Geriatric Society'. At Croydon and Battersea Howell formed the 'British Association for Services to the Elderly', and at the time of his death growth had been such that there were twenty other branches in existence.

Trevor Howell was a voracious reader and owned a unique collection of books. Extremely meticulous, he kept hand-written notes of every book that he read and records of every patient that he had examined.

102

These detailed records were used as the basis of the four books and more than three hundred papers that he wrote during his career. He was a popular teacher and taught students from Bart's, Westminster, Charing Cross and St. George's. After his retirement from the NHS he became a research fellow at St. George's Hospital Medical School in the Department of Geriatric Medicine.

The seminal contributions of Trevor Howell to geriatric medicine were recognised internationally when he was made a Fellow of the American Geriatric Society and awarded the Willard O. Thompson Gold Medal, and in the United Kingdom when he was made the first recipient of the Founders Medal of the British Geriatric Association. Shortly before his death in 1988 Trevor Howell was awarded the F. E. Williams Prize of the Royal College of Physicians.

Outside medicine Trevor Howell enjoyed music, and was for many years President of the Streatham Swimming club, and an Official of the Surrey Swimming and Water Polo Club.

THE ALASTAIR HUNTER ROOM

Mark Ian Alastair Hunter, MD, FRCP

Alastair Hunter was born in 1909 in Sussex, where his father was a general practitioner. He received his education at Winchester, and Trinity College, Cambridge, before entering St. George's Hospital in 1930. After qualifying MRCS, LRCP in 1933, Hunter decided to specialise in cardiology, so, after completing a number of junior appointments at St. George's, he was appointed to the London Hospital, where he received his cardiological training under Sir John Parkinson.

During the Second World War Alastair Hunter served with the Royal Army Medical Corps in the Far East. After peace was declared Hunter returned to St. George's, and was appointed Assistant Physician in 1947, a year later he became a full Physician and was given the responsibility of setting up a Department of Cardiology. In 1954 Hunter was joined by Aubrey Leatham, and the two of them established a department which quickly gained both national and international recognition for its pioneering work in phonocardiography and artificial pacemakers.

In 1956 the kind, considerate and diplomatic Alastair Hunter was the obvious choice to succeed Marriott Nicholls as part-time Dean of the Medical School. During Hunter's fifteen years as the Dean he spent a considerable amount of time persuading the Department of Health and the University of London of the urgent necessity of establishing a much enlarged medical school on the Tooting site. By 1971 the main arguments were resolved and planning for the new St. George's Hospital Medical School was well underway. Hunter had cause for self-congratulation, in spite of the delays. Regrettably a number of junior consultants, who by now had become frustrated waiting for the Department of Health and the University of London to give their blessing for the rebuilding of hospital and medical school at Tooting, mistakenly heaped the blame for this procrastination on to Hunter's shoulders. As a consequence he was forced to resign and Robert Lowe was appointed as the first whole-time Dean. Hunter was devastated, bitterly disappointed and probably he never recovered from this savage blow to his self-esteem, together with the gratuitous disregard for all that he had achieved on behalf of St. George's Hospital and its Medical School.

From 1971 until his retirement from St. George's in 1974 Alastair Hunter devoted his energies to the Royal College of Physicians, where he became Senior Censor and Vice President in 1974-1975, to the Conjoint Board, and to the University of London, where he was a member of the Senate and the Academic Council. After retirement from St. George's Hunter served from 1972 until 1976 on the General Medical Council, and from 1976 until his death in 1983 he was chairman of the Professional and Linguistic Assessment Board.

Outside of medicine Hunter was a keen sportsman and continued to play cricket for the Sussex Martlets, and against the students well into his retirement. He was a first class wicket keeper and a useful batsman. He also played squash and was always keen to take on the students, who, even if he did not beat them, were well aware that they were up against a formidable opponent. Once a student from another hospital was caught out when he turned up for a United Hospitals Cross Country Race and met Hunter in running kit. The student asked Hunter which hospital he belonged to. When Hunter replied 'St. George's', the student asked if he was in the same year as a friend of his, and was met with the reply 'No, I am afraid I am the Dean'. The student suffered further humiliation when he was well beaten by Hunter. Another major interest was in modern art, and Hunter's personal and unique collection contained works by Dali, Picasso and Sutherland, which on his death were given to the Fitzwilliam Museum, Cambridge, where he was honorary adviser on contemporary art. It was said that if Hunter had not been slighted by the more junior members of the consultant staff he would have left his collection to his beloved St. George's. That is open to conjecture, but what is certain is the fact that Hunter's determination and steadfastness in adversity ensured not only the survival but the eventual transfer and rebuilding of the Medical School. The present School at Tooting stands as an apposite memorial to Alastair Hunter who was a highly popular consultant, a good teacher, a genuine and kindly friend, an approachable, honest and respected adviser to students and junior doctors, and an outstanding Dean of St. George's Hospital Medical School.

HUNTER WING

John Hunter

Until the 19th century surgeons were regarded as being inferior to physicians. The reason for this lay in the diverse pathways they had taken to arrive at their respective qualifications. Physicians obtained their doctorate in medicine from the existing universities and considered themselves superior by virtue of the intellectual qualities required for this task, although examination of patients did not form a major part of the curriculum. Thus diagnosis was the outcome of an intellectual process rather than occurring as a result of the laying on of hands, and in the absence of a scientific foundation the process lent itself to deeply serious mumbo-jumbo. Their station, several notches higher than surgeons, was confirmed by the fact that they did not get either their hands or clothes dirty, and in this respect they were akin to the lilies of the field. Surgery on the other hand had always had a practical journeyman sort of background. And surgeons were primarily technicians learning their trade through an apprenticeship, and thereafter honing their skills with constant exercise of the very few operations that were safe enough to do on a regular basis, in the days before anaesthesia they had to be deft, or their patients suffered alarmingly. It was as late as 1747 that they broke away from the barbers, with whom they had shared a guild, and struck out on their own to improve their image, and to acquire a degree of social respectability, even if much of what they did lacked any scientific validity. John Hunter spent his life attempting to place surgery on a more scientific footing, and in doing so automatically improved the surgeon's social lot.

Little is known about his early years, but he was born into a farming family in February 1728, at Long Calderwood, near Glasgow, the youngest of 10 children. There is some anecdotal evidence that his special position in the family hierarchy led to him being 'spoiled and idle', but it would have given a very unflattering glimpse of his personality if he had not been indulged. His father died when John was 14; the lad appears to have had no firm ideas as to the sort of career he wanted to pursue, but he helped out with some farm work when he was unable to avoid it. He was not regarded as being in any way gifted, indeed, he had considerable difficulty in learning to read, and only did so long after his peers; it seemed that he was quite happy to sit and dream. It was noted that he was fascinated by the wonders of the natural world, and was a keen and shrewd observer, so his intelligence in this respect at least was not in question. It may be inferred that he was not constitutionally idle, as he became the most industrious of people. Did his problems with reading perhaps stem from a mild form of dyslexia?. Whatever the reason his apparently aimless existence drifting around the vicinity caused his mother and older siblings much anxiety, so they were delighted when his elder brother, William, wrote to them stating that John's presence in London was required to act as his assistant in the flourishing Anatomy School that he owned. John was 20 when he left home to work with his brother, and quickly developed an aptitude for the dissection and preparation of specimens. Lack of suitable preservatives meant that it was difficult to keep specimens in the summer months, and their fragility and smell made the study of anatomy very much an occupation for the cooler weather. When teaching was at an end for a while, John would attach himself to one of the leading surgeons: for a while he attended operations conducted by William Cheselden, and after his death he went to watch Percival Potts. His initial association with St. George's Hospital began in 1754/5 when he underwent short courses of study as his dissecting duties permitted, by this time he was giving lectures and living in his brother's school, so that life must have seemed a continuous tutorial for the resident students.

The diligence and skill he showed in the anatomy theatre rapidly gave him a profound knowledge of the human body, and he extended his studies and the course of lectures to include comparative anatomy and embryology. Turning from structure he began to take an increasing interest in function (physiology), and he investigated bone growth, placental function, the role of the gastric juices, and many other topics. In 1760 he became a Governor of St. George's by donating a subscription, but later that year his health began to suffer. It was thought that he had tuberculosis, and advised to get away for a while. He lacked the means to take an protracted holiday, so he became a surgeon in the army, and went with the British forces to Belle Isle and then Portugal during the Seven Years War. New lands with new creatures gave added impetus to his natural history studies, and he seems to have been doing about the same amount of work as he did back in London before his illness! So much for the rest, but presumably the climate was better.

He returned to England in 1763, and little is known about his activities for a time, but that he was busy goes without saying. When he was jumping up and down one day he ruptured his Achilles tendon, which set him off to study the repair process of tendons in dogs where first he had divided the tendon by a tiny subcutaneous incision. Shortly after he embarked on a study of the course of the clinical events in syphilis and their response to mercury treatment by inoculating himself with the disease. All the experiments he performed were carefully annotated and recorded for future reference, many of his ideas and theories could not be tested at the time due to technical limitations, but were subsequently shown to be correct over a century later. And his achievements are well known even to the laity. There is an old chestnut of a story current at St. George's concerning two South London ladies walking past his bust in Tooting one day. One said to the other 'Oos 'at then', the other replied 'That's John Hunter, the first bloke to catch syphilis'. His endeavours were widely reported in the scientific circles in which he moved, and he was well known for his integrity, in 1767 he was elected to a Fellowship of the Royal Society, earlier than his elder brother William.

During these years his surgical practice continued to grow, but he lacked a senior hospital post that would set the public seal on his achievements. To this end in 1768, at the age of 40, he put himself forward for the diploma examination of the Company of Surgeons in which he was successful; later in the same year Thomas Gataker, one of the St. George's surgeons, died. This made an opening for a new appointee. At a special court of the Governors, held in December, John Hunter received 114 votes, beating David Bayford, the other candidate, by 72 votes. Hunter had conquered another major obstacle, and he was elated because he could now teach surgical students, which he continued to do with his usual zest for the rest of his life. During the winter months he lectured in public three evenings a week so that a larger audience could be reached.

In 1771 Hunter published the first scientific treatise on teeth in the English language, the first volume dealt with the development and structure of the jaws and teeth, and the second part released seven years later described the disease of the jaws, gums, and teeth; noting with his usual prescience the potential for fillings with heavy inert metals, and bone grafting. It was over a century before his ideas could be translated into reality. It was said that the reason why the first volume saw the light of day so much earlier than the second was because he needed the money to marry, Anne Home, a 29 year old, to whom he had been engaged for several years, their first child was born almost a year to the day after the wedding, and they went on to have four others.

Edward Jenner became one of Hunter's resident pupils in 1770, and they rapidly became close friends and collaborators in their shared interest in the natural world, even when Jenner turned his back on London and returned to the country he was bombarded by requests for specimens, and while Hunter was commiserating with Jenner on the break up of a courtship, he could not resist using the opportunity to make a forceful plea for more hedgehogs! It was to Jenner that Hunter made his famous comment: 'Don't think, try the experiment'.

A vertiginous illness in 1777 led Hunter to begin the mammoth task of cataloguing all 700 of his specimens, together with the experimental results. Before his death more than a 1000 others were added to his collection. In this area he must be regarded as the first experimental

108

pathologist. Further honours were given to him, including the Copley lectureship, the highest honour of the Royal Society, and soon after he became the Surgeon General and Inspector of Hospitals in 1790, this gave him the opportunity to revolutionise the army medical services; from 1776 he had been Surgeon Extraordinary to King George III. His declining years were dogged by ill-health, but he devoted himself to improving the education of medical students at St. George's. He suffered from angina, and his sudden death in the hospital is said to have occurred after a stormy meeting, where his wish to admit two young men as students was thwarted because they had not produced evidence that they had completed their preliminary studies. He died in 1793 and was buried in the vaults of St. Martins in the Fields, but in 1859 Frank Buckland conducted an exhaustive search through 3000 coffins over 16 days before his coffin was identified, so that he could be reinterred with due honours in the North Aisle of Westminster Abbey. It is perhaps as well that we do not have Hunter's comments on this curious episode, though it is unlikely that he would have approved. His portrait was painted by his neighbour and friend Sir Joshua Reynolds (1723-1792), and now hangs in the Royal College of Surgeons. It is said that Reynolds found Hunter a bad sitter and could not produce a true likeness, but one day Hunter lapsed into deep thought, and the artist immediately turned the half completed portrait upside down and made a quick sketch of Hunter on top of the original, so forming the basis of the finished portrait. The story is not quite correct in detail as radiological examination has confirmed. Reynolds certainly did repaint Hunter's head but he did not invert the canvas but overpainted the original face. The copy of the portrait which hangs in St. George's Hospital was painted sometime about 1834. Mr. Nussey on behalf of the Board of Governors sought permission from the Royal College of Surgeons in that year for an artist to take a copy of Reynolds's original. In 1843 the Board resolved 'that Mr. Smith, the artist be empowered to provide a frame for the picture of John Hunter, the cost of which is not to exceed £6'. It is likely that Mr. Smith was Herbert Luther Smith (1811-1870). Stone busts of both John Hunter by Thomas Woolner and Joshua Reynolds by Henry Weekes stand on the north side of Leicester Square where they both lived. John Hunter lived at No. 28 Leicester Square which had previously been owned by

John Singleton Copley, the American painter (1738-1815) who feuded with the Royal Academy. The house next to Hunter's, No. 27, had been previously occupied by Nathaneal St. André, a surgeon and colleague of Claudius Amyand and Ambrose Dickins at the Westminster at the time of the 'split'. St. Andre looked after Mary Tofts, who after having been frightened by a rabbit in a field went on subsequently to give birth to a litter of fifteen rabbits. The surgeon claimed that he had personally delivered two further rabbits. King George I asked Sir Hans Sloane, President of the Royal Society to investigate the matter, and he reported that he also witnessed the birth of a rabbit. Mary Tofts was later caught secretly buying rabbits in the market. One wonders what Hunter's opinion was of this strange affair.

The bust of John Hunter which stands in the foyer of the Medical School at Tooting was sculptured by Sir Alfred Gilbert, and commissioned by St. George's Hospital, to mark the one hundredth anniversary of the surgeons death. Funds were raised to pay for the sculpture by Charles Slater, the bacteriologist, and Clinton Dent, the surgeon.[1] Having completed the sculpture Gilbert went overseas as his affairs had become involved and there was some anxiety at the hospital that the bust might disappear. Legal opinion was sought and the advice given was 'that although no doubt the friends and relatives of Mr. Hunter would put a high value on the bust, it was not likely to be a great attraction to others, and Clinton Dent and Charles Slater need not therefore be afraid of its confiscation'. The bust was duly delivered and placed in the Boardroom where it remained for many years, before it was transferred to the arch leading to the entrance of the Medical School in 1924. It was moved to

---

[1] Clinton Dent (1850-1912) was a superb surgeon and a brilliant mountaineer. A bachelor and deeply religious, Dent was passionately fond of St. George's, and gave the church window which is displayed in the front entrance at St. George's Hospital at Tooting. His executors presented his portrait painted in 1887, when he was President of the Alpine Club, now sadly missing and the water colour painting by Arthur McCormick 'John Hunter leaves St. George's Hospital' which is displayed in the Boardroom. Dent wrote 'Above the Skyline' and was an excellent photographer. Several examples of his expertise with the camera can be seen around the hospital. In the English Church in Zermatt there is a memorial plaque to Clinton Dent, President of the Alpine Club, and First President of the Swiss Alpine Club.

1. St. George's Hospital, 1745 - This engraving is earlier than the date given, as Isaac Ware had completed his extensions by 1744. The men talking are standing in what is now Knightsbridge, and to the right of the hospital stands the cottage belonging to Huggitt, the cowman

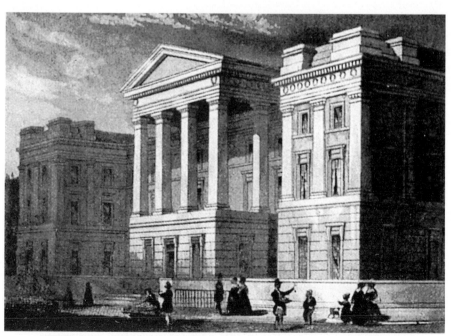

2. Wilkins' completed St. George's Hospital, 1836. Note the absence of the attic floor - it was not added until 1859

3. St. George's Hospital ready for the Coronation, 1953. The scaffolding erected on the roof of the hospital was for the television cameras and commentators

4. Outside Victoria Children's Hospital 1938. Children returning from convalescence to their waiting mothers. Less than five years later mothers were standing in the same place waving goodbye as children were evacuated to Windsor and Basingstoke

5. The Dispensary, Victoria Children's Hospital, 1910. How things have changed!

6. Aerial view of the Grove and Fountain Hospitals, 1953. The Fountain Hospital
can be seen in the top left hand corner, the Nurses' Homes towards the top right and
Blackshaw Road curving around the bottom right hand corner

7. The Weir Hospital, Balham

8. St. James' Hospital, Balham

9. The opening of the new Casualty Department at Hyde Park Corner, 1958. From the left are Alexander Gray, the architect, Dame Muriel Powell, the Matron, with Lord Ingleby the Chairman of the Board of Governors standing behind, E. K. M. Hilleary, a Board member, Philip Constable, the House Governor and Hugh Gainsborough, the senior physician

10. Norman Tanner

11. Ruth Myles

12. Sir Humphry Rolleston

13. Sir Marriott Nicholls

14. William Heberden

15. Sir Frank Holdsworth

16. Henry Gray

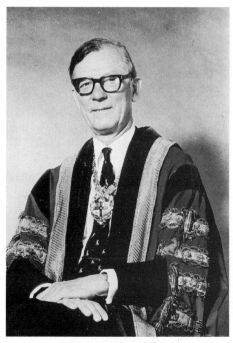

17. Lord Smith of Marlow

18. Clinton Dent

19. Calvert Gwillim

20. Charles McEntee

21. John Hunter. Taken from the copy of
the Reynolds Portrait which hangs in St.
George's Hospital

22. Edward Wilson

23. Sir Stewart Duke-Elder

24. Sir Claude Frankau

25. Albert Tarrant

26. Dame Muriel Powell

27. William Dakin

28. Sir Benjamin Brodie

29. The Anaesthetists - 1904. Pictured from the left: Sir Frederick Hewitt, Joseph Blomfield, Llewelyn Powell and Henry Menzies

30. James Hope

Tooting by the Special Trustees in the late '70's. John Hunter was the Founder of Scientific Surgery. A colleague said of him 'He alone made us gentlemen'.

INGLEBY HOUSE

The Right Honourable Viscount Ingleby of Snilesworth, PC
The Right Honourable Viscount Ingleby was Chairman of the Board of Governors of St. George's Hospital from 1956 until 1966.

Viscount Ingleby was born plain Osbert Peake in 1897, a cousin of the Earl of Halifax, and a great grandson of Lord Grey, the Prime Minister under whose guidance the great Reform Bill of 1832 was passed. Peake was educated at Eton and served in the first World War, before entering Christ Church College, Oxford, where he took an honours degree in history. In 1922 he was elected as a Conservative Member of Parliament, and served, in turn, as Under Secretary of State to the Home Office, Financial Secretary to the Treasury, and Minister of National Insurance, where his major contribution was to changes in the social services. Peake decided to retire from politics in 1956, and in recognition of his public service he was gazetted Viscount Ingleby of Snilesworth in the East Riding of Yorkshire. Almost immediately he was appointed Chairman of the Board of Governors of St. George's Hospital in succession to Sir Malcolm Trustam Eve, who resigned following an acrimonious meeting of the Board of Governors at which he had attempted to push through radical changes, but realised that he did not have the confidence of the Medical Staff. Trustam Eve had been both Chairman of the Board of Governors and the Medical School Council.

Viscount Ingleby, although new to the hospital service, very quickly established himself as a most able and popular Chairman. The medical staff warmed to his enthusiasm and willingness to do whatever he could to help St. George's achieve its aim of building a new hospital at Tooting, and affectionately called him Lord 'I'. Ingleby showed a great interest in all details of hospital life, and was keen to meet all disciplines, and staff at every level, to try to understand their concerns and difficulties. He regularly visited the wards where he spent time talking to both patients

111

and staff. Ingleby made everyone feel at ease with the combination of his charm and excellent sense of humour.

Lord and Lady Ingleby always found the time to join in the many social activities of the hospital, and both were regular attendees at the Sunday morning service held in the Chapel at Hyde Park Corner. A man of deep religious conviction, Lord Ingleby attached great importance to the spiritual aspects of healing, and gave the utmost priority to the building of a Chapel at the Grove Fever Hospital as soon as he became Chairman. As soon as the Chapel building was complete Viscount Ingleby gave the 'Mouseman' Thompson[1] oak chairs which survive today, for use in the Chapel.

Viscount Ingleby's death in 1966 was a tragic and grievous loss as he was universally regarded as one of the finest leaders that St. George's has had in its long history.

THE URSULA JAMES ROOM

Ursula James, MB, BS, FRCP
When the National Health Service was introduced in 1948 St. George's took over the responsibility for the administration of the Victoria Children's Hospital. The staff from the latter joined that of the parent hospital, and none was more welcome than the very popular, Ursula

---

[1] Robert Thompson (1876-1955), born in Yorkshire, the son of a joiner and wheelwright was apprenticed to an engineer in Cleckheaton but loathed it. He persuaded his father to let him work in his carpenter's shop. Soon, he received commissions for wood carving in Ampleforth Abbey, Workington Priory, Fort Angus, Ampleforth College, Peterborough Cathedral and Frampton Court. By 1919 he was developing his own ideas and designs based on 16th and 17th century styles. As well as undertaking commissions in York Minster, Upsall Castle and Brough Hall, Thompson was turning out good solid furniture usually in oak. The story goes that whilst carving a beam in a church roof in his younger days, he heard a fellow craftsman remark that in spite of all their hard work they were as poor as church mice. This caught Thompson's imagination and he carved a mouse on the beam. From that day on 'Mouseman' Thompson carved a busy little mouse chewing away at the wood with its chisel-like teeth on every piece of his work. The beam on which Thompson carved his first mouse has never been found.

James, a superb paediatrician, an excellent teacher, a courteous and charming lady.. Ursula James was educated at Fontainbleu in England and qualified MB BS, and MRCS LRCP from the London School of Medicine for Women in 1938. She obtained her MRCP in 1941, and four years later was appointed Consultant Paediatrician to the Victoria Children's Hospital. Ursula James was later appointed similar posts at the Elizabeth Garrett Anderson and Lambeth Hospitals, before becoming Consultant Paediatrician to St. George's. In 1958 she was elected a Fellow of the Royal College of Physicians, by which time she was closely involved with the discussions which led to the closure of the Victoria Children's Hospital and the eventual transfer of its beds to the new hospital at Tooting.

The Victoria Children's Hospital had been originally founded as a result of a meeting held early in 1866 at the home of Dr. Edward Ellis, in Pimlico, with a Mr. B. R. Green in the chair. A motion was carried that a children's hospital was badly needed in the neighbourhood of the King's Road, Chelsea, and that it should be called the South London Hospital for Children, even though it was to be situated north of the Thames!

During the spring of 1866 various premises were visited and inspected in Sloane Street, Wellington Square and Battersea Bridge Road; but by the autumn Mr. Green and his colleagues had decided to rent Gough House, which was situated in Queen's Road West, Chelsea, at a cost of £65 a year. The committee met at Gough House on the 11th. October 1866, and agreed that the hospital should now be named 'The South Western Hospital for Children', and that a 'Ladies Committee' should be established.

The out-patient department of what was to become known as the Victoria Hospital for Sick Children was opened on Guy Fawkes day, well within the same year that the hospital was first conceived. By April in the following year the first six in-patient beds were opened. Under the chairmanship of Sir William Ferguson, the leading London surgeon of that time, over £1500 had been collected within the year. As the donations poured in so did the patients, and by 1872 the Committee was concerned about the adequacy of the building as a hospital. Certainly a better site could not be found, and having secured the freehold for £1500, along with some additional land, it seemed an opportune moment to redevelop. At the time approaches were made to the Belgrave Hospital for Children to see whether the two could amalgamate, but it was decided to go it alone, and new wards were put into commission in 1874. Florence Montgomery, a famous authoress in her day, wrote a story called 'Wild Mike' in 1875, proceeds from the sale of which were donated to the building fund, and the hospital was enlarged to include an operating theatre, ten additional cots and staff accommodation. HRH Princess Louise, the Marchioness of Lorne, opened the extension in 1876, and this event was commemorated by naming a ward after her.

To ease some of the pressure on cots, four convalescent cots were acquired in Sydenham, but in 1876 Mr. Dalton offered a large house, 'Churchfield', in Margate, for use as a convalescent facility. In 1877 the Metropolitan Board of Works was planning a new street, to be named Tite Street, which was to run from Queen's Road (later to be named Royal Hospital Road) to the Embankment. The Board of Works found itself in a position to offer some additional land to the front and rear of Gough House to the Committee, and this was purchased for possible future development.

It was during this period that Oscar Wilde, the playwright, dramatist and leader of the aesthetic movement lived opposite the hospital at No. 34 Tite Street at which time the out-patient facilities were becoming increasingly cramped. In 1885 the foundation stone of a new wing, lying just south of Gough House, was laid by HRH Princess Louise. The wing was opened by the Prince and Princess of Wales in the following year. The hospital continued to thrive, and in 1890 the St. Gabriel Home for Infants was taken over, and the ever present Patroness of the hospital, Princess Louise, opened a new convalescent home in Broadstairs in 1891. At this time the hospital was supported by Sir Henry Rider Haggard (1856-1925), who wrote a short story 'A Visit to the Victoria Hospital' which was used in order to raise funds for the additional wings, which were added in 1903 and 1905, giving a total of six wards, a new operating suite and an X-Ray department. In order to maintain these additional facilities more funds were required, and the Ladies Committee under the presidency of Princess Louise, now the Duchess of Argyll, responded and covered the increased

114

costs. Haggard continued to support the hospital up to the time of his death.

During the early part of the First World War part of the hospital was assigned as the 2nd. London General Hospital, but by 1916 it was fully functioning again as a paediatric hospital. In 1921 the house next door to the hospital in Tite Street came on the market, and the Board of Management, realising at once that this was a wonderful opportunity to further enlarge the hospital, felt it must be purchased. So strong was this feeling that they took a calculated risk to run into debt, but quite fortuitously the 'Daily Mirror' decided to launch a 'Princess Mary Wedding Gift Appeal' to commemorate the marriage of her Royal Highness. The appeal was very successful and both Great Ormond Street and the Victoria Hospital benefitted to the tune of over £5000 each. The Princess Mary Home was opened in 1922, and contained another new operating theatre, a physiotherapy department and two wards, the smaller of which was named the 'Daily Mirror' ward. Alfred Noyes wrote a poem especially for the occasion.

Mr William Shepherd, the builder, who was also a great benefactor to the Bolingbroke Hospital provided a Tonsil and Adenoid ward in 1926. After almost seventy years as the ever attentive and loyal Patroness of the Victoria Hospital for Children, Her Royal Highness Princess Louise, died in 1939. The Princess, who had allowed her name to be associated with a ward in 1876, had given annual gifts since the foundation of the hospital. She was always available to lay foundation stones, or open extensions and wards, and had served as President of the Ladies Committee since 1904, was greatly missed.

The Second World War disrupted the work of Tite Street. The children were sent away to the 'sector' hospitals at Windsor and Park Prewett, Basingstoke, and the out-patient department was used by the local authority as a casualty and decontamination centre. The hospital survived a number of incendiary attacks, and escaped major damage when a large bomb fell and flattened the cylinders in the oxygen store. By a miracle none of the cylinders exploded!

After the end of the Second World War the Committee of Management saw the need to re-organise and amalgamate with another hospital. Discussions were held with the Belgrave Hospital for Children, but for

115

the second time in its history these came to nothing as the Ministry of Health began to prepare for the introduction of the National Health Service. The Ministry decreed that small specialised hospitals, should be integrated with the larger Teaching Hospitals, so Tite Street, as the Victoria Children's Hospital was known, became part of the St. George's Group.

During the early 1960s, as plans for the re-building of St. George's at Tooting were beginning to be finalised, it was decided that the Victoria Hospital for Children should close, and its cots transferred to Tooting. The hospital in Tite Street closed in 1964, but it was not until after an intermediary decantation to St. James' Hospital, that the paediatric beds were opened in Lanesborough Wing in the new St. George's Hospital at Tooting.

The Board of Governors promised that a Princess Louise ward would be established in the new hospital, and, although the name was used for a short period of time in Knightsbridge Wing, it has now disappeared. It was also promised that two of the paediatric wards in the new building would be known as 'Victoria Wing'. Regrettably these promises were broken, but the Ursula James Room and Pinckney Ward serve as reminders of the children's hospital in Chelsea, which paved the way for the establishment of the large and successful department of paediatrics that is now established at Tooting.

JENNER WING

Edward Jenner, MD, FRS
Edward Jenner was born on 17th of May, 1749; he was the ninth and last, but only the sixth surviving child of the Rev. Stephen Jenner, Vicar of Berkeley, Gloucestershire. At the age of five young Edward was orphaned, after this tragedy he was brought up by his eldest sister, Mary, and her husband, the Rev. George Black, who had taken over their father's living, but the greater part of his care was undertaken by his Aunt Deborah who had married a farmer.

At the age of seven he was sent to Cirencester Grammar School, some years later in anticipation of a smallpox epidemic he and his fellow pupils were forced into smallpox inoculation, a savage form of prophylaxis of uncertain efficacy, which was preceded by six weeks of debilitating preliminaries which included bleeding, purging and a far from nourishing vegetarian diet, which left the body with impaired resistance. The technique of inoculation, or variolation as it was better known, had been brought into Britain by Lady Mary Wortley Montagu in 1721, as a result of her own experiences in Turkey. The basic idea was that one had an attack of the disease under 'optimal' conditions, thus becoming indefinitely immune, but there was no guarantee that the procedure would be safe, particularly as those who had been inoculated were herded into 'smallpox stables' for a time to see if it had 'taken'. Jenner, who was rather below average stature, suffered rather a bad bout of the illness, and was left rather delicate so he was placed in a less arduous school, where he showed great interest in all aspects of natural history, a fascination which lasted to the end of his days.

Perhaps it was the prominence of these interests that led his guardians to think that he would make a surgeon. Whatever the reason when Jenner left school at the age of 14 he was apprenticed to Mr Ludlow, who was a surgeon in Sodbury, with whom he served the customary seven years, during which time he is alleged to have heard the famous claim by a milk maid that because she been infected by cowpox she was immune to smallpox. A saying he never forgot. The next step in his career was of enormous importance because this took him under the wing of one of the finest surgeons and medical scientists of his day, John Hunter, who proved to be the seminal influence in Jenner' life, as Hunter taught him to refine his powers of observation, and to submit these to experimental verification wherever possible. In addition to helping Hunter in the anatomy theatre, he prepared specimens for him, 'walked the wards' at St. George's with him to increase his surgical experience, and he also lived with him. Hunter was impressed by his young protégé, and the two began a lifelong friendship that saw Jenner diagnosing his teacher's angina from a distance and correctly predicting that the autopsy would show the constriction of the coronary arteries that he had been the first to demonstrate in other sufferers. At the conclusion of Captain Cook's long voyage of Pacific exploration in 1771, Joseph Banks, the expedition's scientist returned with vast quantities of specimens which he was anxious to catalogue, he sought Hunter's advice as to who would be equal to the task, as a result Jenner was invited to undertake the commission, which he did with great success and skill. Banks was sufficiently impressed to invite Jenner to accompany him on the next expedition, but the former's extravagant demands for more space, personnel and facilities appalled the Admiralty, and Cook sailed without him on his second great voyage of exploration; and after two years in London at his brother's expense Jenner decided to return home and become a country doctor.

His early years brought medical recognition on a growing scale, but these responsibilities did not stifle his curiosity about the natural world, and in his spare time he became the first person to describe the nesting habits of the cuckoo, although his observations were ridiculed in some quarters, it was on the strength of these that he was elected to a Fellowship of the Royal Society – a rare honour for a country doctor. Together with the Earl of Berkeley, his close friend, they were the first people in England to fly a hydrogen balloon, they followed on horseback until it came to rest in the gardens of Kingscote, in high excitement they were prevailed upon to repeat the experiment in front of the Kingscote family, one whose daughters, Catherine, he courted against opposition from her parents, who finally were reconciled to the match after a five year battle. The young couple made their home in the Chantry at Berkeley, which he always called his 'little cottage' despite its fifteen rooms! This is now the Jenner Museum. He is said to have dressed in a neat and almost fastidious manner, kept a good table, an excellent cellar, and was always on the look out for new recipes.

Smallpox in Jenner's day was the most serious illness threatening mankind, mortality was high, and a legacy of severe and permanent disfigurement faced the survivors. No one was exempt from its ravages, but anecdotal tales existed of milk maids spared its worst consequences. In the literature of the bucolic they were typically denoted by the prefix 'fair'. This was not due to the fact that were all blondes, but because they were not pockmarked. Jenner kept this in mind together with the comments of the girl he had seen during his apprentice days, and spent much time collecting and collating evidence from country sources concerning the protective powers of the relatively mild cowpox infection against the much more devastating smallpox. In 1796 he had an opportunity to test this theory when Sarah Nelmes, a local milkmaid, developed a cowpox infection, and, on May 14 he was able to transfer material from a pustule on her hand into a small incision on the arm of an 8 year old boy, James Phipps, who was inoculated with smallpox shortly afterwards by another practitioner. There was no reaction! With delicious irony the experiment had been completed by this unexpected twist of fate. It appeared that immunity had been conferred from one individual to another. It was two years before he had a chance to repeat the work. The results together with his meticulous records of other cases were published privately, as the Royal Society had declined the opportunity, and there was a tremendous demand for them throughout Europe.

Quite soon there were clashes in the press between those for and against the concept of vaccination (vacca, Latin, = a cow). Opposition to the method was inflamed by ignorance, fearing that those inoculated would assume bovine characteristics, and by the profit motive (always a potent ingredient in medical disputes). Those who favoured variolation charged fees, as did those who were happy to vaccinate but use contaminated material and keep inadequate or erroneous records. These threatened the future of vaccination and Jenner stoutly defended his position, to such effect that within a few years he was renowned throughout the civilised world as a great benefactor of mankind. The fact that he was burdened by correspondence led to his practice suffering, and he complained of being 'the vaccine clerk to the world', in a letter to his lawyer he remarks that 'honours won't buy mutton'; and at this time he was being inundated with them. His friends petitioned parliament for help, and he was granted the sum of £10,000 in 1802, though his affairs failed to recover and he was awarded twice this sum 5 years later, but as he did most of his work for free he was insolvent when he died. He fell out with institutions set up to promote and control vaccination, usually for personal profit, but had to be satisfied when these were gathered together under the aegis of the Royal College of Physicians. His later years were saddened by the death of his eldest son in 1809, and his beloved wife in 1815; he continued his mission to convert his opponents, contribute to the study of nature, and work in his Berkeley practice until the end of his life. He had been to see an old patient on 24th January 1823, and next morning was found with a major left hemisphere stroke from which he died in the early hours of the 26th, without regaining consciousness.

Both during Jenner's lifetime and since, there has been active controversy as to who was the very first person to vaccinate. This is a question beyond resolution: oral evidence points to an obscure and long-standing rural tradition amongst certain countryfolk which bears witness to its efficacy; and to these unsung observers belongs the credit. In this sense there are no discoverers, and the question is otiose. Since Jenner's day there has been an opposition camp which claims the palm for a Dorset farmer named Benjamin Jesty, who, in 1774, successfully vaccinated his family on the strength of the country tale and local evidence in the shape of his maids, who had both been infected with cowpox, and then gone on to nurse relatives with smallpox without ill effect themselves. It was a bold step to take without knowing the consequences of failure. His activities became known in the locality, as a result he was subjected to a considerable degree of obloquy. Perhaps for this reason he did not bring his experiences to a larger audience, and he remained silent about his doings until 1803 at the time when Jenner's name, parliamentary gift, and vaccination principles must have been widely known. Jesty's story was noted by Dr. Bell, appointed in 1801 as vicar of Swanage, and he wrote to connections in the capital to tell them of Benjamin's claim. Two years later in 1805 Benjamin went to London at the invitation of the Vaccine Pock Institute to speak to the members, he was feted and flattered, but no financial rewards followed his return to Purbeck. His visit had achieved little, except exciting the animosity of Jenner and his allies, who felt that he was being manipulated to embarrass Jenner rather than being lauded for his own sake. Benjamin probably cared nothing for these medical intrigues, with his sturdy independence intact he continued to farm in the area until his death, respected by all for his integrity and honesty, and his wife made sure that posterity could read of her husband's deeds by having them carved on his gravestone.

So who should take the laurels? There is no reason to doubt Jesty's claim, but this was a single event, with no contemporary documentary evidence, which remained unpublicised for 25 years despite the continuing ravages of the disease, and he may have come forward at last in anticipation of a reward, though this may be doing him an injustice. Jenner, on the other hand, was a trained observer who recorded multiple experiments in writing as they happened, who published when he thought his findings justified such a course, defended them against criticism, and devoted his life to the crusade of vaccination without thought of personal gain to such good effect that in 1980 the World Health Organisation could say that for the first time in human history a major disease had been eradicated completely, and 1996 was the 200th anniversary of the vaccination performed by Jenner.

The skin of 'Blossom', the cow from which Mary Nelmes contracted cowpox is displayed in the Medical School at Tooting but for some curious reason the real horns have been replaced by two carved out of wood. An excellent bronze statue of Edward Jenner by William Calder Marshall (1813-1894), the Scottish Sculptor stands in the Italian Garden, Kensington. The statue was originally erected in Trafalgar Square in 1858, but was moved to its present site in !862.

KEATE WARD

Robert Keate, FRCS

The name Keate is associated with two distinguished surgeons who served St. George's Hospital in very different ways during the late eighteenth and early nineteenth centuries. The younger, Robert, served the hospital with distinction, whereas his uncle, Thomas, was never on time and remiss in the performance of his hospital responsibilities.

Thomas Keate, the son of a Somerset vicar, was born in 1745, and entered St. George' Hospital in 1765 as a pupil under John Gunning, and then, just two years later, he became Gunning's assistant. In 1787, Thomas Keate was appointed Assistant Surgeon to St. George's and then on the resignation of Charles Hawkins in 1792, Thomas Keate defeated John Hunter's favoured candidate and brother in law, Everard Home, in the contest and was elected Surgeon to the hospital.

The following year Keate succeeded John Hunter as Surgeon General to the Army, a post he held for twenty years until 1813. Keate became an examiner to the College of Surgeons in 1800, and was Master of the College in 1802, 1809 and 1818. By all accounts he was an excellent surgeon, and was the first to tie the subclavian artery for the treatment of an aneurysm. In 1800 his nephew, Robert Keate, was appointed assistant surgeon to St. George's and thereafter he carried out all his uncle's work, a form of surgical simony not unknown in the recent past! Thomas Keate resigned his appointment to St. George's in 1813, and thereafter continued in his private practice and as surgeon to the Chelsea Hospital. Keate served as Surgeon Extraordinary to King George IV and Queen Charlotte, and was a member of the Court of Assistants of the Corporation of Surgeons. Thomas Keate was not interested in writing and thus published little. He died in the Chelsea Hospital aged seventy six in 1821.

Robert Keate, the fourth son of William Keate, a doctor of divinity and rector of Laverton in Somerset was born in 1777. Robert's elder brother, John became the Headmaster of Eton, and Canon of Windsor. Robert Keate was educated at the grammar school in Bath until 1793, when he enrolled at St. George's under his uncle, Thomas. At the same time he was made 'hospital mate' at the Chelsea Hospital. At St. George's he benefited from the teaching for a short while of John Hunter, then John Gunning, William Walker and Everard Home.

Within six years Keate became a member of the Surgeons' Corporation, and was appointed staff surgeon to the Army. He retired from this post in 1810, when he went on half pay and became the Inspector General of Hospitals. Nepotism was rife in those days and his uncle probably had considerable influence on his appointment to the army, as well as young Keate's election to the post of Assistant Surgeon to St. George's in 1800. Robert then began carrying out all his uncle's hospital obligations so that when Thomas retired in 1813, Robert was the obvious choice to succeed him as Surgeon, having had 13 years in which to practise the role. Robert Keate was, according to Sir Benjamin Brodie, a good surgeon and an excellent colleague, but inclined to be irritable. Robert was a member of the Council of the College of Surgeons, an examiner from 1827 to 1855, and president in 1830, 1831 and 1839. Keate also held the appointment of Inspector General of Hospitals.

Keate was described as being 'a square, compact little man, with a rough complaining voice', who was well liked by his pupils, yet, like his Uncle Thomas he contributed little to the medical literature.

Robert Keate was the surgeon to a number of members of the Royal Family during his professional career including: Queen Charlotte, Queen Adelaide, Princess Amelia, George III, George IV, William IV and

Queen Victoria. He was Sergeant-Surgeon to the latter two monarchs. In later life he said 'I have attended four sovereigns and have been badly paid for my services. One of them now deceased owed me nine thousand guineas'. His royal appointments caused considerable interference to his practice, as he was often called to Windsor at short notice.

Keate had the rare distinction of being offered a baronetcy twice, and by different prime ministers, on both occasions he refused. On the first occasion, Robert Peel, when offering the baronetcy indicated that there would be no more medical baronetcies. Keate considered this decision derogatory to his profession, and refused to accept the honour of being the last medical baronet.

Robert Keate held his appointment as surgeon to St. George's for forty years, and did not resign until 1853, by which time he was seventy six. He died in Hertford Street, Mayfair, in 1857.

KNIGHTSBRIDGE WING

Knightsbridge
This wing takes its name from the street known as Knightsbridge which was situated to the south of Hyde Park, and ran from the toll gate at Hyde Park Corner to Kensington Road. The name Knightsbridge originates from the eleventh century, when there was a bridge which crossed the River Westbourne close to the present Albert Gate. Legend has it that two knights fought to the death on the bridge. The village which grew up around this structure became known as Knightsbridge, and over the years it was renowned for its many and excellent taverns, which included 'The Swan', which was mentioned in 'The Soldier's Fortune' by Thomas Otway, 'The White Hart', 'The Fox and Bull', and a favourite of Samuel Pepys: 'The World's End'. The 'White Horse' stood to the west of Lanesborough House on the site which is now occupied by the National Farmers Union building and close by were 'The Triumphant Chariot' and the 'Pillar of Hercules' which was mentioned in 'Tom Jones' as the place where Squire Western stayed when he came up to see Sophia.

Knightsbridge was a frequent haunt of thieves, cut-throats and high-waymen, and, as it was a lonely and inhospitable place but yet conveniently near to the growing capital, it was often chosen as a duelling ground. In 1740 the Bristol Mail was robbed in Knightsbridge and in 1774 Hawke, a highwayman was hanged for a murder and robbery committed there. Despite its reputation as a somewhat raffish and dangerous area, it gained a reputation for the freshness and purity of its air, and, over time, people began to move out of the noisome conditions in the centre of London to build and live there.

In 1719 James Lane, Second Viscount Lanesborough, was one of the first to be attracted to this 'bracing and healthy' part of London, and built Lanesborough House on the south side of Knightsbridge Road, at Hyde Park Corner, which was later leased to the breakaway group of the Westminster Infirmary to house their newly established hospital, which was named St. George's. The 'clean' air in this part of London was due to its close proximity to Hyde Park, the largest of London's parks covering nearly 350 acres. It was confiscated in 1536 by Henry VIII for hunting, and Elizabeth I also hunted there, but by the end of the seventeenth century it was plagued by highwaymen, and in 1689 William III ordered 300 lamps to be hung from the branches of the trees between Rotten Row and St. James.

By the time St. George's Hospital was established at Hyde Park Corner the area was becoming respectable. Over the next one hundred years Knightsbridge became one of the most fashionable streets in London and many of the resident 'housemen' at St. George's proudly gave their address as 'The Cottage', Knightsbridge. 'The Cottage' built for the resident medical staff alongside the hospital in 1892 was quite inappropriately named as it was eight stories high. The junior doctors were always of the view that 'The Cottage' had a greater claim than Apsley House to the prestigious address of No. 1 Knightsbridge.

When Grosvenor and Lanesborough Wings were opened in 1980 in the new St. George's, the name Knightsbridge was given to the Long Corridor, which gives access to the Victorian wards of the old Grove Fever Hospital that are still in use. This wing dates back to 1898 and was originally made up of eight ward blocks which were linked by the Long Corridor. The corridor was raised above ground level, open at the sides, but covered by a slate roof. The roof was supported by upright wrought iron pillars to which were attached wrought iron balustrades to prevent people falling over the edge. Three of the ward blocks were demolished in the 1960s to make way for the building of Ingleby House, and the experimental 'race-track' design ward that eventually became the Trevor Howell Unit, having previously housed the Intensive Therapy Unit, the Communicable Diseases Unit and the orthopaedic beds. During the 1960s the draughty open corridor was completely enclosed, a move which delighted the patients who had found transfers between wards and the operating theatres to be often a damp and chilling experience, but this modification was not universally welcomed. Many medical students disapproved, as the alterations reduced the width of the corridor and obscured the view of its junction with the side corridors, so it was no longer possible to spot visitors and staff debouching into the corridor from the wards, as a result it became far too dangerous to motor cycle up and down the corridor at night, which had previously been an exhilarating experience for the riders, albeit an extremely annoying and irritating one for the patients who were attempting to sleep. The reduction in width of the passageway caused further difficulties for one student who is now a well established and highly respected general practitioner, who had the misfortune to find that his Austin Seven could not be turned at the first attempt at the far end of the corridor. There was great concern amongst his colleagues and well-wishers that it might prove to be irretrievable, but by a stroke of good luck after further increasingly manic efforts it was turned around and driven out, before it was spotted by the Night Sister, who was bustling around the corridors doing her rounds.

LANESBOROUGH WING

Lanesborough

Lanesborough Wing takes its name from Lanesborough House which St. George's occupied when it was first founded in 1733. The name Lanesborough originates from the title which George Lane adopted when he was created a Viscount in 1676.

George Lane's grandfather, another George, had been a Captain on the side of the Royalists during the Civil War in Ireland, and it is recorded that he 'served Queen Elizabeth well'. Captain George Lane's son, Richard, having been deprived of his estate in 1641 became a Member of the Council of Connaught and Sheriff of County Roscommon of Tulske in 1651. For his public service to the Royalist cause he was created a baronet in 1660 at the Restoration. For strategic military reasons he had demolished his own castle, so his son, George, inherited little other than a title.

George Lane was born in 1621 and at the age of seventeen he entered Trinity College in Dublin. Soon after leaving Trinity, he was elected as Member of Parliament for County Roscommon and he held this seat until 1666. Like many senior adherents to the Royalist persuasion he went into exile to serve as secretary to King Charles II in 1655, and he was knighted at Bruges in 1657. On the death of his father, Richard in 1668 he succeeded to the baronetcy. He became a senior figure in the administration of Restoration Ireland, and between 1666 and 1671 he held the Clerkships of the Privy Council of Ireland, the Parliaments of Ireland, and the Crown and the Star Chambers of Ireland. In 1664 he was appointed a Privy Councillor in Ireland, and became Joint Secretary of State for Ireland in 1676. The Duke of Ormonde recommended him for a peerage, and he was created Viscount Lanesborough in County Longford in 1676. In spite of his onerous public duties George Lane still found time to marry on no less than three occasions, firstly to Dorcas, the daughter of Sir Anthony Brabazon of Tallaghstown, the brother of the First Earl of Meath in 1644; then Susan, the daughter of Sir Edward Nicholas, the Secretary of State, in 1653; and lastly Lady Frances Sackville, the daughter of Richard , the Earl of Dorset in 1673. Lane died in Lanesborough in 1683, and his son, James, from his marriage to Dorcas, succeeded to the title.

James Lane was the fourth, and only surviving, son of George and Dorcas. He was born in 1649 and matriculated from Oxford University in 1667. Following in his father's footsteps he was appointed Joint Clerk of the Parliaments of Ireland in 1669, and served Charles II in this post until 1683. James did not attend the Irish Parliament of James II in 1689 (perhaps he saw which side his bread was buttered on!), and from then on he drifted out of the public eye. There were no children from his third marriage in 1676 at Fulham Chapel to Mary, the daughter of Sir Charles Compton. Mary and James lived at this time in Golden Square, but in 1720 they decided to build a country house at Hyde Park Corner to reap the benefit of the country air and where 'out of the sound of the noisy streets Lane could pursue in quiet his favourite recreation' – dancing. James Lane was immortalised in Pope's line *'Sober Lanesborough dancing with the gout'* and he had the singularly bad taste to advise Queen Anne when she lost her husband to whom she was devoted, to apply herself to dancing as the best method of dispelling her grief. Sad to relate, despite his energetic life style in the country air, James Lane only lived in the house for four years before he died at the age of seventy four in 1724. He was buried in St. James', Westminster, and although his wife, Mary, lived until she was ninety three, she was quite happy for the Board of Governors to acquire the lease of Lanesborough House, and she lived to see it open as a hospital. As James Lane left no heirs his titles became extinct at his death.

When St. George's Hospital was opened the Board of Governors resolved that 'Mr. Johnson and his wife (caretakers for Lady Lanesborough) be continued in the house at Hyde Park Corner as messenger, or porter, and matron, until Christmas next'. Mr. Johnson was paid £6 0s 0d a year and Mrs. Johnson, £10 0s 0d. Mrs. Johnson was given wide responsibilities including taking care of all the furniture, seeing that 'inferior' servants did their duty, taking charge of all keys, making sure that no patients left the house without the permission of the physicians or surgeons, played cards dice or other games, drank gin or other strong liquors or wander into a ward designated for the opposite sex. Mrs. Johnson served as matron for six years during which time there was only one complaint recorded against her. Because Johnson, the porter was married to matron he was privileged to dine with her and the apothecary, but on his death the Board resolved that his successor should be unmarried and able to write. Clearly Johnson's conjugal and literary demands were considered to be prejudicial to matronal dignity and efficiency.

The present Viscountcy of Lanesborough in County Longford was created in 1731 when Brinsley Butler, the Gentleman Usher of the Black Rod, and member of Parliament was honoured for his public service. Brinsley's son, Humphrey, who was Member of Parliament for Belturbet, Sheriff of County Cavan and County Westmeath, Governor of County Cavan, and a Privy Councillor, was created Earl of Lanesborough in 1757. This title of Lanesborough has no connection at all with

127

the old Lanesborough House at Hyde Park Corner or St. George's Hospital.

When St. George's Hospital vacated its building at Hyde Park Corner and it was converted into a luxury hotel, the hotel was given the name of Lanesborough thus re-establishing its links with the past.

MARNHAM WARD

Sir Ralph Marnham, KCVO, MA, MChir, FRCS
Sir Ralph Marnham was the twelfth of the general surgeons from St. George's Hospital who became Sergeant Surgeon to the reigning monarch, but the only one to achieve the honour in this century.

Ralph (pronounced Rayf) was born in Stellenbosch, South Africa in 1901, and was educated at the Diocesan College, Rondebosch, before becoming an undergraduate at Gonville and Caius, Cambridge, where he excelled at rowing. Having obtained his BA in 1923, he began his clinical training at St. George's Hospital, where he excelled both in sport and academic studies. Marnham was a fast and solid wing forward, and played off an eight handicap at golf. He was awarded the Allingham scholarship in surgery in 1927, and the Francis Laking research prize in 1930.

After qualifying MRCS, LRCP in 1925, Marnham undertook his house appointments, and then became assistant curator of the museum. He travelled to Toronto to obtain his primary FRCS examination, before returning to the United Kingdom, where he became a clinical assistant at St. Mark's Hospital. Marnham's next post was as a medical registrar at St. George's Hospital, before becoming surgical registrar, and finally resident assistant surgeon. He obtained his final Fellowship examination in 1930, and his MChir in 1933. In 1934 Ralph Marnham was elected Assistant Surgeon.

Soon after the beginning of the Second World War Marnham joined the RAMC as a surgical specialist, and was appointed officer in charge of the surgical division at No. 62 and No. 6 general hospital. The story is told that Marnham spent the first few months of the war as Chief Surgeon at what became known as the Casualty Clearing Station, under the control of the Emergency Medical Services at Hyde Park Corner, but on seeing Dr. Desmond Curran (the psychiatrist) in a Surgeon Captain's uniform he became so enraged that he appealed to Sir Claude Frankau, who was the sector officer in charge of the Emergency Medical Services, to be transferred immediately into the Army proper.

As the war progressed Marnham was promoted to the rank of Brigadier, he became surgeon to the 9th Army, and was twice mentioned in despatches. On demobilisation in 1945 he returned to St. George's Hospital as a Consultant Surgeon, and was also appointed to the surgical staff of: King Edward VII Hospital, Mount Vernon Hospital and the Royal Canadian War Memorial Hospital at Taplow.

In 1946 Ralph Marnham became surgeon to the Royal Household of King George VI. Later he was appointed Surgeon to Queen Elizabeth II, and then Sergeant Surgeon from 1967 to 1971. Her Majesty honoured Marnham with a KCVO in 1957.

Marnham examined regularly for the University of Cambridge in surgery, and was a member of the Court of Examiners of the Royal College of Surgeons. In 1935 Ralph Marnham was elected Moynihan Fellow of the Association of Surgeons of Great Britain and Ireland, and became its President in 1965. From 1970 until 1976 he was President of the Medical Defence Union.

Marnham who had a very large private practice, was never known to neglect his responsibilities to St. George's or to his patients there. He published very little, but will be remembered as a very quiet, dextrous and safe surgeon, an amusing and charming colleague, an excellent and stimulating teacher who was with justification very popular amongst his colleagues, his theatre staff and his students. Sir Ralph Marnham was an fine doctor, and his patients were all treated with exemplary kindness, gentleness and sympathy.

Sir Ralph Marnham died in London in 1984.

McCALMONT WARD

Hugh McCalmont
Mr. Hugh McCalmont was a wealthy business man who lived at 9, Grosvenor Place, Hyde Park. He became a Governor to St. George's Hospital in 1861, and continued to pay an annual subscription of £10.00

each year thereafter until his death. When this occurred on July 13th, 1886, it was discovered from his will that he had left nearly £100,000 to the hospital, which equalled the previous largest legacy, given in 1885, by the late William King. Two conditions were attached to Hugh McCalmont's will: firstly, the legacy was not payable and no interest was allowed to accrue until twelve months after his death; and secondly, there would always be a ward bearing his name at St. George's Hospital.

The earlier wills of William King and Thomas Apreece contained similar provisos to the McCalmont document, as a result all these benefactors had wards named after them at St. George's Hospital whilst it was situated at Hyde Park Corner.

To comply with the terms of the bequest McCalmont was substituted for York as one of the ward names. Of the original legatees whose names were celebrated only the name of McCalmont survives in the new St. George's at Tooting. Once McCalmont's legacy became accessible a year after his death it was divided and invested equally between India 3% stock and Metropolitan Board of Works 3% stock. McCalmont's closest surviving male relatives were made Life Governors of the charity. The William King and the McCalmont legacies became a major part of the Endowment Fund which survives to the present day as The Special Trustees General Fund.

McCalmont ward at Hyde Park Corner was initially a male general medical ward, but as the heart became open to investigation the speciality of cardiology developed, and it became in time the name of the male cardiac ward under the aegis of Dr. Alastair Hunter and Dr. Aubrey Leatham. This ward adjoined Fuller ward on the first floor at the southern end of the easterly aspect of the hospital. Both wards shared a common staff, as Fuller ward was used for female cardiac patients. The names Fuller and McCalmont survive at Tooting, and appropriately enough both are within the Cardiac Unit.

McENTEE WARD

John Charles McEntee, MA, MD, FRCP, DPH
Dr. Charles McEntee was born in Sligo, Southern Ireland in 1900, the son of an Inspector in the Royal Irish Constabulary. He was educated at

Clongowes Wood School, and Trinity College, Dublin, where he graduated MB, ChB, BAO, in 1922. At this point he migrated to England and joined a general practice in a coal mining district of Derbyshire, after a couple of years he moved into hospital practice in London, and obtained his MD in 1926. In 1928 McEntee was appointed as assistant medical officer at the Royal Western Hospital in Hampstead. After passing the Membership of the Royal College of Physicians examination in 1933 he was appointed Senior Assistant Medical Officer at the London County Council's Northern Hospital, Winchmore Hill, and later he was promoted to Deputy Medical Superintendent. In 1936 McEntee took his Diploma in Public Heath, and then worked for short periods of time at the West End Hospital for Nervous Diseases, the Metropolitan Hospital and St. John's Hospital for Diseases of the Skin. By 1938 McEntee had returned to work for the London County Council, where he was a Divisional Medical Officer at County Hall, on the Embankment, before being appointed at the end of the year to the Grove Fever Hospital, Tooting, where he was to stay for the remainder of his professional life. At 'The Grove' he became Deputy Medical Superintendent to Dr. John Anderson.

John Anderson joined the services in 1940, and Charles McEntee became acting medical superintendent at 'The Grove'. He enrolled as a private in the local Home Guard, where he found himself subservient to the hospital's head porter, who had been given the rank of Company Sergeant. McEntee had a marvellous sense of humour; he was highly amused by this reversal of seniority, and took every opportunity to exploit the humour latent in this unusual situation, though never with malice. There were times when there was nothing amusing in life at Tooting during the war years. Whilst the blitz on London raged, bombs fell on the Grove Hospital, and six wards were destroyed. All the staff, including McEntee, worked furiously together, and made sure that casualties were minimal. On another occasion McEntee came to believe that he really was blessed with the luck of the Irish, when a bomb just missed his flat by fifteen feet causing only a small amount of damage.

At the Grove Fever Hospital Charles McEntee, or 'Dr. Mac' as he was known, developed his great expertise in the treatment of infectious diseases. As a teacher he was outstanding, and successive generations of medical students from St. Thomas' and St. George's Hospitals flocked to his ward rounds to benefit from his encyclopaedic knowledge and wide experience. The 'Fever' Registrars and Senior Registrars rightly idolised 'Dr. Mac' and they all acknowledged their debt to him as a friend and mentor. McEntee retained a fatherly interest in his students and junior doctors and was always, even in retirement, readily available for good, kind and wise advice. Charles McEntee, blessed with an easy Irish charm and eloquence, could entertain for hours, discussing literature, whiskies, wine, ceramics and antique furniture, which were his non-medical interests of later years, although in his younger days he had been a keen sportsman, and was once chosen as a reserve for the Irish international cricket team.

The Grove Fever and Fountain Hospitals had been chosen as the site for the new St. George's Hospital by Aneurin Bevan, the Minister of Health in Clement Attlee's post-war Labour Government, and it is more than likely that this decision had a demoralising effect on the staff of the Grove Fever Hospital, who saw their independence being subordinated to the demands of an alien teaching hospital, with its powerful Board of Governors. If Charles McEntee entertained the slightest concern with these developments he never let it show, and, indeed, it was fortuitous for St. George's that he was at Tooting at that time. With his natural diplomatic skills in overdrive he went out of his way to welcome his new colleagues. His charm, kindness and sound constructive advice facilitated the smooth transition of the Grove Fever Hospital into a large district general hospital with its attendant medical school to take place smoothly and without any upset or acrimony. Later changes and closures would well have benefited by the presence of a 'Dr. Mac'. Charles McEntee was appointed consultant physician to St. George's Hospital in 1954, and given responsibility for the infectious diseases unit.

Charles McEntee was Consultant to the Ministry of Health on Small-pox, and belatedly he was elected FRCP in 1960. He was also a Lecturer in Communicable Diseases to St. Thomas's Hospital, and Consultant in Infectious Diseases to the Victoria Children's Hospital, Tite Street. He died at the age of 69 in 1969, and never saw the redevelopment of the Grove and Fountain Hospitals sites, but both St. George's Hospital as a whole, and the speciality of communicable diseases, have many good reasons to be grateful to Charles McEntee.

Charles McEntee published a number of erudite papers including *Observations of the Dick Test* (1928), *Diphtheria Today* (1947), *Pertussis and Measles* (1949) and *Diarrhoea in Children* (1959).

THE EMMANUEL MILLER UNIT

Emmanuel Miller, MA, FRCP, DPM

Emanuel Miller was one of the leading figures in the development of the speciality of child psychiatry. He was born in Whitechapel, London, of Lithuanian Jewish parents, in 1892, and was educated at the City of London School, and St. John's College, Cambridge, where he read Natural and Moral Sciences.

Miller completed his medical studies at the London Hospital, and after qualification in 1918, he embarked upon a career in psychiatry. The first hurdle was the Diploma of Psychological Medicine which he obtained in 1919; and after a series of junior posts he was appointed a lecturer in psychology at Cambridge five years later.

After developing a keen interest in child psychiatry he returned to London, where he helped to found the Child Guidance Unit at the West End Hospital for Nervous Diseases, of which he became the Director. Miller was also Honorary Director of the East London Child Guidance Clinic, the first institution of its kind in the United Kingdom. His wise supervision of these two units provided the impetus for them to develop into models of good sound psychological practice for the treatment of children, who up to that time had been regarded as merely delinquent. In 1939 Miller passed the examination for the Membership of the Royal College of Physicians, and was appointed physician to the Maudsley Hospital where he served with distinction, as he did at the London Jewish Hospitals and the Tavistock Clinic where he also held appointments.

Emmanuel Miller's reputation as an outstanding child psychiatrist continued to spread, and before long St. George's Hospital were fortunate enough to tempt him with the offer of an appointment at the Victoria Hospital for Children, and in due course he was appointed Director of Child Psychiatry to St.George's Hospital.

Miller was awarded the FRCP in 1946, and retired from hospital practice in 1958. During his professional career he wrote extensively on the psychological disorders of childhood, and his papers included 'Types of Mind and Body' and 'Insomnia and Disturbances of Sleep'. He was editor of the 'British Journal of Criminology' and the 'Journal of Child Psychology and Psychiatry', and he edited two books: 'Neurosis and War' (1940) and 'Foundations of Child Psychiatry' (1967), to which he made original contributions.

On a more practical level Miller actively supported medical and welfare work in Israel, and was elected president of the Friends of Magen David Adom in 1953, and was chairman of the Medical Friends of MDA in Britain. He was a frequent contributor of the 'Jewish Chronicle', writing articles on subjects which included parentcraft, aesthetics and backward children, as well as reviewing books.

On a personal note he was gifted as an artist, sculptor, musician, linguist; he was a voracious reader (he owned an extensive collection of books), and an authority on a wide range of subjects. He was married to Betty, the authoress. Many of his talents have been passed down to his son, Jonathan, who after qualifying and beginning a career in psychiatry at University College Hospital, London, moved away from medicine to become the well known actor, writer, raconteur, producer and theatrical director.

Emanuel Miller had the misfortune to suffer from severe arthritis in his later years, which at times he found an extremely depressing burden to bear. He died in 1970.

THE MONCKTON THEATRE

Walter Turner Monckton, KCVO, KCMG, KC, MC, 1st Viscount Monckton of Brenchley

The large lecture theatre at St. George's Hospital is named after Walter Monckton, who was appointed as the first chairman of the twenty eight strong Board of Governors by Aneurin Bevan after the introduction of the National Health Service. Under Monckton's leadership the Board of Governors forged strong links with the medical staff gaining in the process their fullest respect The Board had individual members of

134

great distinction such as: Sir Hugh Lucas-Tooth, MP; W. E. Meade OBE, formerly secretary of the Post Office Workers Union, who was an outstanding Chairman of the Grove Hospital Development Committee; Anthony Greenwood, MP; E.K.M. Hilleary, Chairman of the White Heather Laundry Company, and a former distinguished amateur English International footballer, was the forthright and determined Chairman of the Works and Buildings Committee, later the New Hospital Executive Committee; Mrs. Feiling, the wife of Anthony Feiling, the physician, who chaired the Nurse Advisory Committee and concerned herself with aspects of patient welfare; and Lady Monckton, a former Chief of the Women's Royal Army Corps, who was Chairman of the Council of the Royal Dental Hospital School of Dental Surgery.

At the first meeting of the Board Philip Constable's appointment as House Governor was confirmed, and so was that of W.E. Hall as Finance Officer. The Board also established a General Purposes and Finance Committee, as well as a Medical Advisory Committee under the chairmanship of Philip Jory DSO, FRCS, the very popular Ear, Nose and Throat Surgeon. These arrangements set up under Monckton's leadership were to last for twenty six years until 1974, when the Board of Governors was disbanded and replaced by Area Health Authorities. The relationships between the medical staff and the 'management' were undoubtedly happiest and most harmonious under the benevolent regime introduced by Walter Monckton, who also quickly abolished the historical, but by this time otiose, distinction between Physicians and Assistant Physicians and Surgeons and Assistant Surgeons.

Walter Monckton was born in Plaxtol, Kent in 1891 and educated at Harrow and Balliol College, Oxford. On the outbreak of war in 1914, Monckton joined the Royal West Kent Regiment, and for four years served in the trenches in France winning the Military Cross in 1919. As soon as the armistice was signed, Monckton was called to the bar, and in 1930 he became a King's Counsel. It is recalled that the monocled Monckton was a quiet, courteous, non-theatrical advocate, who seldom resorted to long and detailed cross examinations. In 1932 he became Attorney-General to the Duchy of Cornwall, and it was in this post that he had the responsibility for advising Edward VIII on the legal, financial and constitutional aspects of abdication, and he had the additional task of drafting the Instrument of Abdication. His probity and diplomacy stood him in good stead, and he emerged from the dark days of crisis with an unscathed reputation, indeed it was enhanced. He was held in high regard by both the departing Edward and King George VI, who on succeeding to the throne immediately gave Monckton a knighthood.

Monckton continued to advise the Duke and Duchess of Windsor, and he persuaded the Duke to take up the Governorship of the Bahamas in 1940. By this time Monckton had supported Neville Chamberlain's policy of appeasement with the Nazi Germany, and had been appointed Director-General of the Press and Censorship Bureau in the Ministry of Information. As soon as Winston Churchill became Prime Minister of the wartime coalition government Walter Monckton was appointed Director-General of the Ministry of Information. Although Monckton found favour with the Conservatives, and had been offered two safe Tory seats, he was, in fact, well to the left of them and his views were markedly socialist. In 1941 Monckton was appointed Director-General of British Propaganda in the Middle East working in Cairo. On returning to London in 1942 he undertook a number of public duties, for which he was awarded the KCMG in 1944. Monckton continued to be courted by the Conservatives and was made Solicitor-General in the post war Caretaker Government, but he refused to take a seat in the House of Commons. On the defeat of the government Monckton, after a brief spell advising the Nizam of Hyderabad returned to his legal practice, becoming one of the highest paid barristers in England, but by 1951 his socialistic views had changed and he was persuaded to take the safe Conservative seat of Bristol West. On Churchill's return to power Monckton was made Minister of Labour in the hope that by using his charm and tact as a negotiator he would be able to avert potential conflict with the unions.. Monckton's reward for achieving this goal would be the post of Lord Chief Justice. There were many who would oppose this appointment, as Monckton had a reputation as a womaniser. After separating from his first wife it is said that he had a number of affairs, before he obtained a divorce and married Lady Carlisle.

During his time at the Ministry of Labour Walter Monckton dropped the Workers' Charter and the Industrial Charter, which had been drawn up previously by the Conservatives to curb the power of the Unions, as well as arguing in support of the workers against derationing and lowering of food subsidies. Also he supported the unions in their arguments that wage increases should not be linked to productivity. Monckton appeared to defer to the Unions at every turn, which caused Churchill to remark 'Monckton has gone on holiday – he is worn out by giving way'. The Unions were allowed to become disproportionately powerful and Monckton must take the major share of responsibility for allowing them to disrupt the post-war recovery, and to threaten the British economy for many years to come by their militancy. It was not until the Unions began to act as a state within a state, and interfere directly with government in the 1970's, that steps were taken to curb their power and influence. Even so, Anthony Eden who took over the premiership from Churchill in 1955 asked Monckton to continue as Minister of Labour, but the Party Conference in the October of that year was concerned about an excessively conciliatory attitude to industrial relations that failed to provide a dividend, and called for more rigorous action against union militancy. Walter Monckton was appointed Secretary of State for Defence, but the Suez crisis developed quite soon and Monckton with Richard Austin, 'Rab' Butler, the Lord Privy Seal and Leader of the House of Commons, let it be known that they disapproved of the use of force. Monckton would not resign his post for fear of upsetting Anthony Eden who then offered him the Paymaster-General portfolio.

Walter Monckton left politics in 1957 to become Chairman of the Midland Bank. He continued to act as advisor to royalty and the establishment, and was involved in the cover-up of the Duke and Duchess of Windsor and their secretary's illegal currency transactions, the Duke of Kent's marriage settlement, and the position of Group Captain Peter Townsend, Equerry to King George VI, if he had married Princess Margaret.

For his public service Walter Monckton was given a Viscountcy in 1957. Monckton took the title of Viscount Monckton of Benchley. He died in 1965. An excellent photograph of Viscount Monckton which was presented by his son, the second Viscount hangs in the large Lecture Theatre that bears his name.

THE RUTH MYLES UNIT

Ruth Kathryn Myles BA

Ruth Kathryn Myles was born at Royal Leamington Spa on 25th August, 1964, the only daughter of Margaret and David Myles, the latter being a Solicitor practising in the town. Her brother, Peter, was just over two years older. From her earliest days Ruth was a happy and contented child, and as she grew and mixed with other children she began to display a genius for friendship which remained throughout her life. In her first few years there were various family moves, but when Ruth was nine the family moved to Boylestone, a very small village about 14 miles west of Derby, where they settled for the next twelve years.

Ruth had a great rapport with animals, not only the family pets, but also horses, and she was very fond of riding, to the point where she became a competent and often successful performer at Pony Club and Riding Club events and shows, learning to lose as well as to win, and to bear disappointment with good grace

Neither at school nor in her extracurricular activities was Ruth in the 'brilliant' category of those who excel without effort, but whatever could be attained by application and perseverance, based on a good level of intelligence, she attained- without ever losing her sense of humour and capacity for fun. She attended the School of St. Mary and St. Anne at Abbots Bromley. Here, as well as a sound education, she gained an affection for the dignified forms of worship of the Church of England, which was coupled with a deep and real personal faith in Christ which enlightened and inspired her whole outlook on life. Her genius for human friendship blossomed also, and she made further deep and abiding friendships, male and female, both at Repton College where she completed her sixth form studies, and later at Bristol University, where she studied law with a view to qualifying as a solicitor. Ruth always had the rare gift, even though absorbed in the multifarious activities of everyday life, of being able to be concerned for those she loved, and, even more importantly, to make time to keep in touch with them.

After graduation, Ruth became an Articled Clerk with the firm of Maxwell Batley, Solicitors of Chancery lane. She entered on this new experience with the whole-hearted enthusiasm and transparent enjoyment that was her hall-mark. She made a favourable impact on all her colleagues. So much so, indeed, that although she was only with the firm for just over a year before she fell ill, the Partners and Staff have made donations to St. George's in her memory ever since.

A few months later Ruth became very tired, with aching limbs and a feeling of great coldness, the sudden development of spontaneous bruising led to her rapid admission to McEntee ward at St. George's Hospital on 12th December 1988. Acute lymphatic leukaemia was diagnosed the next day.

From that time, until her death exactly six months later, her mother was with her every day, and often by night as well, and she had much loving support from friends and relatives, to each one of whom she was a very special person. Ruth's genius for friendship was unaffected by her illness, and many doctors and nurses gained a deep and abiding affection for her, and received the same in return.

Unfortunately serious life-threatening complications developed, but she recovered and the disease went into remission Ruth was advised that a bone marrow transplant held the only chance of long-term cure, her brother proved to be an ideal and willing donor, and this was duly undertaken at the Royal Marsden Hospital at Sutton. Once again, however, her body could not tolerate the immuno-suppressive drug regime and after several weeks of terrible reactions and much suffering, borne with great fortitude, the time came when it was bluntly put to her that her chance of survival was negligible. Having considered this shattering disclosure, Ruth decided that she wanted to return to St. George's for palliative treatment, as she had serene confidence in the loving and skilful care she had received there previously.

It was so arranged, and her return to McEntee ward was like a home-coming, with a welcome beyond words. The psychological boost from this, coupled with a skilfully applied change of drug treatment, brought about an almost miraculous temporary improvement, but early in June 1989 she lapsed into a coma and on 13th June at 7.50 am, in the presence of her parents, her brother and her closest friend, she left her pain-racked body and entered into the peace of her God.

This tragically short but beautiful life is fittingly remembered in the unit that is named after her. Would that it were given to all of us to give so much without seeking equivalent returns, and to suffer with such ineffable grace.

NICHOLLS WARD

Sir Marriott Fawckner Nicholls, KBE, CBE, BA, MB, BCh, MChir, FRCS

Marriott Nicholls and Alastair Hunter were two of the most popular deans in the history of the Medical School. They differed from each other in so many respects but each stamped their own individual mark on the school; and the students in the four decades leading up to the beginning of the 1970s were extremely fortunate to be able to call on the wisdom and experience of these two great men for friendly counsel. Both men played key roles in the academic development of the school and its successful transfer to Tooting.

Sir Marriott Fawckner Nicholls was born in London in 1898, and educated at the City of London School, Clare College, Cambridge, and St. George's Hospital. In 1915, having gained a place at Clare College at the age of seventeen, he enlisted in the Royal Fusiliers and served in France throughout the First World War. In 1919 Nicholls was demobilised with the rank of Captain. Back in civilian street he resumed his studies at Cambridge and graduated BA in 1921. Nicholls then entered St. George's and qualified MRCS, LRCP in 1923. After qualification he served in a number of junior posts including that of Curator to the museum. In later life he never seemed to be happier than when he was sitting in the pathology museum demonstrating specimens as he lectured to his students – he was a first class teacher, an outstanding clinician, and brilliant administrator. Marriott Nicholls took his FRCS in 1926, and then graduated MB, BCh in 1928.

In 1932, the same year in which he was appointed Assistant Surgeon to St. George's, he obtained his Mastership in Surgery (MChir). With exemplary speed Nicholls established himself both as a successful surgeon, and a popular and perceptive teacher, and was appointed full Surgeon within four years. 'Nick', as he was affectionately known, held similar appointments to the Royal National Orthopaedic Hospital, The Royal Chest, and the Belgrave Children's Hospitals. His main interest was in genito-urinary surgery, and he was at various times on the council of the Association of Urological Surgeons, and President of the Section of Urology of the Royal Society of Medicine.

Nicholls became Dean of the Medical School in 1936 and served in this post for a record spell of twenty years, which is all the more surprising when one recalls that he was a busy surgeon. He was away in the RAMC from 1940-1946 when Dr. Hugh Gordon MC, FRCP, the dermatologist, deputised for him. During the Second World War he served as a Lieutenant Colonel in Freetown, and later as a Brigadier to the 14th Army, South East Asia Command. He was made a CBE in 1946.

On his return to St. George's as Dean he was faced with difficulties arising from uncertainty as to the future location of the expanding hospital and medical school. A new site had been provisionally identified in Tooting, but it was geographically far removed from Hyde Park Corner, and presented problems with regard to accommodation and transport for the students and teachers alike. With tact, delicacy, and steady diplomacy he overcame these obstacles, and St. George's has good reason to be grateful to him for his skill as an administrator. Nicholls was the first to move his clinical department to Tooting, demonstrating by his decisive leadership his conviction that the new arrangements would work; it was the great respect, trust, and esteem in which he was held by his colleagues that helped to overcome difficulties as they arose. Nicholls was one of the visionaries who pursued a policy of academic development in the school, and he was the driving force behind the gradual evolution of a series of new university departments and their academic staffs. Undoubtedly 'Nick' was one of the greatest deans in the history of St. George's and it was a sad day when his beloved Lagonda was no longer seen on the forecourt outside the school at Hyde Park Corner. In 1956 he relinquished the post of Dean, but with undiminished zeal it was only natural that he should turn his attention to establishing a Department of Academic Surgery, so by the time he took retirement at the age of 64, its foundation was recognised by the University, and a Chair in surgery had been established. After his retirement Marriott Nicholls succeeded Julian Taylor as Professor of Surgery in the University of Khartoum, where he was held in the same warmth and high regard that he had been at

141

St. George's. For his work there he was awarded a KBE in 1969. Nicholls was a tall man of distinguished military bearing who could appear to be aloof, but, in fact, he was one of the most approachable of men and was held in the greatest of respect by all who worked with him. He had a love for cricket and fishing, and he was a staunch supporter of the school cricket club, and often turned out for the team when it played on tour in Northleach, where he had a home, as well as playing in the annual Staff versus the Students cricket match regularly until his retirement. 'Nick' was noted for his genial hospitality.

Marriott Nicholls served as a Member, and, for two years, as Chairman of the Court of Examiners of the Royal College of Surgeons. It was said that he gained the universal respect of his fellow examiners for his ability to put even the most nervous candidates at ease and to bring the best out of them. To mark this admiration they took the unprecedented step of presenting him with a silver cigarette box in which he could keep his favoured 'Players' cigarettes.

Sir Marriott Nicholls died in Khartoum aged 71, his wife Norah Schuster, past president of the Association of Clinical Pathologists, died aged 98 in 1990.

A cartoon of Marriott Nicholls by Elliott Blake, the plastic surgeon hangs in the Medical School library. It portrays 'Nick' in the guise of a conjuror wielding his cystoscope like a magic wand so as to produce a rabbit out of the hat.

THE GROVE HOSPITAL NURSES HOMES

Bronte, Clare and Dorcas

When the Grove Fever Hospital was built in 1901 provision was made for eight nurses homes, all of which remained in use until the hospital was handed over to St. George's Hospital in 1953. The Board of Governors of St. George's decided that only six of these homes, which were identified by the letters A, B, C, D, N and S would be required. The Nursing Committee, under the chairmanship of the Matron, Muriel Powell, was asked by the Board of Governors to chose suitable names for the homes. The Nursing Committee agreed that the homes should be named after famous women, and that the name should begin with the same letter as the existing designation. The proposal placed before the Board of Governors was that the homes should be called Austen, Bronte, Cavell, Dorcas, Nightingale and St. Clare. It is clear from the annotations to the minutes of the Board of Governors that reservations were expressed over the names Dorcas and St. Clare, but the Governors eventually accepted Dorcas, and, after much deliberation, Clare was adopted also, but without her saintly prefix. Nightingale and Austen Houses were pulled down in the late 1970s to make way for the construction of the peripheral hospital road. Only Bronte and Dorcas remain in their original form; Cavell and Clare were joined together by the construction of extensions to both buildings in the early 1970s. Nightingale was named after Florence Nightingale (1820-1910) who was an honorary member of the Board of Governors of St. George's in the latter part of the nineteenth century. Austen was named after Jane Austen (1775-1817), the novelist whose books included *Love and Friendship*, *Sense and Sensibility*, *Northanger Abbey* and *Pride and Prejudice*.

Bronte

Bronte House is named after the Bronte sisters, Anne (1820-1849), Charlotte (1816-1855), and Emily (1818-1848), the daughters of an Irish clergyman, Patrick Bronte, and a Cornish mother, Maria, who were born in Thornton, Yorkshire. Two other sisters, Maria and Elizabeth, died in childhood of tuberculosis, and a brother, (Patrick) Branwell (1817-1848), a bright child who later wasted his many talents with an increasingly dissolute lifestyle, which brought shame and sadness on the family. When their father was appointed rector of Haworth in 1820, the young Bronte sisters moved there with him, but unfortunately their mother died soon afterwards, and the girls grew up very much in each others company, lacking suitable companions of their own age and station. They were, however, free to wander over the Yorkshire moors, and their austere beauty much influenced the content and Romantic style of their literary work. The girls attended schools at Cowan Bridge and Roe Head, until they were forced to leave the latter because of Branwell's mounting debts.

The straitened financial situation at home in the Parsonage meant that on leaving school Anne and Emily had to seek work. There were few areas of employment for ladies from a genteel background, except as companions to elderly ladies, or private governesses; and they both took posts in the latter occupation, as befitted their educational standing. Anne was forced to leave one post because her brother, Branwell, fell in love with the mistress of the household. Charlotte became a teacher for a brief time, but soon the three sisters returned to Haworth, where they planned to open a school. This plan failed to materialise, and Charlotte took a post in Brussels for a short period between 1843 and 1844. At this point Charlotte returned to Haworth, where, by chance, she found Emily's poems, and this stimulated the three girls to write more of them. In 1846 the collected *Poems* were published under their pseudonyms: Acton, Currer and Ellis Bell. As only two volumes of their joint venture were sold the Bronte sisters decided that they should each go their own way and turn their hands to writing novels.

Anne wrote *Agnes Grey* in 1845 and *The Tenant of Wildfell Hall* in 1848 but neither were successful at the time; Emily wrote the powerful tale of love and vengeance, *Wuthering Heights* in 1847, but it was Charlotte who received the greatest public recognition in her day. Anne, Emily and Branwell, who by this time was an alcoholic and an opium addict, all died in 1848 – 1849 from tuberculosis. Charlotte completed *Jane Eyre* in 1847, *Shirley* in 1849, *Villette* in 1852 in which she satirized M. Heger, a married man who had been head of the school she had taught at in Brussels, and *The Professor* which was published in 1857 after her death. Charlotte had fallen hopelessly in love with M. Heger but he had failed to reciprocate her affection. Charlotte married her father's curate, the fourth man to propose to her, Arthur Bell Nicholls in 1854 but she died of tuberculosis during pregnancy the following year. Two of her stories *The Secret* and *Lily Hart* were not published until 1978, almost a century and a quarter after Charlotte Bronte's death. On sober reflection it appears no less than a literary miracle that three apparently repressed sisters living in genteel poverty in a remote corner of Yorkshire should each be capable of writing avant-garde novels with a passion which amounted to genius.

Clare

Clare House takes its name from St. Clare who was born in Assisi in 1194, a daughter of a nobleman. When she reached the age of twelve

144

her father sought to give her away in marriage, Clare refused, and ran away to Portiuncula where she became a nun under the instruction of Francis of Assisi. As Francis did not have a convent he placed Clare in a Benedictine convent in Bastia. Her family attempted to remove her, so Francis moved her to the convent of Angelo di Panzo, where Clare was joined by another fugitive, Agnes, her elder sister. Again, their family tried to remove the two sisters, but, at this critical point, Clare performed her first miracle by rendering Agnes too heavy to be bodily lifted and moved. Francis made Clare the Superior at St. Damiano in 1215, and she remained there for the next forty years as head of the newly founded Order of Poor Clares. Clare was eventually joined by her mother and younger sister, Beatrice, and all vowed strict poverty, a vow which was sanctioned by Pope Innocent III. In 1228 Pope Gregory IX attempted to persuade the Poor Clares to accept the ownership of buildings and land, but Clare argued her case so well that the Pope was forced to accept defeat, and granted the convents of St. Damiano, Perugia and Florence the 'privilege of pauperism'. A second attempt to make the Poor Clares accept ownership of property was made by Pope Innocent IV in 1245. It is generally recognised that it was mainly Clare and St. Francis who were responsible for the growth of the Franciscan Order. Clare was credited with a number of miracles during her lifetime, the most notable occurring in 1241 when she saved Assisi from Emperor Frederick II's troops. Clare was canonised in 1255, two years after she died in Assisi. St. Clare is the patroness of television.

Dorcas

The story of Dorcas is told in The New Testament of the Holy Bible, Acts 9, Verses 36 to 43. Dorcas, meaning gazelle in Greek or Tabitha in Aramaic, was a Christian lady living in Joppa who performed many acts of kindness in helping the sick and providing clothing for the poor. In time she fell sick herself and died. Her body was washed and laid out in an upper room of her house. At this time the Apostle Peter, was close to Joppa in Lydda where he had been spreading the gospel and curing a number of people who were suffering from chronic illness, including Aeneas who had been bedridden with paralysis for eight years. Peter's fame spread through the district, and two men from Joppa were sent

145

to him inviting him to visit Dorcas and restore her to health. Peter hurried to Joppa and went to the upper room where Dorcas was laid out and surrounded by many people whom she had helped. Peter asked them to leave him alone with Dorcas. Peter knelt by her bedside and said 'Tabitha, rise'. Tabitha or Dorcas opened her eyes and holding Peter's hand she stood up and went to the window where Peter showed everyone below that Dorcas was alive. Word spread fast and many people in Joppa were persuaded to believe in Jesus Christ. The word dorcastry is sometimes used to describe a church function at which women gather to make clothes for the poor.

OGLE WARD

The Ogle Family

Three Ogles, all physicians, served on the staff of St. George's, John William, his son Cyril, and a distant relative, William. A fourth Ogle, another William (1824 – 1905), who became a physician to the Derbyshire Royal Infirmary, was a contemporary of John William when they were both students at St. George's, and oddly enough they were distantly related.

John William Ogle was born in Leeds in 1824 and educated at Wakefield and Oxford, where he took his BA in 1847. Ogle studied medicine firstly in Leeds, and later at St. George's Hospital, where he took his MB in 1851. After the usual junior appointments as house physician, demonstrator, and curator, Ogle was elected assistant physician in 1857, the year in which he obtained his MD. He was elected physician in 1866, but was forced to retire through ill-health in 1876 after only ten years in the post, amazingly he continued to serve as a consulting physician for nearly thirty years thereafter. In his relatively short period of time as a physician at St. George's, Ogle played a very active role. He began the Hospital reports with Timothy Holmes, and the first seven volumes were published under their joint editorship. From the School Gazette columns of the period it is clear that John William was a kind, generous, considerate and friendly man, who had 'no enemies and bore no malice'. Of deep religious convictions, John William Ogle was keenly interested in the affairs of the Royal College of Physicians. He was elected a Fellow in 1855, Censor in 1873, Senior Censor and a Vice President in 1885. Ogle, a man of enormous industry successfully managed to combine these responsibilities with a large and lucrative private practice. Dr. J. W. Ogle died in Highgate at the age of eighty one.

Cyril Ogle was the third son of John William, born in 1861, and educated at Westminster School and Trinity College, Oxford. Cyril Ogle graduated in Natural Sciences in 1884 and then enrolled at St. George's Hospital as a student from where he qualified in 1888. He was appointed Assistant Physician in 1897 and Physician eight years later, by which time he had gained his MD.

Dame Fortune certainly smiled on Cyril, who stood barely five feet in height, as not only did he appear to have inherited his father's capacity for work, but, in addition, it was said that he had an 'uncanny clinical sense'. A formidable combination of talents! As curator of the museum he carried out his duties 'with conspicuous ability', often referred to as 'our friend Dr. Ogle' he was 'loyal to the Corner' and regarded as 'the doctor's doctor' and many said that 'no one could wish for a truer friend'. Dr. Ogle had a reputation of being infallible, and the story was told that when he attended a post-mortem carried out by a senior pathologist who had once taught him, the pathologist when verifying Ogle's correct diagnosis, remarked 'Right again you little b——r but don't forget who taught you medicine!'. Ogle often described himself as a 'West End cockney' which he felt was apt description for one born within the sound of the door bells of Harley Street.

Cyril Ogle, like his father before him, involved himself in the affairs of the Royal College of Physicians. He was awarded his Fellowship in 1899, examined for the Conjoint Board, and Cambridge University, before becoming Censor of the College in 1924, a post his father had held forty years previously. To the end of his days he had no interests outside medicine, and remained a modest and reticent individual. He never married and died in Folkestone in 1931. The Medical Gazette paid tribute to Ogle on his death with 'Modest in his opinions, he was never heard to make a disparaging remark about any colleague or student. Neither sport or worldly pleasures had any attraction for him and a more unselfish life was never lived, a truer friend was never known. His private life was lonely, almost ascetic. Much worried by sick relations under his care, he gave himself unto others'. A portrait of Cyril Ogle, by Ernest Moore, shows him indulging in his one worldly pleasure, smoking a cigarette, hangs in St. George's.

William Ogle, the fourth son of J. A. Ogle FRCP, Professor of Medicine at Oxford, was born in 1827, and took holy orders before deciding to follow a career in medicine. William Ogle enrolled at St. George's in 1855, and took his MB in 1858. After a number of junior posts he was appointed Assistant Physician to St. George's Hospital in 1869, but surprisingly for a robust man blessed with a strong physique who lived to the age of 85, he was forced to give up this appointment in 1872 due to ill health; only one of three Assistant Physicians who did not ascend to senior status, all due to illness. Others will be encountered in this book (like the first Ogle in this section) who were advised to retire early and then went on to an enviable longevity, perhaps these rather imprecise predictions occurred as a result of incorrect diagnosis, it would be interesting to learn the retrospective views of the victims. After his departure from the hurly burly of clinical life William Ogle devoted his energies to public health. In 1880 he became Chief of the Statistical Department at the General Register Office, where he was responsible for Census reports and Occupational Mortality figures.

After retirement in 1903, William Ogle who counted Darwin, Hooker and Lankester among his close friends, translated many of the works of Aristotle into English, as well as producing an English edition of Kerner's 'Flowers and their Unbidden Guests'. William Ogle died in 1912.

Several well known names in medicine shared the name Ogle but the ward at St. George's hospital is named after Cyril Ogle, who George Edwards, the anaesthetist and medical historian, described as 'probably the most gifted physician that St. George's has ever known'.

> Ogle's Drops were famous in their day, and consisted of a linctus of morphine, hydrocyanic acid and squill – presumably used for coughs but deemed to be so potent that the formula was withdrawn.

148

PINCKNEY WARD

Charles Pinckney FRCP

Charles Pinckney, or 'Charlie P' as he was affectionately known by colleagues, friends and countless students of St. George's Hospital, was the first paediatrician to be appointed at the hospital, as previously one of the general physicians had been in charge of diseases of childhood.

Charles Percy Pinckney, to give him his full name, was born in 1901, and educated at Cambridge, and then at St. George's Hospital. After qualification, he undertook a number of appointments at St. George's before becoming Resident Assistant Physician in 1929.

In 1931, Pinckney was appointed as a neurologist to King George V Hospital at Ilford, and in 1932 he became Physician to the Victoria Hospital for Children, Tite Street, where he served until the hospital closed in 1964, when he helped to transfer the beds to the new St. George's Hospital at Tooting. Charles Pinckney also held appointments to the Windsor Group of Hospitals, and to the Chailey Heritage Hospital for Handicapped Children.

In 1938 he was appointed Physician in Children's Diseases to St. George's hospital, in succession to Dr. T. F. McNair Scott, a general physician with an interest in paediatrics, and he remained in this post until his retirement at the age of 65. Soon after his retirement, he was persuaded to return to look after the staff, which he did so far a further four years, in the process endearing himself to another generation of St. George's nurses and students.

Charles Pinckney was a most engaging and delightful man, it was said he never lost his temper, and always appeared to have time for everyone. He loved his hospital, and it was only during Wimbledon fortnight which he adored that he was not seen regularly. Sadly, he died in 1982, two years after the ward was named for him.

MURIEL POWELL WARD

Dame Muriel Powell, DBE, CBE, SRN, SCM

Muriel Powell was an outstanding figure among the nursing leaders of her era. She had all the old-fashioned virtues associated with being a humanitarian, which were rather unusually coupled with her being very definitely a woman ahead of her time. Muriel or 'Betsy' as she became known, was born in Cinderford, Gloucestershire and educated at the Cinderford East Dean Grammar School, before entering the School of Nursing at St. George's Hospital in 1934, and such was her progress that in less than thirteen years she became its Matron.

After qualifying as a State Registered Nurse and a State Certified Midwife, in 1939 Miss Powell left St. George's Hospital, where she had become a Ward Sister, to take up an appointment as Sister in Charge of the County Maternity Hospital, Winchcome. She then worked for a short while at Postlip Hall, Gloucestershire, which had been made an Emergency Hospital during the Second World War, before becoming a District Nurse in her home county. By the time she was 28 she had obtained a Sister Tutor Diploma, and the Diploma of Nursing of the University of London. Muriel Powell was then appointed to the Ipswich Borough General Hospital as Nursing Tutor, before she became Principal Tutor at the Manchester Royal Infirmary.

In 1947 Helen Hanks retired as Matron of St. George's Hospital and the vacancy was advertised. The 33 year old Muriel Powell applied for the post, and despite some misgivings that she might prove to be too inexperienced, the majority view was that with the imminent introduction of the National Health Service, it was essential to have a youthful, forward looking and progressive leader for a large nursing staff. Muriel Powell was appointed, and over the next twenty three years that she remained in post she fully justified the confidence of those who had taken the bold step of appointing her. Straight away she began to demonstrate her great managerial ability together with a passionate commitment to improve the welfare of both the patients and her nurses.

Muriel Powell revolutionised established practices. She recognised the importance of involving the patient in the process of decision making, and, despite some raised eyebrows amongst the medical staff, she implemented it. With great courage she introduced questionnaires on medical and nursing care, and invited comments on other aspects of the service, to see where improvements could be made. Her other innovations included changes in the patients day; she stopped the early wakening, and ruled that patients should be allowed to sleep on until a more acceptable hour. The off-duty rotas for nurses were changed to their advantage, internal rotations for night duty were introduced, she promoted the status of the enrolled nurse, and abolished the practice of nurses having to resign when they married. Muriel Powell's vision was to humanise the whole atmosphere of St. George's Hospital, which she considered to be far too strict. There is no doubt that she succeeded so well in the task she had set herself that St. George's became the role model for other hospitals to emulate.

Muriel Powell's achievements were nationally and internationally recognised. She became President of the Association of Hospital Matrons (1958-1963), President of the National Association of State Enrolled Nurses (1965-1967) and Deputy President of the Royal College of Nursing (1963-1964). She was Chairman of the Standing Nursing Advisory Committee at the Ministry of Health (1958-1969), a member of the Central Health Services Council for many years, as well as serving as a member of many national and international commissions and committees.

In 1970 Muriel Powell left St. George's Hospital to take on the demanding post of Chief Nursing Officer for Scotland, and, for her services in this role, and also in recognition of her enormous contributions to the development of nursing, she was made a Dame of the British Empire. It was a sad blow for nursing when her wonderful career was brought to a premature close in 1976 by an illness which led to her death two years later.

Dame Muriel was a deeply religious person, and her books *Patients are People* and *Called to Serve*, in which she collaborated with the Reverend Paul Glidden, underline her strong principles and convictions; they remain popular and should be essential reading for nurses and other health professionals. Away from work she had a love of music, and was never happier than when she was at her home in Cinderford, where she was close to the River Severn as it meandered its way through the magnificent Gloucestershire countryside close to the Forest of Dean.

The portrait of Dame Muriel which hangs in the Philip Constable Boardroom was painted by Dot Nassim, the wife of Dr. J. R. Nassim MD FRCP, Physician to St. George's Hospital from 1946 to 1973, and was presented to the hospital by Mrs Terry Pickthorne, the sister of Dame Muriel.

HUMPHRY ROLLESTON WARD

Sir Humphry Davy Rolleston, Bart, GCVO, KCB, CB, Hon. FRCS, PRCP, MD, Hon. FRCPI, Hon. MD (Dublin) (Bordeaux) (Jefferson) (Madrid) (Padua) (Paris) (Pennsylvania), Hon. LLD (Birmingham) (Bristol) (Edinburgh) (Glasgow), Hon. DCL (Dublin), Legion d'Honneur
Rolleston and Duke Elder are probably St. George's Hospital's most honoured consultants. Sir Humphry Rolleston was the eldest of the five sons and three daughters of George Rolleston, MD, FRS, a Professor of Anatomy and Physiology at Oxford University. It would appear that George Rolleston had little say in the choice of forenames for his first son, clearly these were chosen by his wife who was the niece of Sir Humphry Davy, President of the Royal Society. Burdened with such distinguished forenames it was obligatory for the young Rolleston to succeed. And succeed he did. He was the only St. George's physician to become President of the Royal College of Physicians, President of the Royal Society of Medicine and Acting President of the British Medical Association. Rolleston also received almost every honour open to a British physician, including honorary degrees and diplomas from most of the major universities and colleges around the world.

Born in Oxford in June 1862, Humphry Rolleston was educated at Marlborough and St. John's College, Cambridge, where he obtained first class honours in the Natural Sciences Tripos in 1886. At Cambridge, he played as a forward at rugby football for the University, and later he was a member of the St. Bartholomew's Hospital XV, which won the Inter Hospital's Cup. Following his medical training at St. Bartholomew's Hospital, Rolleston obtained his MRCP in 1889, before being elected FRCP in 1894, and he was awarded a Cambridge MD in 1891. Following qualification, he became house physician to Sir William Church at Bart's, and next he became a demonstrator in anatomy and assistant physician at the Metropolitan Hospice. Aware that there was no imminent vacancy for a physician at Bart's, Rolleston applied for, and was appointed to, the post of Curator of the Museum at St. George's in 1890, and three years later was appointed Assistant Physician. Soon afterwards, he became Assistant Physician of the Victoria Hospital for Children, and in 1898 he was appointed Physician to both St. George's and the Victoria Hospitals. Rolleston took an active part in the principal medical societies making a name for himself as a physician, pathologist, teacher and researcher. His research work on the adrenals, the mechanism of the heart, and the anatomy of the appendicular region were undoubtedly some of his greatest contributions to medicine.

In 1901, Rolleston was found to be suffering from tuberculosis, but he volunteered for service with the Imperial Treasury in the South African War. Restored to health in that country's kinder climate he returned to London where he built up a large practice and continued his research and writing. Among his many contributions to both medical and general literature were his editorship of *The Practitioner*; his co-editorship of *System of Medicine, Manual of Practical Morbid Anatomy, Diseases of the Liver, Gall Bladder and Bile Ducts*, as well as his authorship of *The Two Heberdens, Sir Thomas Clifford Allbutt, Medical Aspects of Samuel Johnson* and *The Cambridge Medical School*. In total he wrote over 600 papers and twenty books.

Humphry Rolleston served in the First World War as a Surgeon Rear Admiral, and was appointed CB in 1916, and KCB in 1918. In 1923, he was appointed physician to King George V. A year later he was created a baronet, and in 1929 he was appointed GCVO. Rolleston's presidencies of the Royal Society of Medicine (1918 - 1920), Royal College of Physicians (1922 – 1926), and the Medical Society of London (1926 – 1927) illustrate his commanding position in medicine.

Rolleston retired to Haslemere in 1932, but even in retirement he continued to be at the forefront of medical matters as editor of both the *Practitioner* and the *British Encyclopaedia of Medical Practice*. Away from medicine he was president of the London Council Association, the Papworth Village settlement, and he was a trustee of the British Museum. He died at the age of 82 in 1944.

Humphry Rolleston had two sons, one of whom was killed in Flanders in 1915, and the other in Zanzibar in 1916. His brother, John Davy Rolleston, had tenuous links with St. George's through serving as a medical officer to the Grove Fever Hospital throughout the First World War.

According to Blomfield 'Rolleston with his slim figure and fresh complexion looked very young and blushed readily which made him look younger' Apparently, any interruption during one of his lectures, or a stupid or unexpected answer to a question, would cause him to blush furiously. Blomfield recalled that he and some of fellow students 'used to give an occasional weird reply to call forth this phenomenon'. Humphry Rolleston when describing the size of a tumour or organ often compared it with a familiar object, often edible, such as an orange, or a tomato. In one class he asked for the size of the spleen, the answer came back 'the size of a half boiled turnip'. Rolleston coloured to the roots of his fair hair and replied 'That answer was more culinary than correct'.

The Hunter Arch which stands in front of Grosvenor Wing at St. George's Hospital, Tooting, was originally unveiled by Sir Humphry Rolleston when it was first erected at Hyde Park Corner in 1924. A portrait of Sir Humphry Rolleston dressed in his robes as President of the Royal College of Physicians by George Henry painted in 1925 hangs in St. George's Hospital.

RODNEY SMITH WARD

The Rt. Hon. Lord Smith of Marlow, KBE, PRCS, MS, Hon DSc (Exeter) (Leeds), Hon FRACS, Hon FRCS (Glasgow) (Edinburgh) (Canada) (South Africa), Hon FACS, Hon FRCSI, Hon FDSRCS, Hon MD (Zurich)

Lord Smith of Marlow who as Rodney Smith was Consultant Surgeon to St. George's Hospital from 1946 to 1978.

Rodney Smith, born in 1914, was a child prodigy as a violinist, but, after losing to the young Yehudi Menuhin in a competition at a music festival (surely nothing to be ashamed of), he realised that he would never attain the same heights in music as Menuhin. By nature Rodney could never accept being second best at anything so he looked for an alternative career, one in which he was determined to reach the pinnacle. He chose medicine.

In his younger days, Rodney Smith was a superb all round sportsman. He boxed for Westminster School, and St. Thomas's Hospital, where he was educated. On a number of occasions he fought in the famous

Blackfriars Ring, and as a cricketer he played for Surrey at the Oval. 1934 was a year of multiple triumphs for Rodney Smith. Just twenty years old, and still some way off qualifying in medicine, he obtained the primary Fellowship of the Royal College of Surgeons, scored two hundred runs in the United Hospitals Cricket Cup match against the London Hospital, ran the half mile in one minute and fifty seconds, and was the soloist in Mendelssohn's Violin Concerto at a concert in the Great Hall, Westminster. Rodney Smith qualified MB BS and MRCS LRCP in 1937.

In 1941, he enlisted in the Royal Army Medical Corps and served in the illustrious Eighth Army in both North Africa and Italy. He was wounded at Anzio. After demobilisation he was appointed Assistant Surgeon to St. George's Hospital in 1946, and from then on his career was meteoric, yet he still found time to become an international bridge player, and on many occasions he partnered the Right Honourable Ian MacLeod, the Conservative Cabinet Minister. Many years later as Lord Smith he captained the House of Lords Bridge team.

Rodney Smith's chief surgical interest centred upon the hepato-biliary tract, where he made great advances in both knowledge and operative technique. His reputation for reconstruction of the bile duct was international, and surgeons from around the world regularly elbowed one another around operating table to watch the master at work. No one could match his manual dexterity or had a greater knack of making all operations appear to be such models of simplicity. Smith was always punctual, to begin his day he would arrive in his Rolls Royce, and latterly his Mercedes, gliding into Grosvenor Crescent from Hyde Park Corner he would quickly sweep into a U-turn and park outside the Casualty Department. Swiftly entering the hospital his progress to the operating theatre was clearly audible to those familiar with his habits, as his metal tipped and heeled shoes clipped along the corridors. Everyone was aware that 'Hot Rod' as he was known by both his juniors and students was arriving and itching to begin operating. He occasionally displayed impatience with his juniors and the scrub nurses, who were rebuked with a 'Like that, doctor', or 'Oh, come on, ducky'.

Rodney Smith was elected President of the Royal College of Surgeons in 1973, and during his presidency he was made a Knight of the British

Empire. On completion of his term of office as president of the college in 1978 he retired from the staff of St. George's Hospital, and was created a Life Peer taking the title of Lord Smith of Marlow, which was where he had his country home. As Lord Smith he became President of the British Medical Association and was awarded the Gold Medal in 1982. Other presidencies included that of the Royal Society of Medicine and the British Association of Surgical Oncologists. He was also Chairman of the Conference of Medical Colleges, Chairman of the Armed Forces Medical Advisory Committee, and Emeritus Consultant Surgeon to the Army.

Rodney Smith wrote and lectured widely on his surgical interests and his numerous publications include *Surgery of Pancreatic Neoplasms* (1953), *Surgery of the Gall Bladder and Bile Ducts* (1964), and, with Charles Rob, the multi-volumed hand book *Operative Surgery*. After retiring from public life and not in robust health Rodney Smith took up oil painting, and still exercising his formidable gifts is now recognised as an accomplished artist.

A cartoon of Rodney Smith by Elliott Blake hangs in the Medical School library. It shows the surgeon juggling with a cricket bat and playing cards in front of a Rolls Royce.

JOHN SNOW WARD

John Snow, MD

John Snow achieved fame in two fields of medicine: anaesthesia and epidemiology. His outstanding research in both subjects tend to be overshadowed by the two unconnected events for which he is instantly remembered namely: being the first doctor to give an anaesthetic to a reigning monarch when he administered chloroform to Queen Victoria; and his insistence on the removal of the Broad Street pump-handle.

Snow, the eldest son of a farmer, was born in Heyworth in 1813. At the age of fourteen he became apprenticed to Mr. William Hardcastle, a surgeon in Newcastle-on-Tyne. It is one of those fascinating oddities that occur from time to time to note that Snow began his medical career in a town which gave its name to the public house in Broadwick Street that now bears the name of John Snow. One wonders whether Snow, as a man who practised absolute alcoholic abstinence, would have approved! It was while he was with Mr. Hardcastle that he first encountered a cholera epidemic at Killingworth Colliery.

By 1833, John Snow was engaged as an assistant to Mr. Walls in Barnopfield, and a year later he moved to Pateley Bridge in Yorkshire, where he worked with Mr. Warburton. In 1836 he walked to London and enrolled as a student at the School of Anatomy in Windmill Street. Snow qualified as a member of the College of Surgeons in 1838, and began to practice in Frith Street, Soho. At the same time he continued his clinical studies at Charing Cross and passed the MB in 1843, and was awarded the MD in 1844, and became a lecturer in forensic medicine at the Aldersgate School of Medicine from 1844 to 1849, but in addition from 1838 until 1846 he carried out some original research on asphyxia and ether. In 1847 he was invited to give ether anaesthetics to dental outpatients at St. George's Hospital. Following the successful introduction of his own apparatus for giving ether he was invited to extend his practice to include the inpatients. The publication of his book on ether followed in 1847. Soon afterwards, Snow turned his attentions to chloroform and devised an inhaler. Such was his reputation as an anaesthetist and researcher that William Ferguson, Robert Liston's successor as the leading London surgeon, made Snow his colleague at King's College Hospital and in private practice. Snow continued his research into the dosage and toxicity of chloroform and his work on the subject was published in 1858. Already Snow was regarded as the leading anaesthetist in London when he wrote 'On the Inhalation of Ether in Surgical Operations' in 1847. Later Snow was to abandon ether in favour of chloroform, although he was well aware of its dangers. So high was his reputation that he was asked to anaesthetise Queen Victoria for the birth of Prince Leopold in 1853, and Princes Beatrice in 1857; and on both occasions he gave the Queen fifteen minim doses intermittently on a silk handkerchief, after which Her Majesty said 'Dr Snow gave that blessed chloroform and the effect was soothing, quieting, and delightful beyond measure'. Snow's administration of chloroform by this method became known as 'Chloroform *à la reine*'! John Snow's last paper which was published after his death was *On Chloroform and other Anaesthetics*.

John Snow's pioneer research work in anaesthetic agents and his skills as a clinical anaesthetist were only part of his claim to fame. He had long held the belief that cholera infection was water borne, and from this it followed that the disease could be controlled by improved sanitation. He deduced that cholera entered the body via the alimentary tract and was prevalent in crowded areas especially those lacking proper sanitation. Snow was convinced that cholera was water borne by 1848, and from 1849 onwards he investigated the particulars of every case of cholera in London, as well as extensively examining Thames river water at those places from where the supplies were taken. In 1854 the infamous Golden Square epidemic of cholera erupted, leading to five hundred deaths within ten days. Snow's research convinced him that contamination of the water was the cause of the epidemic, and he carefully detailed the deaths and found that the outbreak was centred around the Broad Street pump, the site of which was at the junction of Broadwick and Lexington Streets. He found that people using other nearby pumps, such as the inmates of the workhouse in Poland Street, which later became the site of the Marshall Street Baths, and the brewery workers in Broad Street largely escaped the epidemic, and he concluded that, as their daily lives were identical in every other way, they were spared precisely because they were taking their water from those other pumps. Snow examined the water from the Broad Street pump and found that it was contaminated. He was convinced that this was the source of the epidemic, and asked the Board of Guardians of St. James parish to remove the pump handle, but by the time they did so the cholera epidemic had begun to recede naturally. This should not detract from his triumph, however, because his painstaking epidemiological detective work showed that he was right on both scores: firstly, that, in general, the disease was water-borne, and then, in particular, that the water from the Broad Street pump was the cause of the current outbreak. Later it was found that the sewer ran within a few feet of the well supplying the pump, and a small crack in the sewage pipe could well have led to the contamination.

Ultimately he was able to demonstrate conclusively that cholera was water borne in the South London epidemic, when he compared the incidence of cholera between the Southwark and Vauxhall areas, with the Lambeth area. The former was supplied with Thames water taken at Battersea Fields, whereas Lambeth's water came from the Thames much further upstream at Thames Ditton. By investigating every household where there was a case of cholera, he showed that the incidence was nearly fifteen times greater in those houses which received water from Battersea Fields. His work on this subject was published in 1855.

Unfortunately John Snow had been in poor health for many years suffering from tuberculosis and nephritis, for which he was treated by Robert Bright (1789 – 1858), but, as if this was not enough, he developed a brain tumour, which in those days was inoperable, and died at the relatively early age of 45, on the 16th June 1858. During his short professional career he made momentous scientific contributions to both anaesthesia and epidemiology, and St. George's may proudly boast of its connection with this great medical pioneer.

John Snow was buried in Brompton Cemetery. The original gravestone, which was damaged in an air raid in 1941, was replaced by the Association of Anaesthetists in the 1950s. The 'John Snow' public house on the corner of Broadwick Street and Lexington Street in Soho, London, was built in the 1870's as the 'Newcastle-upon-Tyne' and is within a stone's throw of the site of the Hunter's School of Anatomy. Its name was changed to the 'John Snow' in 1955 to mark the centenary of Snow's researches into the causes of the cholera epidemic of 1854. In the saloon bar there is an account of John Snow's life and his work, along with a copy of the letter written to 'The Times' by a few of the local residents complaining of the appalling condition of the drains at the time of the cholera epidemic. In the bar there are displayed two other photographs, one is of the unveiling of the 'John Snow' sign in 1955 by Professor Sir Austin Bradford-Hill, who was then President of the Section of Epidemiology and Preventive Medicine of the Royal Society of Medicine. The other photograph concocted by some wag is of the 'ghost' of the old Broad Street pump. Outside the 'John Snow' a red granite kerbstone marks the original site of the infamous pump.

ST. JAMES' WING

St. James' Hospital

The name of this large wing in the new St. George's Hospital at Tooting acknowledges the long standing association of the old St. James' Hospital, Balham with St. George's Hospital.

The land on which St. James' Hospital was built was formerly part of Wandsworth Common, which by 1850 had become a cultivated field. In 1851 the Parish of St. James', Westminster purchased 20 acres of the field for £500, and on it they proceeded to build an industrial residential school for juvenile offenders . By 1868 St. James' Parish had merged with the Parish of St. Ann's, Soho, under a new Westminster Board of Guardians for Poor Law purposes, and, having sold 14 acres of the site for a handsome profit of £14,000, the school was enlarged so that it could accommodate nearly 200 children.

The Westminster Board of Guardians sold the buildings and the land to the Board of Guardians of Wandsworth, who used the buildings as a branch workhouse for a short period to ease the problems of overcrowding in the main workhouse in Swaffield Road, and the Tooting Home for the Aged in Church Lane. It had already been decided that the site would be used for the new infirmary, which was essential to overcome the inadequacies of St. John's Hospital, Battersea.

St. James' Hospital was opened in 1911 and was managed by the Wandsworth Board of Guardians until 1930, when they were superseded in accordance with the Local Government Act of 1929 by the London County Council. On the introduction of the National Health Service in 1948 the control of the hospital passed from the London County Council to the Wandsworth Hospital Group Management Committee, which was responsible to the South West Metropolitan Regional Hospitals Board. In 1974 St. James' and St. George's Hospitals were brought together under a District Management Team responsible to the Merton, Sutton Wandsworth Area Health Authority, and then in 1982 the Wandsworth District Health Authority assumed the Management responsibility. By this time the medical staff of the two hospitals had integrated, and plans had been finalised for the two hospitals to be combined on the St. George's Hospital site.

160

St. James' Hospital finally closed in 1985, and the old site is now used for residential purposes. There were a number of eminent medical men and women who worked at St. James' Hospital, and two of these: Norman Tanner and 'Pop' Vernon now have wards named after them at Tooting.

The Foundation Stone laid by the Rev. Canon Hubert Curtis MA, the Chairman of the Board of Guardians of the Wandsworth Union, on 15 December 1908, and the stone which was laid in 1879 by Henry Cooper MRCS, and fifteen fellow Westminster Union Guardians of the Poor, were set into the perimeter wall which enclosed the school building built on their land; they are situated now in the grounds of St. George's Hospital close to the Accident and Emergency Department. [The Boards of Guardians responsibilities were eventually taken over by the London County Council]

TANNER WARD

Norman Cecil Tanner, MB, ChB, FRCS
Born in Bristol in 1906 Norman Cecil Tanner was educated at the Merchant Venturers School, and Bristol University, where he qualified both MRCS, LRCP, and MB, ChB, in 1929. After qualification he held resident posts at Bristol Royal Infirmary, the West London, and Putney Hospitals before passing the final part of the Fellowship of the Royal College of Surgeons in 1931. Tanner then joined the London County Council hospital service, working at Lambeth and then Highgate, before he was appointed Senior Resident Surgeon to the latter hospital. In 1939 he was transferred as Senior Resident Surgeon to St. James' Hospital, Balham, where he remained until his retirement in 1971, during this time he saw the demise of the London County Council Hospital Service with the introduction of the National Health Service. These changes failed to interfere with Norman Tanner's tremendous accomplishment of making his unit at St. James' Hospital a centre of excellence in gastric surgery, which went on to achieve an unrivalled international reputation. Such was Tanner's personal reputation and standing that he received an unprecedented invitation to join the staff of Charing Cross Hospital in 1953. Tanner accepted this invitation, but never turned his back on

St. James', where he continued to devote his considerable energies to his patients, his teaching, his writing and helping both his senior and junior colleagues.

Norman Tanner was a superb teacher and a highly skilled surgeon, who, with his burgeoning reputation, naturally attracted large numbers of post graduate visitors from all over the world. They probably cared very little for the physical surroundings. One of Tanner's most remarkable achievements was his ability to prosper although being forced to work under the direst handicaps at St. James'. Tanner's operating theatre opened out on to a public corridor, and on one occasion a major operation was interrupted by the intrusion of a bowler hatted gentleman carrying a furled umbrella. Tanner politely asked the reason for this visitation but the gentleman left without answering. Who he was, or why he wandered into the theatre remained a mystery. If it was an interloper from the Ministry of Health wishing to see at first hand just how bad conditions really were at St. James he had arrived fortuitously in the right place, but nothing was done to improve things until just shortly before Tanner's retirement when a new theatre suite was built, including an excellent viewing gallery. The famed American surgeon Frank Lahey once visited St. James' to watch Norman Tanner operate, and on leaving the hospital he was heard to remark that he had never seen better gastric surgery performed despite the most appalling and discouraging conditions.

Norman Tanner was extremely popular with both under- and post-graduates. He was a sound and effective teacher whose knowledge was based on his exceptional and unique experience, and personally he was a kind and compassionate man who was held in the highest esteem by all who came into contact with him.

Tanner's publications were abundant, and he wrote or contributed to twenty classical surgical textbooks. His name will always be associated with the repair of inguinal herniae, and operations on the stomach. Norman Tanner was President of the British Society of Gastroenterology in 1967, the West London Medical Society in 1968, the Clinical Section and the Surgical Section of the Royal Society of Medicine in 1961-63 and 1965. He examined in surgery for the Universities of London, Cambridge, Singapore and Khartoum, he served on the editorial board

162

of both the 'British Journal of Surgery' and 'Gut'. Tanner was also a member of the Council of the Royal College of Surgeons from 1963 to 1971, was elected an Honorary Fellow of the American College of Surgeons in 1964, and received a similar honour from the Royal College of Surgeons of Ireland in 1969.

Outside medicine Norman Tanner had a deep and abiding interest in music and opera, was a keen and expert skier, and after retirement became a golfing fanatic!

Norman Tanner died suddenly aged seventy six in 1982. Today his name is remembered not only at St. George's but around the world where there are still many surgeons who are proud to acknowledge the part he played in their training.

TARRANT WARD

Albert 'Tim' Tarrant

Mr Albert Tarrant was born into a London working class background in 1879, and like so many of his fellows there was no extended educational programme for him, except in the 'University of Life', wherein he appears to have achieved First Class Honours. After leaving school at the age of 14 he held a variety of jobs including a spell in the army before he was appointed to a porter's post at the Hospice in Hendon which was near the family home. In 1906 he was appointed as a general porter at St. George's Hospital, Hyde Park Corner, for a wage of £1-1s a week, with an additional eighteen pence in lieu of beer! Tarrant was a highly popular and industrious member of the portering staff, but despite his obvious qualities it was not until 1926, nearly twenty years after he had joined the hospital, that his salary was increased to £2-2s a week.

At this stage in his career Tarrant was transferred from the pool of general porters to the Casualty Department, where he was known as the 'Surgery Porter', working with his colleague, Drury. It was in this department that 'Tim' Tarrant's real abilities, based on his thoughtful observations of life allied to a good memory, proved valuable in solving clinical problems and being the discrete and diplomatic adviser. And as he honed these innate skills his popularity rose with the medical and nursing staff, and he was quietly encouraged to take on increasing responsibilities. When he retired in 1945 his salary had risen to the princely sum of £5-5s a week plus specialist pay, but his opinion and advice was sought on many clinical problems by quite senior members of the medical staff.

Sir Ralph Marnham, Consultant Surgeon to St. George's Hospital wrote at time of Tarrant's retirement :-

> As I did not come to St. George's until 1923 you will appreciate that the earlier part of Tarrant's career has had to be glossed over, and I can only speak from personal knowledge of the finished product, but remembering that the child is indeed father of the man, I and all those who have known him can assess fairly accurately what he must have been like at all stages of his career. 'Gloss' therefore is intended to convey an apology for the absence of those intimate details so popular with the modern biographer, how for instance, Tarrant acquired his uncanny skill at shove-halfpenny, and not to suggest the need for any particular discretion.
>
> Looking back over our professional lives we can all of us remember a few teachers whose words of wisdom did not fall on barren ground, perhaps some question of personality, perhaps an unusual clarity of expression, or maybe an innate appreciation of the fundamentals win them pride of place. Be it what it may, I feel sure that countless generations of Housemen will number Tarrant among the valued few. His bandaging classes were profitable to the harassed examinee, his advice on the disposal and treatment of a difficult case must have adverted many a tragedy, his manner in dealing with patients and their relatives was in itself a valuable lesson, and his unfailing tact and discrimination must, over the course of years, have brought much credit to the institution he served so well.
>
> Tarrant was the mentor and friend of many St. George's men, all of whom benefited from the association.

On occasion throughout the Hospital's long history one finds that several members of the same family have been amongst its employees, either simultaneously or at different times. For example Albert Tarrant's brother, Charles, served as the gateman, and his son, Ralph, was an electrician's assistant for a number of years. Often successive generations followed their forebears and amongst these family groups were the Elliotts, the Howes and the Hathaways. Nurses and doctors rely heavily on all the other disciplines in the hospital in their attempt to provide high quality care, and thus the naming of the Day Surgery ward after a highly regarded porter recognises and acknowledges the invaluable contribution of those staff who have proudly served the hospital with little reward, yet always appeared grateful for the opportunity to work at St. George's Hospital. One of Tarrant's predecessors, John Attwood who was appointed a porter in 1887 and promoted Head Porter in 1900 was described as 'a man of fine presence and is possessed of a courtesy and charm of manner which never deserts him under the most trying pressure' wrote on receipt of a gift from the medical staff to mark his retirement in 1902

> Please accept my deep appreciation to you and all the gentlemen and ladies who subscribed to my testimonial I can assure you it came as a great surprise to me. Words fail me to express my gratitude to you all, if I have done any little service to anyone it has always been done with pleasure and I have been doubly repaid for it. It shows that there is that spirit of friendship in the past and present ladies and gentlemen of St. George's Hospital that cannot be equalled elsewhere and which will live when we are no more. Please accept my humble thanks.

The ward name 'Tarrant' serves as our humble thanks to all the unsung Tarrants and Attwoods for their unique contribution.

TATUM WARD

Thomas Tatum FRCS

Thomas Tatum was the eldest of the three sons of Captain Thomas Tatum of the South Wilts Militia, who lived in Salisbury. Thomas, was the forename given to the eldest male in line so young Thomas was the grandson of Thomas Tatum, a physician to the Salisbury Infirmary and great-grandson of Thomas Tatum MD, another physician who practised in Salisbury.

The three brothers received their early education in Salisbury. Thomas and his younger brother, George Roberts, decided to follow careers in medicine, whereas the youngest, William, was destined to enter the church and became Rector of St. Martin's in Salisbury. Thomas entered St. George's as a perpetual student in 1824, and George followed him there three years later. They each chose to become surgeons, and received their early training at St. George's, and the Hunter School of Anatomy in Great Windmill Street, before going on to complete their training in Paris. George was actually taught by Dupytrens at the Hotel Dieu. Thomas returned to England in 1828 and was appointed house surgeon to St. George's. The younger Tatum returned to England some time later and returned to his native Salisbury where he served with distinction as surgeon to the Infirmary.

In 1830 Thomas Tatum became a teacher in anatomy at the Hunter School, and in the following year he was appointed as the first lecturer in anatomy at the newly opened St. George's Hospital Medical School in Kinnerton Street, where he later became the lecturer in surgery.

Thomas Tatum was appointed Assistant Surgeon to St. George's Hospital in succession to Robert Walker in 1840, and then on the resignations of both Robert Walker and George Babington as full surgeons, Tatum and Edward Cutler were appointed in their place. Whereas Cutler's appointment was contentious, Tatum's was met with warm approval by the governors and his colleagues.

Described as a brilliant operator, Thomas Tatum's reputation as a skilled surgeon quickly spread. Thomas and his brother George, were both among the three hundred original fellows of the newly formed Royal College of Surgeons, and Thomas served as a member of the Council of the College from 1857 until 1863. Tall, elegant and with a flare for showmanship, Tatum was extremely popular with the students who marvelled at his skill, and especially his speed as a surgeon. Students often had a wager on how quickly Tatum could amputate a leg which was described once as being 'as fast as one could turn one's head'.

Tatum wrote a number of papers including *Removal of Tubero-Cystic Disease of the Breast* (1851), *Autoplastic operation of the Face* (1853) and *Fibrous Tumour of the Pharynx attached to the base of the Skull and Removal of the Upper Jaw* (1858). The latter described his removal of the whole of the upper jaw in order to remove a large naso-pharyngeal polypus which pioneered the way for complicated sinus and skull base procedures. He also contributed a chapter on *Injuries and Diseases of Muscles* to Timothy Holmes' book on *System of Surgery Practical and Theoretical*.

Married twice, Tatum's first wife was the daughter of William Brodie,

166

the Member of Parliament for Salisbury, and brother of Sir Benjamin Brodie, surgeon to St. George's Hospital. These interesting links lead to conjecture as to how Tatum met his first wife. Their son, Herbert Thomas, entered St. George's as a non-paying student in 1866, and qualified MRCS in 1871. Away from his medical duties Thomas Tatum was renowned as a linguist and fluent in several languages, as well as being a naturalist 'of repute'.

Thomas Tatum retired from the staff of St. George's Hospital in 1867, and was replaced by Timothy Holmes, one of his star pupils of whom Blomfield said 'he left as great a name for service to his hospital and school as anyone who ever worked there'. Holmes wrote extensively, served with distinction on every important hospital committee, and his skill as a surgeon earned him the recognition to be elected vice president of the Royal College of Surgeons. It was an open secret at the College that the president's office was his if he chose 'to abandon certain opinions' unpopular with his colleagues on the council. Holmes' character would not allow him to give up his firm beliefs for the sake of office. Timothy Holmes would have been delighted that his mentor at St. George's had at long last been recognised by having the new ear, nose and throat, and maxillo-facial surgery ward named after him in 1996.

In retirement Thomas Tatum served as Consulting Surgeon to St. George's Hospital until his death in Eastbourne at the age of 77 in 1879. He was buried in Brompton Cemetery, the resting place of one of his erstwhile colleagues, John Snow.

VERNON WARD

Henry Kenneth Vernon, FRCS

Henry Kenneth Vernon who was affectionately known as 'Pop' by both his colleagues and juniors, was a Urologist with appointments at both St. Peter's and St. James' Hospitals, London.

Vernon was born in West Hartlepool in 1907, the son of a chemist. On graduation from Durham University in 1931, he was first appointed as a house surgeon at the Royal Victoria Hospital, Newcastle. Other junior posts in Exeter and London followed before he obtained his FRCS in 1935, when he was appointed resident surgical officer at Queen

Mary's Hospital, Stratford. It was there that his interest in urology was stimulated and led to his appointment as resident surgical officer to St. Peter's Hospital, where he remained for two years before going on to a number of other posts with the London County Council, until finally he was appointed to St. James' Hospital Balham in 1940. His appointment was as a general surgeon, but he retained his interest in urology through his association with Professor Grey Turner at the Postgraduate Hospital Hammersmith.

In 1948, with the introduction of the National Health Service, Vernon was appointed Surgeon to St. James' Hospital, and Urologist to the Hammersmith Hospital. In 1950, when he was appointed to St. Peter's Hospital as Consultant Urologist, he gave up general surgery at St. James' and concentrated his attentions on developing the department of Urology which quickly received widespread recognition.

Henry Vernon was founder member of the British Association of Urological Surgeons, and trained many generations of surgeons in the basic principles of urology.

Vernon was a small, wiry man with very dark eyebrows and a droopy moustache His bright eyes peered over half moon glasses. His dress was always conventional – pinstripe trousers, grey waistcoat and black jacket over which he often donned a white coat as he carried out his ward rounds. He was kind, witty and an excellent teacher, an enthusiastic chorister, and a staunch supporter of his local church where he was church warden.

A year before his death in 1983, St. James' Hospital marked his contribution to the hospital by naming a ward in his memory. When St. James' Hospital closed, it was only fitting that the name of Vernon was transferred to designate the urological ward at St. George's Hospital.

BENJAMIN WEIR WARD

Benjamin Weir
Benjamin Weir was a resident of South London, who lived during the last century at 'The Hawthorns', Grove Road, Clapham Park, and became renowned for his generosity in helping the less fortunate in Wandsworth and Streatham. Weir also owned 12, Devonshire Road, Balham.

Weir was born in Southwark in 1809, and built up the family fortunes by investing wisely in land and property, which in time brought him considerable wealth. Although personally an unostentatious man who was content to live modestly with his wife and only daughter, he yearned to contribute his time and money for the public good. He became a member of the old Streatham Vestry (a committee formed from members of that congregation to run parish affairs), and a member of its Board of Works; when the Reverend Erskine Clarke proposed the purchase of Bolingbroke House, and its development as a hospital, Benjamin Weir immediately supported the proposal. His support took the practical shape of a generous donation, with further promises of financial support for the maintenance of the hospital.

Benjamin Weir was a man of the highest integrity and kept his promise to support the Bolingbroke Hospital for the rest of his long life, which ended with his death in March 1902 at the grand old age of 94. His benevolence continued even beyond the grave, for in his Will, he instructed his executors, the Reverend Thomas Bates, who was the Vicar of St. Mary's, Balham, and Adelbert Winfred Zabell, to use his house at 12 Devonshire Road as a Dispensary Hospital, or Convalescent Home, or Medical Charity, to be called the 'Weir Hospital': 'for the benefit of the Parishioners of Streatham and its neighbourhood, until such time as 'The Hawthorns' could be demolished and a new hospital built in its grounds with the money which Weir had left for this purpose. Weir's Trustees felt that the legacy was insufficient to build a new hospital, so they decided that under the terms of the Will they were within their rights to give one half of the capital and the whole of the income to the Bolingbroke Hospital.

The Streatham and Balham Ratepayers' Association and the Wandsworth Borough Council objected strongly to this proposal, and a dispute followed which ground on for the next seven years. Eventually, the Trustees accepted the arguments of the opposition, which by then had been swollen by a large number of local Streatham residents, and it was agreed that a 'Weir Hospital' should be established in Weir Road, Streatham. The hospital was opened in 1913 and flourished for many years. Eventually, it was used as a Maternity Hospital, but its role as a healing institution came to an end and its doors were closed, when the services it provided were transferred to St. George's Hospital in 1978.

The Benjamin Weir Trust Fund still exists, and is managed by four aldermen of the Borough, who ensure that both Wandsworth and Streatham benefit equally from its largesse. Benjamin Weir's portrait hangs in the Boardroom of the Bolingbroke Hospital, and in the ward which bears his name at St. George's Hospital. His daughter, who predeceased him, wove a number of very fine tapestries in Berlin wool, and examples of these hang in the Staff Sitting Room at the Bolingbroke Hospital. Weir also left three paintings by Saddal Hopkins, who was his wife's grandfather, which he desired to be hung in the Board Room of the hospital which bears his name.

Benjamin Weir's Mural Tablet and Memorial are in St. Mary's Church, Balham, but he was actually buried in Nunhead Cemetery.

THE EDWARD WILSON ROOM

Edward Adrian Wilson, BA, MB, ChB

A number of St. George's students achieved fame outside medicine: Clinton Dent in the Himalayas, Monier Williams for his skate, Hartley, who was awarded the Victoria Cross in Basutoland, and more recently Peter Steel in the Himalayas, and Mike Stroud in Antartica. Edward Wilson was another doctor in this group who are remembered principally for their non-medical attainments.

Edward Adrian Wilson was born in Cheltenham in 1872, the second son and fifth child of Edward Thomas Wilson, MB, a consulting physician to Cheltenham General Hospital. Young Edward Wilson was educated at Cheltenham College, and then in 1891 he entered Gonville and Caius College, Cambridge, where he rowed for his college and read for the natural science tripos successfully taking his BA in 1894. Wilson then entered St. George's Hospital where he qualified in 1900. While studying at St. George's Wilson worked at the Caius College Mission. The house in which he lived during this time still stands in Vicarage Crescent, Battersea.

In the year he qualified, Wilson applied for a post on the National

Geographical Society's Antarctic Expedition, led by Commander Robert Falcon Scott, RN, and was appointed junior surgeon.

The Discovery left England in 1901 but was frozen in McMurdo Sound for two years. During this enforced halt to their travels Edward Wilson took the opportunity of painting many delightful scenes of the Antarctic landscape, as well as researching the habits and breeding of the Emperor Penguin. Once freed from the grip of the ice Scott explored the Ross Sea area and discovered King Edward VII land. Before the Discovery sailed for home, Wilson accompanied Scott and Shackleton on the sledge journey over the ice barrier. The return journey was difficult due to all three developing scurvy. On his return to England Edward Wilson published his researches on the birds and mammals he had collected. This work led to him gaining national recognition as a naturalist, he went on to serve as a member of the Royal Commission on Diseases of Grouse, and he also illustrated Barrett-Hamilton's *History of British Mammals*.

In 1910, Scott having been promoted Captain in 1906, invited Edward Wilson to become Chief of the Scientific Staff on his ill fated Antarctic expedition in the 'Terra Nova'. Having reached the Antarctic, Scott, Wilson, Oates, Bowers and Evans set out for the South Pole on the 1st November 1911; they reached it on 18th January 1912, only to find that Roald Amundsen, the Norwegian, had beaten them by just a month.

Scott wrote of the pole 'Great God, this is an awful place', and, thoroughly dejected that they had lost out to Amundsen, the party set off back for base. The Antarctic conditions worsened and they were delayed by severe blizzards, during which time Evans fell ill, eventually dying on 17th February. Oates then recognised that he was weakening, and fearing that he might act as a drag on the rest of the party and put them all at risk, gallantly wandered away from the tent to perish of hypothermia in the dreadful conditions. Scott, Wilson and Bowers finally managed to get back as far as One Ton Depot, tantalisingly close to base, but by then they were perilously weakened by their exposure to the elements, suffering from scurvy due to a failure to take vegetables and fruit with them, and starving from a lack of food. They expired at the end of March 1912.

Eight months later their bodies, diaries and a number of Edward Wilson's drawings were found by a search party. Wilson received the Polar Medal in 1904 and the Patron's Medal of the Royal Geographical Society posthumously in 1913, his statue stands in Cheltenham, and St. George's is fortunate to possess a number of his paintings. 'Pen' Pendlebury, the St. George's surgeon wrote on Wilson's death 'We have good fortune at St. George's; we possess a Frank Buckland and an Edward Wilson' and continued 'So lived and died a very gallant gentleman'. Scott was posthumously knighted and his wife, Kathleen's, statue of him stands in Waterloo Place, London, his son, Sir Peter Markham Scott (1909-1989) was a well known artist, ornithologist and broadcaster.

WRIGHT WARD

Wright

Doubts exist as to why the name 'Wright' is attached to one of the wards at St. George's. The sub-committee set up by the Board of Governors in 1876 to review the policy regarding the naming of wards stated categorically that: 'Harris, Crayle, Wright, Hollond, Hudson, and Williams were taken from individuals who bequeathed money to the hospital'; whereas Philip Constable, the House Governor, writing in 1946, claimed that the name Wright was adopted in memory of a Mr. and Mrs. Wright who were Governors of the hospital. George Edwards in 1940 evaded the issue when he included the name Wright in the list of other ward names, and stated that 'they were given to commemorate some distinguished benefaction, patronage or service, and in no case is there any question of the appropriateness of the honour'. Unfortunately, when the Board of Governors chose the name Wright for one of the wards in the second phase (completed in 1831 – the third and final phase was not opened until 1834) of the William Wilkins version of the new St. George's they did not include in their minute the reasons for their choice, and now over one hundred and sixty years later, which Wright gave his or her name to the ward is open to speculation.

It is very doubtful that Wright ward took its name from Dr Richard

Wright, MD, Cantab.; FRCP, who was a physician at St. George's from 1769 to 1785, and does not merit a mention in W.E. Page's *Some Account of the Hospital and School* which was published in 1866.

Richard Wright was in fact, born in Derbyshire, and educated at Emmanuel College, Cambridge, where he obtained a BA in 1762. His MA followed in 1765. Wright was never a pupil at St. George's, but he was appointed a physician to the hospital in 1769, before gaining his MD in 1773, two years before he was admitted as a Fellow of the Royal College of Physicians. At some time he became a Fellow of the Royal Society. Wright was Censor of the Royal College of Physicians in 1775, 1779 and 1783, so he was clearly respected at the College, and Page may have been a little unkind to one of his predecessors, or perhaps there was some other reason for overlooking him, as Richard Wright, who lived in Knightsbridge, died at the early age of 45, just one year after he left his post at St. George's, in what was described as 'in deep decline', which gives few clues as to the real diagnosis; though this may be intentional, and meant to cloak a situation which could conceivably have contained a whiff of scandal, and brought shame or harm to those with whom he was connected. Apparently Wright kept 'a select and curious library' 'the strength of which lay chiefly in publications relating to drama and romance', which may imply, in the code of the times, that he had a collection of obscene books.

It is much more likely that the ward takes its title, Wright, from one or possibly two of the lay Governors who shared the same name. Anyone of moderate means could apply to become a Governor of St. George's Hospital. Once an application had been made, the candidate's name was posted in the Boardroom for one month, and then a ballot was held amongst the existing Governors. If the applicant secured a majority of the vote, then he or she was admitted as a Governor or Trustee, on condition that they subscribed at least five pounds a year. The Governor could then put his or her name forward as a representative of the Governors at the Weekly Board, which was also attended by the senior physicians and surgeons. All Governors were also entitled to attend any extraordinary meeting held, for example, to elect the surgeons and physicians. A Governor who subscribed £5 per annum was entitled to one vote, and those who subscribed £10 or more were entitled to two votes. A subscription of £100 secured a life Governorship. Peers who contributed £10-10 per annum became Governors without election.

The lists of Governors from 1733 to 1831 contains a number of people who share the name Wright. Most subscribed for a very short period, but between 1750 and 1770 a William Wright was a regular attendee at the Weekly Board meetings, often chairing the meetings, and from 1760 to 1775 the name John Wright figures prominently in the lists of subscribers. However, inspection of the lists of Governors from 1767 to 1831 instantly reveals the name of Mrs. Barbara Wright, who subscribed to St. George's Hospital for no less than 64 years, as well as making a number of contributions to the convalescent fund. Renowned for her generosity, and as she was an active governor during the period immediately prior to the rebuilding of the hospital at Hyde Park Corner, it is more than likely that she contributed generously to the Rebuilding Fund. Unfortunately, the Weekly Board Minutes do not include the names of all the Governors who attended the meetings, they record only the numbers; so it is impossible to determine whether Mrs. Wright matched her many years of financial support to the hospital with an equivalent degree of interest in its affairs. It would be very strange for someone to make such a long term commitment financially and yet remain indifferent to the welfare of the hospital and its future development. The writers believe that Wright ward is named to commemorate the benefaction, patronage and service of Mrs. Barbara Wright; and, of course, this does nothing to invalidate Philip Constable's view that the ward is named after a husband and wife team, as it is quite plausible that either John or William Wright was the husband of Barbara. Of course, if Philip Constable was correct then it is possible that John may have been the husband of Barbara, and she might well have been William's daughter in law.

Whoever was the benefactor of Wright ward, he, she, or they, would not have known that the ward bearing their name was to suffer the brunt of the 5000 gallon torrent of water that was to cascade through the ward in 1876 from the ruptured water tank on the roof, tearing holes in its floor, and swirling four beds, along with their unfortunate occupants,

174

down through Holland ward onto the ground floor. Wright ward at Hyde Park corner was to see happier times in 1887, when its windows were let out at five guineas each to those who wished to watch the passage of Queen Victoria's jubilee parade.

THE YOUDE HEART CENTRE AND THE LADY YOUDE UNIT

Sir Edward and Lady Youde

The Youde Heart Centre and the Lady Youde Centre are named after Sir Edward Youde GCMG, KCMG, CMG, MBE and his wife, Lady Pamela Youde who developed links with St. George's Hospital during the 1980s.

Sir Edward Youde was born in 1924 and received his later education at the School of Oriental and African studies before he was called up into the Royal Naval Volunteer Reserve in 1943. As soon as he was demobilised in 1947 he joined the Foreign Office. Youde's knowledge of the Orient and its languages singled him out for appointment to Nanking and Peking in 1948 as Third Secretary where he served until 1951. During his tour of duty Edward Youde was involved in the negotiations which took place when HMS Amethyst was trapped on the Yangtse River deep in China by the advancing Communist armies. During the shelling her captain was killed but the Chinese would not release the frigate. On July 30, 1949 as the ship's rations and fuel supplies were running low Lieutenant-Commander John Kerans slipped anchor under cover of darkness and sailed HMS Amethyst at full steam down river. Amethyst returned fire as she was bombarded by the shore batteries but after a 140 mile dash Kerans signalled the Admiralty 'Have rejoined the Fleet south of Woosung. No damage or casualties. God Save the King'. Kerans received the Distinguished Service Order and Edward Youde was given an MBE.

In 1951 Youde returned to Britain to the Foreign Office and in the same year he married Pamela Fitt. Within two years he was posted back for a further three year tour of duty as Second Secretary. After promotion to First Secretary Youde was posted first to Washington and the back to Peking where he served from 1960 until 1962. From

1962 until 1965 he served at the Foreign Office before being appointed Head of Chancery for the UK Mission to the United Nations. Youde received the Commandership of St. Michael and St. George in 1968 and in the following year he was appointed Private Secretary to the Prime Minister, Harold Wilson and served in this post until after the general election in 1970 when Edward Heath led the conservatives to victory.

Edward Youde was then appointed to the Imperial Defence College, after which he was successively Head of Personnel Services and Under Secretary of State at the recently merged Foreign and Colonial Office. In 1974, it might have been felt that Edward Youde had achieved all of his career aspirations when he was appointed Her Majesty's Ambassador to China. For his services in China as the Queen's representative Youde was created a KCMG in 1977 and in the following year he returned to the Foreign and Colonial Office, firstly as Deputy Under Secretary of State and then as Deputy to the Permanent Under Secretary of State.

Sir Edward Youde reached the pinnacle of an illustrious career in the Diplomatic Service when he was appointed Governor and Commander in Chief of Hong Kong in 1982. In 1984 Sir Geoffrey Howe announced a framework of the deal for the handover of Hong Kong to China and Sir Edward led a number of the early negotiations which were hailed in Whitehall as a triumph. In December 1984 Britain and China signed the Treaty in Beijing returning Hong Kong to China in 1997. Sir Edward Youde was elevated to GCMG in 1983 and in 1986 he was in attendance when the Queen made her visit to China, the first by a British monarch. Sadly, Sir Edward Youde's health began to fail soon afterwards and he was forced to retire in 1987 and died shortly afterwards. From 1951 Sir Edward was greatly supported by his charming and gracious wife, Lady Pamela. Away from the endless rounds of diplomatic gatherings they both enjoyed walking, music and when they had the opportunity, the theatre.

Sir Edward and Lady Youde were responsible for ensuring that the cardiac and geriatric departments of St. George's Hospital were the fortunate recipients of most magnanimous donations from an anonymous Hong Kong businessman.

176

YOUNG WARD

Thomas Young, MD, FRS

Thomas Young was regarded by his contemporaries as probably possessing the greatest intellect ever to practice medicine, and he was a Physician to St. George's Hospital from 1811 to 1829.

Young was born in 1773 at Milverton in Somerset, and his parents were members of the Society of Friends, though this did not prevent the child from singing, dancing, and playing the flute. However, it was not long before his serious and scholarly aspects began to blossom. By the age of two he could read fluently, by four he had read the bible twice, and at six he could recite many poems from memory. When he first went to school the teacher wishing to test his handwriting skills asked him to write out a short phrase. Young was so insulted to be asked to carry out such a simple task, that he wrote out the phrase in nine different foreign languages. He was a formidable linguist, and before he was twenty he had mastered many ancient and modern languages including Latin, Greek, Hebrew, Arabic, Persian, Syriac, Chaldee, Aramaic, French, Italian and German. Before leaving school the precocious boy had translated Shakespeare into Greek.

In 1787 Thomas Young was employed by a Mr. David Barclay of Youngsbury, as resident companion and teacher of classics to his grandson, Mr. Hudson Gurney. At the age of eighteen Young was admitted to the Society of Porson, which had been established by Richard Porson (1759-1808), Professor of Greek at Cambridge, to enable scholars to meet and discuss the finer points of Greek literature. After looking after Hudson Gurney for four years Thomas Young at the suggestion of his uncle, Dr. Richard Brocklesby, attended lectures given by John Hunter, Matthew Baillie and other distinguished London doctors, before he entered St. Bartholomew's Hospital in 1793 as a pupil. Before he had completed his first year he had written and presented a paper describing his theory that the process of accommodation in the eye was achieved by an alteration in the thickness of the lens, and so disproving the old theory that it resulted from a lengthening of the eyeball. For this paper he was immediately elected to the Fellowship of the Royal Society at the age of twenty one. Next Young went to Edinburgh, where he helped to compile *An Anthology of Greek Poets*, and it was at this time that he severed his links with the Quaker movement. In 1796, having travelled to Gottingen, he drew up an alphabet of 47 letters which represented all the human sounds, as well as qualifying as a doctor of medicine. Young spent the next two years at Emmanuel College, Cambridge where he was known as the 'Phenomenon Young'.

Thomas Young was appointed Professor of Natural Philosophy at the Royal Institution in 1801, and it was here that he gave his lectures in physics, which was known as 'Natural Philosophy and Mechanical Arts ' at the beginning of the nineteenth century. These popular lectures, which covered a wide diversity of subjects ranging from musical instruments to astronomy, and including hydraulic machines, weights and measures, climate and wind, gravitation and other physical subjects, were published in two volumes in 1802, and, as a result, Young was appointed Foreign Secretary of the Royal Society, a post he held until his death in 1829

Having qualified MB at Cambridge in 1803, Thomas Young took over his uncle's practice in Welbeck Street, which he combined with his Professorship of Natural Philosophy at the Royal Institution. In 1808 he obtained his MD, and the following year he was admitted as a candidate of the College of Physicians. In 1811 Thomas Young was appointed Physician to St. George's Hospital, an appointment he held until his death in 1829, although for much of this time he was fully occupied by his many other interests.

Young's genius and insatiable interest in a vast range of scientific and classical subjects, caused him to flit from one topic to the next. Once he had made a fundamental discovery in a subject he would move on restlessly to something quite different. It is likely that he only took up medicine as a challenge, and having satisfied his curiosity in a few matters, he lost interest in the subject after fifteen years. Certainly Young required scientific evidence of the benefits of a treatment before he was prepared to prescribe it. This is probably the reason that he was not popular amongst his colleagues at St. George's Hospital, where he distrusted (rightly) some of the contemporary treatments such as bleeding, cupping, leeching, mercury and antimony that they were practising, preferring to leave well alone and letting nature take its course. Sir Benjamin Brodie, a surgeon at St. George's in Young's time said that 'Young was not fitted

178

for the profession which he had chosen and he was too engaged in other pursuits'. The students regarded him as 'a great philosopher but a bad physician' whereas Dr. Dickinson said he was 'the most comprehensive genius and greatest man of science who ever held the office of Physician to St. George's, or indeed to any other hospital'. It is clear that most of Young's contemporaries, although admiring his wide intellectual abilities and interests, remained unimpressed by him as a medical practitioner, though he undoubtedly had an interest in the development of medicine and was a Censor of the College of Physicians in 1813 and 1823, as well as being the Croonian Lecturer in 1822 and 1823.

Thomas Young's contributions to Egyptology and science were astonishing. Probably one of his most outstanding achievements was his analysis and subsequent deciphering of Egyptian Hieroglyphics. In 1802 a stone found at Rosetta in the Nile delta was brought to the British Museum. On examination it was found to be covered with Hieroglyphics and Greek writing. Young using his knowledge of languages, especially Chinese, discovered that the Hieroglyphics were phonetic, and this discovery led to the interpretation of all earlier Egyptian writings. Thomas Young completed his rudiments of an Egyptian Dictionary on his death bed. In 1818, Young became Secretary of the Board of Longitude, and was responsible for the publication of the Admiralty's National Almanac. In this position he came into conflict with his employers, but, he went on to advise the Admiralty on boat design. Later, commissioned by the government, he evaluated the dangers of introducing coal gas as a fuel into London. In 1824 Young was appointed Inspector of Calculations to an insurance company, and for them he produced the first actuarial tables which formed the basis of those that are used today.

The last five years of Young's life were lived at a furious pace, because as his health failed, he attempted to complete all his outstanding tasks. By the beginning of 1829 he was bedridden with repeated attacks of breathlessness, haemoptysis and general debility, and his condition rapidly deteriorated. Thomas Young, died on 10 May 1829 aged 56 and was buried in his wife's family vault at Farnborough, Kent.

A monument by Francis Legatt Chantrey (1781-1841), the British sculptor was erected in Westminster Abbey by his wife. The inscription by his pupil and juvenile companion, Hudson Gurney reads:

Sacred to the memory of
Thomas Young, MD.,
Fellow and Foreign Secretary of the Royal Society,
Member of the National Institute of France:
A man alike eminent
in almost every department of human learning.
Patient of unintermitted labour,
Endowed with the faculty of intuitive perception,
Who, bringing an equal mastery
to the most abstruse investigations
of letters and of science,
first established the undulatory theory of light,
and first penetrated the obscurity
which had veiled for ages
the Hieroglyphics of Egypt.
Endeared to his friends by his domestic virtues,
Honoured by the world for his unrivalled acquirements,
He died in the hopes of the resurrection of the just.
Born at Milverton in Somersetshire June 13th, 1773;
Died in Park-square London May 10th, 1829,
in the 56th year of his age.

The portrait of Thomas Young by Thomas Brigstocke, which hangs in the 'Well' in Grosvenor Wing, is a copy of the portrait originally executed by Sir Thomas Lawrence (1769 – 1830) for Hudson Gurney, Young's classical pupil. Lawrence, a Bristolian had a precocious talent and became President of the Royal Academy in 1820. Hoppner, who painted Matthew Baillie's portrait was a formidable rival to Lawrence.

180

4

Conclusion

The problem of how wards should be designated has been solved in a variety of ways at different times and places: they can be given names of famous people, well-known either nationally or locally; they may be named after inhabitants of the natural world such as flowers or birds; or quite prosaically with letters or numbers. The most important qualifying factor for the use of famous names was the absence of a controversial background, thus at one time members of the Royal Family could bestow their names almost automatically; other naming schemes could involve national heroes or statesmen, but these would appear to be currently in rather short supply, although this deficiency is neatly matched by the poor prospects for hospital building in the near future. Local worthies in the shape of aristocratic families are often called upon, as are leading municipal figures from more democratic origins, such as aldermen and mayors; what these groups usually have in common are a local reputation for the size and frequency of their benefactions.

Men of letters or scientists of international repute are more likely than not to be a safe bet, and even if there were some areas of their life that were better glossed over, these could be attributed to the eccentricities of genius, and forgotten if not forgiven. In so far as famous doctors could loosely be described as men of science their names were suitable, but one then encountered the difficulty that most smaller hospitals would not have a sufficient pool of historic talent to draw from, they could of course, employ the names of nationally known figures within the profession, and this is what many settled for; larger institutions might have enough of their own to go round by dint of including one or two of somewhat lower standard. The age and size of a hospital becomes a positive boon in respect of the number of meritorious former sons, daughters and benefactors they may have at their disposal. This number is clearly directly proportional to the larger it becomes and the length of time it has been in existence. In this respect St. George's Hospital is extremely fortunate, not only has it had a continuous history going back to 1733, but for most of those years it occupied a splendid site in the affluent centre of a capital city, which must have played a part in attracting professionals to work there, and local people to support it.

The various contributions made by members of staff has been the subject of this book, and it has embraced a wide diversity of activity. Turning the pages one will have encountered people who have made major scientific discoveries that have helped to eradicate terrible diseases such as smallpox, or undertaken academic work that has led to an understanding of disease processes, and enabled others to make practical applications of these studies to create important clinical advances. We have been introduced to others who were quite simply the best of their profession in their day, some who were known for the humanity of their approach and almost saintly dedication to patient care, others whose leadership saw the hospital safely through times of crisis, or whose gift was to mobilise support for expansion and rebuilding; we have seen examples of staff at all levels of the hospital hierarchy, from House Governor to Porters, who saw their duty as being to facilitate the work of the healing professions in whatever role they served, briefly we have had a glimpse of the work and personal qualities of a great matron, and the courage and determination of a patient whose life was so tragically ended prematurely. To continue to use this type of nomenclature at present is fundamentally a way of preserving some of the warmth and humanity associated with a hospital, which are in danger of being lost under the new dispensations. These are unquantifiable virtues that are at risk, and we have been saddened to find that in recent years, history, traditions, pledges and great contributions have been largely ignored in attempts to satisfy the personal whims of a few individuals, and the need for political expediency in the search for another name for a new ward.

182

The authors were surprised to find that so many names of those who had generously supported St. George's and its constituent hospitals, who were respected for their eminence or admired for their generosity in their time have been forgotten in the new hospital at Tooting. In the 1990's, once again hospital services are beginning to be partly dependent on voluntary funding for further developments. It is important that the names of these generous benefactors are not ignored or forgotten as has happened in the past. Some of the greatest servants of St. George's, the Royal Dental, Tite Street, St. James', the Weir and the South London Hospitals have been ignored. However, we applaud those who have made the conscious effort to re-introduce names such as McCalmont, Drummond, Wright and Harris as the occasion has arisen, but we remain aware of the fact that past promises to individuals such as Anne Towry Hall, Mrs. Crayle, Sir Thomas Apreece, William King, Mrs. Oliphant, Dr. John Radcliffe, Christopher Salter, Mr. Pike Scrivener, Sir Brownlow Stone and Dame Marie Tempest and others have been forgotten. One is left wondering whether there is any ring of truth in the lines of Samuel Johnson (1709-1784).

> I have two very cogent reasons for not
> printing any list of subscribers;
> one, that I have lost all the names,
> the other, that I have spent all the money

We have found that patients, visitors and staff generally approve of names for wards and buildings, and only a very small minority favour a change to the lettering and numerical system; which could result in just as much confusion when one considers that St. George's is not a single building, but composed of a number of blocks irregularly arranged on a large site, each having multiple floors, with each floor containing a number of wards.

There are, of course, better reasons for linking wards with the names of people. Taken in the spirit in which it was intended the system in operation at St. George's has much to recommend it: with minimal outlay our forebears in the hospital are commemorated for their lives and work: the academic successes, clinical improvements, better buildings, wise leadership, benefactions and more than anything the sacrifices they made for the well-being of mankind on the basis of care they gave to individual patients, which is, after all, the basic relationship most of those who work as or with the hospital staff have with the sick. It would be a useful exercise for the new medical students to have a mandatory lecture on the history of the hospital, and the people who made it great, as from it they may find some inspiration to dedicate themselves to the same goals. If those of us who have passed that stage, and are becoming a little jaded and world-weary, could, instead of just saying the name of a ward, occasionally pause for a moment to reflect on that person's example, and tell our juniors or colleagues about it, everyone would benefit. The ultimate justification for the practice of using names is to remind us constantly of the high standards to which we should aspire. A hospital is a human organisation, and the whole is much greater than the sum of its parts, if this is forgotten our work and our patients suffer. To whatever technological heights medicine develops someone who is sick will always require a compassionate human face in attendance. This human approach is exemplified by the system of giving personal names to the wards. It works and will continue to do so. Let us continue to celebrate their lives. They all have lessons to teach us. If only we are prepared to learn.

> but these are deeds which should not pass away
> and names that must not wither
> > Lord Byron (1788-1824)
> > Childe Harold's Pilgrimage

If it is the case that the decision to name wards after individuals is made, the next and crucial discussion will revolve around how the selection is to be made. In these times a lottery might prove to be a satisfactory solution. A case could be put forward for a ballot of the hospital staff after a suitable list of names has been canvassed, but this begs the question of suitability, and the list could very well contain persons of considerable transient popularity acquired for reasons unconnected with their altruism or example, whose appeal may have dimmed in a very short period, leading to embarrassment all round. Perhaps the youngest of the staff, should do the selecting as they will have little in the way of prejudice against personalities they cannot remember, but youthful irreverence may throw up some dubious choices. Everyone will agree that the task is far too weighty a matter to be resolved by either of the above methods.

By whatever tendentious means the choice is made, we would suggest, as a result of our labours, that there are certain preliminaries to be undertaken before putting the scheme into practice. First of all careful records should be kept of each individual to be honoured, rather as the Roman Catholic Church does prior to Canonisation; and we hasten to disclaim any other similarities between the two processes. The records would include details as to why the person was considered worthy of the honour of commemoration in this way, and the date when the decision was made, in case anything discreditable emerges about them subsequently. After the research has been completed it should be stored on computer disc, perhaps by the Librarian, and be available to anyone genuinely keen to study the people involved. As history is a continuous process there should be facilities for authorised additions and deletions to be made to the stored text if more information becomes available. No mechanism exists at present for testing the authenticity and reliability of this new material, and loath as we are to add to the hospital bureaucracy we would tentatively suggest the creation of a Hospital Heritage Committee which would not be unduly taxed to meet quinquennially to conveniently oversee and deal with such matters.

Inevitably some names will stand the test of time, but others may have a less compelling reason to be maintained into an uncomprehending future, and a periodic review may be a way of avoiding this particular dilemma. We concede that confusion would be rife if it were done too often, and would suggest that an extraordinary meeting of the Hospital Heritage Committee every quarter of a century would probably be often enough to prune out those no longer in fashion, and substitute instead those with an overwhelming claim to inclusion. Another problem surrounds those who narrowly fail be chosen, it may be that some scandal of a non-professional nature has cropped up to tilt the balance away from them, but it is precisely this sign of human frailty that would create sympathy for them in the eyes of the majority of the population; as a generous gesture it could be arranged to reserve a space for an example of this type; it would bring pleasure to a great many in giving another, and less respectful gesture, in the direction of the Politically Correct.

Does all this concern matter? Apparently not. Already the vandals are at the gates, and since the beginning of the 1996 and for the first time in its history St. George's has a ward called 'Jungle'. After much laborious research we have been unable to find a trace of anyone of that name having a meaningful connection to the hospital, and are forced to conclude that it is named after a geographical phenomenon uncommon in the locality. The reason for this crass non sequitur (probably the fruit of extensive consultations) eludes us, but it leaves us with a feeling that names such as this could easily cause offence, which the hospital is wrong to condone.

Before things go too far, we urge those who wish for revolutionary change to read the following letter written in 1860 by a patient who as well as appreciating the care he had received in St. George's Hospital recognised that the hospital was far greater than any one individual and was proud to identify himself with the name of one of its wards:

> To the kind gentlemen and governors of St. George's hospital. I am in rags and very poor but i trust you will pardon me and except my gratefull and heart felt thanks for the spiritual and bodily goodness I have received in this hospital for all i have come in contact with has treated me with kindness even to the medical gentlemen but as for mrs Scott the nurse and her attentant has been unremitting in kindness and attention to me and I might say my fellow patients surely it must be the uneducated or ignorant that would abuse sutch a heavenly blessing as this hospital for its unbounded blessings besttowed on us that is in need of it. My humble prayer is that the allmighty may preserve it unto the end of the world kind gentlemen i return you my grateful thanks for the grayte benefits received by me and the cure of my disease I am kind gentlemen your humble and obedient servant Joseph Read 31 Queen Street or Fitzwilliam ward. To the kind gentlemen of St. George's Hospital.

Index